D0394002

THEY SAW THE ELEPHANT

WOMEN IN THE CALIFORNIA GOLD RUSH

JOANN LEVY

THEY SAW THE ELEPHANT

WOMEN IN THE CALIFORNIA GOLD RUSH

ARCHON BOOKS • 1990

First published 1990 as an Archon Book, an imprint of
The Shoe String Press, Hamden, Connecticut 06514

Printed in the United States of America

Book design by Abigail Johnston

The paper used in this publication meets the minimum requirements
of American National Standard for Information Science—Permanence
of Paper for Printed Library Materials, ANSI Z39.48–1984.∞

Library of Congress Cataloging-in-Publication Data

Levy, JoAnn, They saw the elephant: women in the California gold rush
JoAnn Levy   p.   cm.
Includes bibliographical references.
1. California—Gold discoveries.
2. Women pioneers—California—History—19th century.
3. Women—California—History—19th century.
4. Frontier and pioneer life—California.   I. Title.
F865.L67   1990   979.4'04'082—dc20   89–78223
ISBN 0-208-02273-2 (alk. paper)

For Lucy, Eliza, Susanna, Sophia,
Nancy, Georgiana, Sarah, Mary, Jennie,
Louisa, Margaret—for all of them

CONTENTS

LIST OF ILLUSTRATIONS

PREFACE

Twenty-five years ago, when I first visited California's Mother Lode country, gentrification and suburban housing had yet to overshadow the long, low, wonderfully evocative rocky piles of gold miners' tailings. I was struck by how close to the historical past our paths still take us, not realizing the distance another quarter century could push it back. In those days, for example, boardwalked Folsom felt to me like a 19th-century town where any moment saloon doors might slap the arrival of a poke-carrying prospector. It's spiffier now, but the feeling's gone.

In those days, too, you could still drive across Nevada County's marvelous covered bridge, hearing old timbers thump and echo your passage. Now, instead of a wondrous discovery, it's a state park with rules and a visitors' parking lot. And the feeling's gone.

What hasn't changed in twenty-five years is my enduring fascination for the Mother Lode country and its dramatic history. Many people know the experience of being drawn inexplicably to a place. There's no explaining it, but there's a harmony in being there, a shared resonance. For me the pulse beats a little quicker beneath a Sonora summer sun, among Nevada City's undulating hills, along the cool Mokelumne River.

For most of the past twenty-five years this attachment remained peripheral; there, but unfocused. I'd seek out the odd historical marker or wayside ruin, explore old towns, and read books like J. S. Holliday's estimable gold rush history, *The World Rushed In*, published in 1981.

I no longer remember the passage in that book that sent me to its index, looking for the heading "women." I do remember the moment. The index didn't include that heading, and I was chagrined at its absence. These are the eighties, I said to myself, and women get included in history now.

This was before the terrible fire at the grand old Los Angeles Public

Library, and curiosity about the overlooked women took me to its California Room, a dark-paneled, tall-cased enclave stuffed with the golden state's history. I slowly circled the room, peering through glass doors, head canted to read spine-stamped titles for anything about women in the gold rush. Finding none, I tugged out long card-catalog drawers and one by one thumbed the cards. I found books about Australians in the gold rush, Chileans in the gold rush, blacks in the gold rush, Irish in the gold rush, French in the gold rush. On women in the gold rush—nothing.

Still, a few women's names attached themselves to titles: the classic *Shirley Letters From the California Mines, 1851–1852* by Louise Clapp; Mrs. D. B. Bates's *Incidents on Land and Water, or Four Years on the Pacific Coast*, published in 1858; Eliza Farnham's *California In-Doors and Out*, dated 1856; *Frontier Lady*, Sarah Royce's reminiscence of crossing the plains to California in 1849.

I started with Eliza Farnham's book, hearing in my mind her distinctive voice telling how her ship's captain abandoned her in South America and sailed off with her children, how she built a two-story house with her own hands and planted potatoes and wore bloomers and discussed philosophy. This was California in 1849! A woman on her own, doing what she had to do to support herself and her children! How extraordinary!

And then I listened to Mrs. Bates relate in Victorian astonishment her multiple ship disasters in an amazing journey around the Horn. Then Sarah Royce's voice, a hoarse whisper of dread as she recalled her fearful desert crossing. What remarkable women, and what a remarkable time they lived in.

So began my search for gold rushing women—and my growing admiration for them. I found them in letters, diaries, reminiscences, the rare book, the unpublished manuscript, old newspapers. Gold rush women turned out to have been not "just prostitutes" at all, as many histories assert or imply. They were mule riders across the Isthmus, boardinghouse keepers and miners, missionaries and actresses, church builders and gamblers, school teachers and temperance speakers, even a Wells, Fargo & Company stage driver.

I discovered more surprises. Contrary to common assumptions about suffering pioneers, many women hugely enjoyed their frontier adventures. Some women were as gold hungry as men. Most women worked, not just at housekeeping but for money, and they worked hard. And they divorced at an astonishing rate.

When I was at last convinced that no library held the elusive volume on gold rushing women that I was pursuing, I realized that I could write it.

The journey Dr. Holliday's oversighted index sent me on was an excursion into a past among women I've come to know very well. I know, too, what historian John Caughey meant when he observed, "the author of every book must feel surprised that his subject has waited for him."

I am not only surprised, I am overjoyed.

J.L.

I think that I may without vanity affirm
that I have "seen the elephant."
LOUISA CLAPP

INTRODUCTION

At California's discovery of its golden ground, the shout "Eureka!" was heard 'round the world. As one, argonauts embarked from the States and South America, from Europe and Asia, from Australia and New Zealand, to participate in the great drama of the gold rush.

For Americans, whose fortuitous find it was, every element bespoke the stuff of legends: westward-rolling canvas-topped wagons seeking the setting sun through an unfamiliar landscape vast and barren and beautiful, with brave pioneers daring death at the hands of painted savages; a remote and unknown California beckoning with glittering promises to the frontier spirit fated to embrace its manifest destiny to conquer a continent.

While prior to 1849 most west-heading wagons were for Oregon, it was news of gold that loosed a flood of humanity upon the plains, deserts, and mountains of the American West. More than 25,000 overlanders called themselves forty-niners. In 1850, another 44,000 followed the trail to gold. By the decade's close, those who had trekked half a continent to see California for themselves exceeded 180,000.

So dramatic an enterprise spread across so forbidding and enticing a canvas as the American West at once assumed heroic proportions. The pioneers themselves first endowed their quest with mythic qualities. For, as though the buffalo was not exotic animal enough for the landscape, gold seekers enhanced the wondrous journey with a marvelous and mysterious elephant.

To forty-niners and those following, no expression characterized the California gold rush more than the words "seeing the elephant." Those planning to travel west announced they were "going to see the elephant." Those turning back claimed they had seen the "elephant's tracks" or the "elephant's tail," and admitted that view was sufficient. Wagon drivers painted colorful names like *Prairie Bird* on their canvas covers, and one teamster scribbled on his the words, "*Have You Saw the Elephant?*" Of it another forty-niner observed, "As matters turned out, this last legend, notwithstanding its bad grammar, was the most appropriate and prophetic of all."

The expression predated the gold rush, arising from a tale current when circus parades first featured elephants. A farmer, so the story went, hearing that a circus was in town, loaded his wagon with vegetables for the market there. He had never seen an elephant and very much wished to. On the way to town he encountered the circus parade, led by an elephant. The farmer was thrilled. His horses, however, were terrified. Bolting, they overturned the wagon and ruined the vegetables. "I don't give a hang," the farmer said, "for I have seen the elephant."

For gold rushers, the elephant symbolized both the high cost of their endeavor—the myriad possibilities for misfortune on the journey or in California—and, like the farmer's circus elephant, an exotic sight, an unequaled experience, the adventure of a lifetime.

This dangerous landscape of mythical elephants and hauntingly beautiful but deadly deserts and mountains fairly begged for the fearless bravery of a man of action walking tall. The woman in this picture would be sunbonneted, suffering, peering wearily westward from the creaking covered wagon dragging her from the comforts of home.

These images reside in our national consciousness. Hollywood gave them to us, of course, grabbing the inherently spectacular from the westward migration, embellishing it mightily, and preserving it in film cans.

Among treasured western lore repeatedly reenacted in living color is the grave threat Indians posed to wagon trains. However, among the hundreds of diaries kept on the journey, surprisingly few recount Indian depredations. The late historian John D. Unruh, Jr., tallied them and discovered that of the more than 250,000 pioneers crossing the plains and deserts between 1840 and 1860, Indians killed 362. Emigrants, incidentally, handily held their own, dispatching 426 Indians in the same time span.

Another favorite western myth, not exclusive to widescreen panorama, is that the gold rush was almost exclusively male. Yet, even in 1849 when the most impetuous rushed west first, nearly every trail diary records the presence of families—wives, mothers, sisters, and daughters. After careful study, the editor of J. Goldsborough Bruff's voluminous journal concluded that as many as 10 percent of over-landing forty-niners were female, and expected even that figure to be revised upward.

Motion picture directors do not, however, deserve full credit for tarnishing the silver screen with inaccuracy. Historians helped, sifting misperceptions through unconscious bias. Even contemporary chroniclers may subscribe to the adage that a story worth telling is a story worth exaggerating.

As example, at least three gold rush histories cite the figure fifteen as the number of women in San Francisco in the spring of 1849. That mysteriously exact number of fifteen gained credence from its appearance in Charles Howard Shinn's highly regarded *Mining Camps: A Study in American Frontier Government*, first published in 1885. Shinn probably got it from Peter H. Burnett's *Recollections and Opinions of an Old Pioneer*, which was published in 1880. And Burnett was there.

The *manuscript* of Burnett's recollections, however, does not say San Francisco had but fifteen women. The book's printer apparently filtered the number through his own reduction system, because Burnett's manuscript estimates San Francisco's female population at *fifteen per mille*. Further, *that* figure Hubert Howe Bancroft recognized as absurdly low. In his monumental *History of California* Bancroft cited Burnett's figure of fifteen women per thousand of San Francisco's population as an example of how writers of the period reduced the presence of women in "the usual spirit of exaggeration."

To have accepted that figure of fifteen women in the whole of San Francisco in the spring of 1849, Bancroft would have needed to dismiss San Francisco's census of 1847. For in that early year residents of the village by the bay already included 138 women.

Women had migrated west years before California promised free gold. In 1841 the first organized emigration party crossing the un-mapped west to California included a woman. She was Nancy Kelsey, eighteen years old, mother of an infant daughter. With her husband of two years, Benjamin Kelsey, Nancy had joined the Western Emigration Society organized by John Bidwell, a twenty-one-year-old Missourian spurred by the letters of John Marsh extolling the distant land's fertility and climate.

These people had no map, no guide, no experience. So meager was their knowledge that one later confessed they "smelled" the way west. Despite abandoning their wagons, traveling on foot, and making too close an acquaintance with starvation, all thirty-three of the first emigrant party over the Sierra survived. No diarist mentions that Nancy's baby was ever sick. Of Nancy herself, fellow sojourner Joseph Chiles recalled: "She bore the fatigues of the journey with so much heroism, patience, and kindness that there still exists a warmth in every heart for the mother and her child."

In 1843 Chiles, who had returned to Missouri in '42, came west again to California. With him were, as he promised his friend, California settler George Yount, eighteen-year-old Elizabeth Ann Yount and her older married sister, Frances Vines, with husband, Bartlett, and their two young children. Besides Yount's daughters, Chiles's party included Mr. and Mrs. Julius Martin and their three young daughters Mary, Arzelia, and two-month-old Martha.

Eight women came west in 1844 with Elisha Stevens, whose caravan of eleven wagons also carried twenty-six men and seventeen children. Not knowing that wagons could not cross the high and rugged Sierra, these Missouri flatlanders, who knew nothing of mountains, did it. They left six temporarily at what came to be called Donner Lake. The other five wagons these determined men unloaded and heroically hauled over a thousand-foot-high granite slope inch by inch. The date of that monumental accomplishment is believed to be November 25, 1844.

That date marks the opening of the California Trail.

Once the Stevens party opened the trail, emigration for California gained momentum. In 1845 five identifiable parties trekked overland to the beckoning west, among them one of twenty-four wagons with thirty-one men, thirty-two women, and sixty-one children.

Hundreds followed west to California in 1846, but one name alone remains the measure against which emigrant suffering is judged: Donner.

No Greek tragedy parades the stage with more cumulative misfortune than fate dealt the emigrants known as the Donner party. Inexperience, quarrels, accidents, a disastrous cutoff, an early and deep snowfall—all were signposts on a luckless trail leading eighty-seven emigrants to horror. "Seeing the elephant" is a meaningless phrase for what these people endured.

Of the forty who died, just seven were women, among them Tamsen Donner, comforting her dying husband and refusing rescue. Historians frequently remark the extraordinary hardihood of women pioneers. Ten men and five women formed the desperate Donner

party band of "forlorn hope," who—starved, weak, and freezing—
staggered thirty-three days through deep snow seeking safety and
assistance. Of those fifteen, all five women survived, but only two of
the men.

Hundreds of overland emigrants that year challenged the deserts
and mountains, and Sam Brannan brought some seventy men, sixty-
eight women, and a hundred children around the Horn from New
York, seeking a western refuge for their unpopular Mormon beliefs.
Their ship, the *Brooklyn*, reached the village called Yerba Buena on
July 31, 1846. Six months later residents renamed it San Francisco.

Because of the war with Mexico—ended in California on January
13, 1847, with the signing of the Cahuenga Capitulation—overland
emigration to California dropped significantly. Even so, ninety wagons, belonging mostly to farming families, made the journey in 1847
without serious problems. Several hundred soldiers for the war with
Mexico, including some 350 Mormon volunteers enlisted on the
plains the previous year, also arrived in 1847. With General Stephen
Watts Kearny and his raggedy Army of the West they traveled the old
Santa Fe trading trail, forging from Santa Fe a southern route to
California.

On July 28, 1847, in San Francisco's first newspaper, the *California
Star*, Sam Brannan published the young community's population
figures: 459 residents, among them 138 females, including 66 white
women over the age of twenty, 8 Indian women, 1 Sandwich Islander,
and 1 Negro.

In 1848 San Francisco's population doubled to an estimated one
thousand.

And, of course, in 1848 James Marshall, a carpenter building a
sawmill for pioneer John Sutter, found gold.

"This day some kind of mettle was found in the tail of the race that
looks like goald," wrote Henry William Bigler in his pocket diary for
January 24. Bigler, one of the several mustered-out Mormon Battalion
boys making up Marshall's crew, was the first to note the momentous
event.

For most histories of California, that event and Marshall's name
are sufficient. Almost none note the one woman present and participating on this historic occasion.

She was Elizabeth Bays Wimmer. Most people called her Jennie.

Jennie and Peter Wimmer and their seven children immigrated to
California in 1846 with a party of fourteen families. In June of 1847

Monday 24th this day
some kind of mettle was
was found in the tail race 177
that looks like goald first discov
ered by Jamys Martial, the Bop of the mill.
Sunday 30 clean & has been
all the last week our metal
has been tride and proves to
be Goald it is thought to be
rich we have pict up more than
a hundred dollars woth last
week

February. 1848
Sun 6th the wether has been clean

Henry Bigler's diary documenting date of gold discovery. Jennie Wimmer tested Marshall's find in her soap kettle and pronounced it genuine.

ELEANOR McCLATCHY COLLECTION, CITY OF SACRAMENTO, MUSEUM AND HISTORY DIVISION

Sutter hired Wimmer to oversee a crew of Indians digging the race for his sawmill. With Jennie agreeing to be camp cook and laundress, the Wimmer family moved to the American River.

Six months later, with the mill nearly finished, Marshall found gold, or so he assumed. None of the crew knew what gold in its natural state looked like. A coin someone compared it to looked brighter and whiter. Jennie Wimmer had an idea:

I said, 'This is gold, and I will throw it into my lye kettle . . . and if it is gold, it will be gold when it comes out.' I finished off my soap that day and set it off to cool, and it stayed there till next morning. At the breakfast table one of the work hands raised up his head from eating and said, 'I heard something about gold being discovered, what about it?' . . . I told him it was in my soap kettle. . . . A plank was brought for me to lay my soap onto, and I cut it in chunks, but it was not to be found. At the bottom of the pot was a double handful of potash, which I lifted in my two hands, and there was my gold as bright as could be.

The great rush for gold that inundated California's foothills in 1849 began with the merest trickle in the spring of 1848. Marshall's crew finished the sawmill, using their Sundays to dig for the American River's gold flakes and nuggets. After all, wages from Sutter were steady and the gold might be a mere sprinkle.

Gradually word filtered into San Francisco and Monterey, to general disbelief. Nearly six months elapsed between Marshall's discovery and the stampede on its behalf. It was June 10, 1848, when the *California Star*, after initially pooh-poohing the report, stated:

Every seaport as far south as San Diego, and every interior town, and nearly every rancho from the pass of the mountains in which the gold has been found, to the Mission of San Luis, south, has become suddenly drained of human beings. Americans, Californians, Indians and Sandwich Islanders; men, women, and children, indiscriminately.

On June 20 the Rev. Walter Colton, Monterey's alcalde, wrote in his diary:

The excitement produced [by the discovery] was intense; and many were soon busy in their hasty preparations for a departure to the mines. The family who had kept house for me caught the moving infection. Husband and wife were both packing up; the blacksmith dropped his hammer, the carpenter his plane, the mason his trowel, the farmer his sickle, the baker his loaf, and the tapster his bottle. All were off to the mines, some on horses, some on carts, and some on crutches, and one went in a litter. An American woman, who had recently established a boarding-house here, pulled up stakes, and was off before her lodgers had even time to pay their bills.

When Colton finally sought the mines himself, he found several women gathering gold, among them one who could not stop for idle chatter:

> Monday, Oct. 30. I encountered to-day . . . among the gold-washers, a
> woman from San Jose. She was at work with a large wooden bowl, by
> the side of a stream. I asked her how long she had been there, and
> how much gold she averaged a day. She replied, "Three weeks and an
> ounce."

Letters and newspapers slowly filtered the news eastward, where doubts gradually decreased as testimony mounted. Then, on December 7, 1848, a messenger reached the nation's capital carrying a tea-caddy stuffed with 230 ounces of evidence.

The rush was on.

Most gold rushers were single men, young, unhampered, free to pursue adventure. But, like Nancy Kelsey in 1841, and Jennie Wimmer in 1846, thousands of women decided that where men could go, they could go. Some women came alone, many more with husbands, fathers, brothers. Some came for the gold, to make their "pile." Some came to stay.

How many women participated in the gold rush cannot be known. Like most people, these women lived anonymously, leaving little record of their passing. Yet, surviving letters, diaries, reminiscences, even newspapers and court records, permit a glimpse at the lives of many gold rush women.

The women whose lives contribute to the following pages are but representative of the hundreds more who might be identified. Many women's accounts still reside unnoticed in libraries large and small as well as in historical societies and private collections. Nor have old trunks long lost in dusty attics yet yielded all their treasures.

This then is the story of but a handful of women whose apportioned time encompassed a historic moment. Against an enduring myth that denies their presence, it is a belated acknowledgment of women's participation in the great American adventure that was the California gold rush.

And, finally, through the few, it celebrates the thousands—the women who saw the elephant.

ONE

Over the Plains

*The country was so level that we could see the long trains of
white-topped wagons for many miles . . . it appeared to me that
none of the population had been left behind. . . . And, when
we drew nearer to the vast multitude, and saw them in all
manner of vehicles and conveyances, on horseback and on foot, all
eagerly driving and hurrying forward, I thought, in my
excitement, that if one-tenth of these teams and these people got
ahead of us, there would be nothing left for us in California
worth picking up.* —MARGARET A. FRINK, *Nebraska Territory,
May 20, 1850*

In 1849 some 25,000 people crossed half a continent to look for gold.
They required wagons, horses, mules, oxen, camping supplies, food-
stuffs, clothing. Merchants in "jumping-off" towns along the Missouri River did a land-office business in everything from harness to
bacon. If you sold mules or blankets or kettles in St. Joseph or
Independence that year, you did business you never dreamed of.
And you did well, too, if you sold books—guidebooks to the trail.

A bestseller in 1849 was Joseph Ware's *The Emigrants' Guide to
California*, assuring "every point of information for the emigrant—
including routes, distances, water, grass, timber, crossing of rivers,
passes, altitudes, with a large map of routes, and profile of country
. . . with full directions for testing and assaying gold and other ores."

Among prospective buyers of that list of promises in 1849 was
lawyer Craven Hester, fifty-two, heading west with his wife Martha,
two sons, and daughter Sallie. Newlywed Catherine Haun and her
lawyer husband may have bought a copy for the journey they envi-
sioned as "a romantic wedding tour." So might Luzena and Mason
Wilson or Sarah and Josiah Royce.

In 1850 nearly twice as many overlanders headed west as the year before. The guidebook business boomed, with Franklin Street and Fayette Robinson, among others, offering competing titles. Honeymooners Lucena and George Parsons probably bought one or more; Sarah and Zeno Davis, too, as well as Margaret and Ledyard Frink.

In 1851 emigration dropped to a fraction of the two previous years. None of the guidebooks had prepared travelers for the hardships they wrote home about, discouraging would-be overlanders. Nonetheless, in 1852 another fifty thousand headed west, including the sizable Cooke family, Lodisa Frizzell, Mary Bailey, Angeline Ashley, the Medleys, Eliza McAuley, and Mariett Cummings.

By 1853, although most of the surface gold had been picked up already, families still headed west, many to join members emigrating earlier. Harriet Ward, a grandmother, went west with a husband and daughter to join a gold-rushing son. The Hite and McDaniel families went, too.

Nearly everyone outfitted at the river towns, as the guidebooks advised.

We will leave you to choose your own starting-point, simply stating that Westport, Independence and St. Joseph have facilities peculiar in themselves, for the outfitting of the Emigrant—every requisite for comfort or luxury on the road, can be obtained at either of those places, on nearly as low terms as at St. Louis.—GUIDEBOOK

It took us four days to organize our company of 70 wagons and 120 persons; bring our wagons and animals to the highest possible standard of preparedness; wash our clothes, soak several days' supply of food—and say good bye to civilization at Council Bluffs. Owing to the cheapness of eggs and chickens we reveled in their luxuries, carrying a big supply, ready cooked with us.—*Catherine Haun, 1849*

We got into St. Joseph at 10 o'clock this morning. The whole country around the town is filled with encampments of California emigrants. . . . They have gathered here from the far east and south, to fit out and make final preparations for launching out on the great plains, on the other side of the Missouri River.

Every house of entertainment in the city is crowded to its full capacity. This has been a backward spring season, and thousands are patiently waiting for the grass to grow, as that will be the only feed for their stock, after crossing to the west side and getting into the Indian country.—*Margaret Frink, 1850*

"We enjoy ourselves better as we get used to this way of traveling & living out of doors," wrote Mary Bailey after nearly two months on the trail.
THE BANCROFT LIBRARY

Father & mother went into St. Joseph's bought another tent, heavy canvas for the boys and men to sleep in, using the other tent for an eating place. They also bought a small sheet iron stove, cut a hole in the tent for the pipe, then when it was raining, we could warm up a pot of beans, make a kettle of soup or a pot of coffee, sometimes a pot of mush.—*Mary Hite, age 13½, 1853*

In the evening William got the tent ready for us to occupy, so I took up my abode there. . . . Pa bought it for $10. It is a government tent, second hand, but very strong. . . . This Kanesville is a poor little mean place. I don't think there's a brick house in it. . . . We move out tomorrow (May 6th) and drive to the bottom about ten miles off, where there is a ferry across the river (Missouri).—*Lucy Cooke, 1852*

You now are in the Pawnee country. Watchfulness is required to prevent their stealing your stock.—GUIDEBOOK

I think none of us have realized until now the perils of this undertaking. During the past week not much has been discussed but the Indians and their doings. Printed circulars have been distributed informing the emigrants of many Indian depredations. Now I begin to think that three men, one woman, and one eleven-year old boy, only armed with one gun and one Colt's revolver, are but a small force to defend themselves against many hostile Indian tribes, along a journey of two thousand miles.—*Margaret Frink, 1850*

I had read and heard whole volumes of their bloody deeds, the massacre of harmless white men, torturing helpless women, carrying away captive innocent babes. I felt my children the most precious in the wide world, and I lived in an agony of dread that first night. The Indians were friendly, of course . . . but I, in the most tragi-comic manner, sheltered my babies with my own body, and felt imaginary arrows pierce my flesh a hundred times during the night.

—*Luzena Wilson, 1849*

. . . saw our *first Indian*. We children stayed closer to camp that night, but Father said the Indians were civilized. The Indians were nude save for a throw over one shoulder, & a strap around the loins. The leaders of the tribe would wear a band of feathers around his head—when a young Indian would kill his first bird, it would be tied to his hair and he would wear it for a few days.—*Mary Hite, 1853*

the strangeness of the scene & the wildness of the place, made me conjure up in my mind all the indian massacres of which I had ever read or heard, but . . . my fears were dispelled with the darkness. Seated outside the tent I was amused watching the indians shoot with their bows & arrows for 5 or 10 cts that some men would put up for the purpose of seeing them shoot, or looking at them ride on their ponies in a manner that none but indians can; it is a novel sight to see them. . . .—*Lodisa Frizzell, 1852*

You would be surprised to see me writing so quietly in the wagon alone . . . with a great, wild looking Indian leaning on his elbow on the wagon beside me, but I have not a single fear except that they may frighten the horses.—*Harriet Ward, 1853*

Monday, June 3. In the afternoon we passed an Indian encampment numbering seventy tents. They belonged to the Sioux tribe, but were quite friendly. The squaws were much pleased to see the "white squaw" in our party, as they called me. I had brought a supply of needles and thread, some of which I gave them. We also had some small mirrors in gilt frames, and a number of other trinkets, with which we could buy fish and fresh buffalo, deer, and antelope meat. But money they would not look at.—*Margaret Frink, 1850*

Lodisa Frizzell thought the Sioux the "best looking" Indians she had seen: "tall, strongly made, firm features, light copper color, cleanly in appearance."
THE BANCROFT LIBRARY

Indians came around us in numbers, and begged all the time. Ma gave one old fellow some molasses in a tin cup, he telling her by his signs that he had three papooses. Ma tried to make him understand to bring the cup back, but he failed to do so. Our camp was quite liberal in gifts to the Indians, wishing thereby to keep friendly with them.
—*Lucy Cooke, 1852*

288 miles. FORT KEARNEY.—Good camping place, and good grazing for stock. . . . The Fort is situated near the head of Grand Island.—GUIDEBOOK

All pass through Fort Kearney. We left letter there. It is a military post & quite a stirring place the government built up. The residences of the officers are very fine, some small framed buildings, others built of sod or turf laid up like brick, with windows & doors. . . . We went into the register office & I looked over the names of those who had passed before us. Some 20,000 men, 6,000 women, besides cattle & horses, mules & sheep to almost any amount.—*Mary Bailey, 1852*

The trail across Nebraska Territory was one immense highway jammed with wagons, animals, and people. At Fort Kearny, passed by most emigrants jumping off from Missouri and Iowa, the commandant recorded their numbers, either keeping a subordinate on the road to tally the passing masses or requiring emigrants to report to a clerk their destination, place of origin, number of people and animals in their companies. By July 13, 1852, the Fort Kearny register had recorded 25,855 men, 7,021 women, 8,270 children, 8,483 horses, 5,853 mules, 90,340 cattle, and 2,166 wagons.

You have now been out more than a month, and experienced all the perils and hardships of life on the Plains.—GUIDEBOOK

I think what is often termed suffering is merely a little inconvenience, for I had so often read and heard of the difficulties and dangers of the overland route to California, and I find from experience that the pleasure thus far quite over-balances it all.—*Harriet Ward, 1853*

I do not get tired of the journey, on the contrary, I like it better every day.—*Angeline Ashley, 1852*

When we left St. Joe my mother had to be lifted in and out of our wagons; now she walks a mile or two without stopping, and gets in and out of the wagons as spry as a young girl.—*Sallie Hester, 1849*

Many are no doubt down with sickness, mostly bilious complaints; many with rheumatism, contracted by being in the water much of the time.
—GUIDEBOOK

we camped on the north fork of the plat river and sarah was very sick their was one woman died in the camp of the colera and was buried the next morning when I went to Sarah she was no better and I soon saw she would die and she did die before noon—*Sarah Davis, 1850*

June 23 . . . The boy that was sick died about noon.
June 24 . . . Last evening there was 3 more died out of the same
    family.

June 25 . . . This morning the mother of the 5 children that have died
   was taken sick and died at evening.
June 28 . . . We have some very sick in camp to day. . . .
June 30 . . . Mrs. Crandalls daughter died to day.
July 2 . . . we stopt & buried a girl, daught of Capt. Coon.
                                              —*Lucena Parsons, 1850*

While we were traveling along the Platte River . . . cholera broke out
among the emigrants. Mother was among the first victims. On June 24
at 2 o'clock in the afternoon mother died. . . . I remember every detail
of her death and burial.—*Mary Medley Ackley, 1852*

We again met with the sick woman. . . . She said her husband had just
died of cholera. . . . About an hour after a man rode past us and
informed us that she was almost dead then, and that the men in
whose company she was were stopping to dig her grave, before she
was dead! There's humanity on the Plains!—*Lucy Cooke, 1852*

saw a fresh made grave, a feather bed lying upon it, we afterwards
learned that a man & his wife had both died a few days before, & were
burried together here, they left 2 small children, which were sent back
to St. Joseph by an indian chief.
   . . . it must be expected that from such a number, some would die;
but it is very sad to part with them here. . . .—*Lodisa Frizzell, 1852*

Estimates for trail mortality during the early emigration years range
as high as 6 percent, with cholera the paramount killer. The disease,
of course, was not exclusive to overlanders. In 1849 cholera raged
throughout the States, killing four thousand in St. Louis alone, and
President Zachary Taylor declared a day of prayer against the "fearful
pestilence."

*The trail lies up the south fork of the Platte. . . . There is no fixed crossing
place; it changes frequently during the season; cross where you can.*
                                              —GUIDEBOOK

Have again struck the Platte and followed it until we came to the ferry.
Here we had a great deal of trouble swimming our cattle across,
taking our wagons to pieces, unloading and replacing our traps. A
number of accidents happened here. A lady and four children were
drowned through the carelessness of those in charge of the ferry.
                                              —*Sallie Hester, 1849*

Chimney Rock's composition was so soft, wrote Mary Bailey, "that names that could not be numbered have been left there."

. . . you find a steep hill to ascend and descend; the road is rough, rocky and crooked—half way over, there is a sudden turn in the road that is dangerous, if great care is not used.—GUIDEBOOK

In coming down a steep hill a woman attempted to jump from the wagon with the child in her arms. Her dress caught in the wheel and she was drawn under and crushed to death.—*Eliza McAuley, 1852*

a boy of Lovells . . . fell from the waggon & broke his leg & died soon after. This is the second child that has broke a leg and died soon after. . . .
    a little boy of Captain Maughns, 3 years of age, fell from the wagon. The 2 wheels run over his stomach & he died in about an hour.—*Lucena Parsons, 1850*

524 miles   CHIMNEY ROCK.—From here there are two roads to Scott's Bluffs. . . .—GUIDEBOOK

Came opposite Chimney Rock. . . . It has been seen 30 miles off on a clear day. Three of us went up to it. I was struck with amazement at the grandeur of the scene.—*Lucena Parsons, 1850*

The road we took led us close to the base of Chimney Rock, where we stopped for some time to satisfy our curiosity. The base is shaped like a large cone, from the top of which rises a tall tower or chimney, resembling the chimney of a manufacturing establishment. . . . It is composed of marl and soft sandstone, which is easily worn away. Mr. Frink carved our names upon the chimney, where are hundreds of others.—*Margaret Frink, 1850*

554 miles   SCOTT'S BLUFFS.—This is one of the most delightful places that nature ever formed.—GUIDEBOOK

Passed Bluff Ruins, most beautiful, too. I made a rough draft then I was so charmed that I could not gaze enough. Made our noon halt opposite Scott's Bluff, altogether the most symmetrical in form and the most stupendous in size of any we have yet seen. One of them is close in its resemblance to the dome of the Capitol at Washington.
—*Mariett Cummings, 1852*

604 miles   FORT LARAMIE.—This place is situated in the valley of the Laramie river, on the north side, and about a mile and half above its junction with Platte river.—GUIDEBOOK

At four o'clock we arrived at the place we have so long been anxious to reach,—Fort Laramie. This outpost formerly belonged to the American Fur Company, who built it as a protection against the savages, then very numerous and hostile. After the United States Government bought it, they sent regular troops to protect the emigration.

The fort is one hundred and eighty feet square, having adobe walls fifteen feet high, on the inside of which are rooms built against the walls all around, of the same material. The parade-ground in the center is one hundred and thirty feet square. On top of the wall are wooden palisades. Over the front gateway is a square tower with loopholes for rifles.

As it is not our intention to go by Salt Lake, this is the last human habitation we shall see until we reach Fort Hall, five hundred and thirty miles further on.—*Margaret Frink, 1850*

This morn went to the Fort to get some blacksmithing done but could not they have so much work. This is a very pretty place to look at, it is

Wagon train passing Devil's Gate, painted by William Henry Jackson.
DENVER PUBLIC LIBRARY

so clean. . . . There are 250 soldiers & some 12 families. They have a
saw mill, one publick house, one store. They hold goods high & work
is also high. They offer for carpenter work 60 a month & find them,
& a woman to cook 20 a month. Flour is 18 per hundred & whiskey 8
per gallon in the emigrants store. They are now building severall
fine frame buildings. They say there have 75 thousand pass here this
season & some days there were 1500 here.—*Lucena Parsons, 1850*

At Fort Laramie, emigrants had traversed about one third the distance
between the Missouri River and Sacramento. Most stopped for trading, repairs, and reprovisioning.

Oh, what a treat it does seem to see buildings again. My dear husband
has just been over to the store there to see if he could get anything to
benefit me, and bless him, he returned loaded with good things, for
which he had to pay exorbitantly. He bought two bottles of lemon
syrup for $1.25 each, a can of preserved quinces, chocolate, a box of

seidlitz powders, a big packet of nice candy sticks, just the thing for me to keep in my mouth, and several other goodies. . . . The preserved quinces seemed so grateful to my poor throat, and I took such tiny swallows of them each time, and then hung the can up overhead to the wagon bows.—*Lucy Cooke, 1852*

INDEPENDENCE ROCK is well worthy the attention of the traveler.
—GUIDEBOOK

This rock in shape looks at a distance like a steamboat. There are many names on it both painted & chiselled, many done on July 4, 1850, this year. It is very larg & high composed of gray granite.
—*Lucena Parsons*

DEVILS GATE, five miles above the Rock, is a singular fissure through which the Sweet Water forces its way.—GUIDEBOOK

It is a grand sight! Surely worth the whole distance of travel. The "Sweetwater" rushes through an opening in the rocks, the walls on each side rising several hundred feet perpendicularly, and as though riven in two by some great convulsion of nature. . . . Oh, it was a most wonderful and sublime sight. . . . I bathed dear little Sarah's feet in the rushing waters, and only wish she had been able to realize the grand occasion. . . .—*Lucy Cooke, 1852*

886 miles   SOUTH PASS, distant from Fort Laramie three hundred miles . . . is about nineteen miles in width, without any gorge-like appearance.
—GUIDEBOOK

Ate luncheon on the south pass of the Rocky mountains. Altitude seven thousand, four hundred feet, but the ascent is so gradual, that one scarcely knows when one is at the summit. The headwaters of the streams flowing eastward to the Mississippi and those flowing westward to the Pacific are but a few feet apart.—*Eliza Ann McAuley, 1852*

906 miles   Fork of the Salt Lake and Sublette Routes.—GUIDEBOOK

Took Salt Lake City road. . . . Passed the most magnificent curiosity I have ever seen on the road. It was a stupendous rock of petrified clay and sandstone of blue and light and dark brown color. There were spires and domes, grottoes and caves of every form and size. It was immensely high and colonnaded.—*Mariett Cummings, 1852*

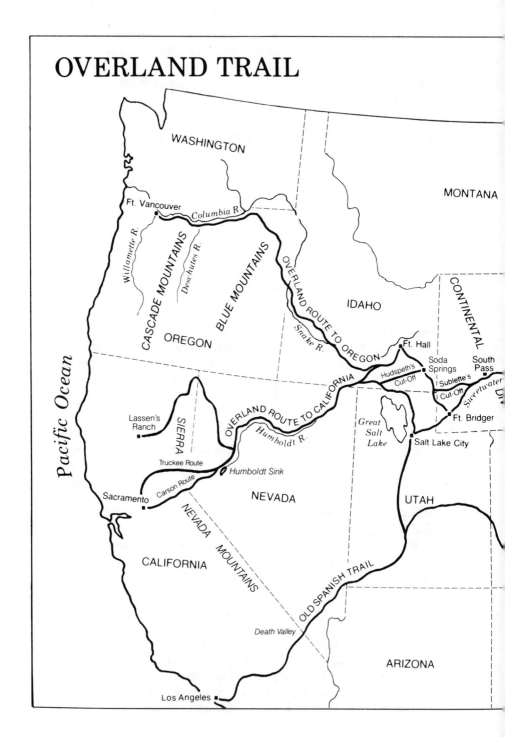

OVERLAND TRAIL

WASHINGTON

MONTANA

Ft. Vancouver

Columbia R.

Willamette R.

Deschutes R.

CASCADE MOUNTAINS

BLUE MOUNTAINS

OVERLAND ROUTE TO OREGON

IDAHO

CONTINENTAL

Snake R.

OREGON

Ft. Hall

Soda Springs

South Pass

Hudspeth's Cut-Off

Sublette's Cut-Off

Sweetwater

Pacific Ocean

Lassen's Ranch

SIERRA

OVERLAND ROUTE TO CALIFORNIA

Humboldt R.

Great Salt Lake

Ft. Bridger

Truckee Route

Humboldt Sink

Salt Lake City

Sacramento

Carson Route

NEVADA

UTAH

NEVADA MOUNTAINS

CALIFORNIA

OLD SPANISH TRAIL

Death Valley

ARIZONA

Los Angeles

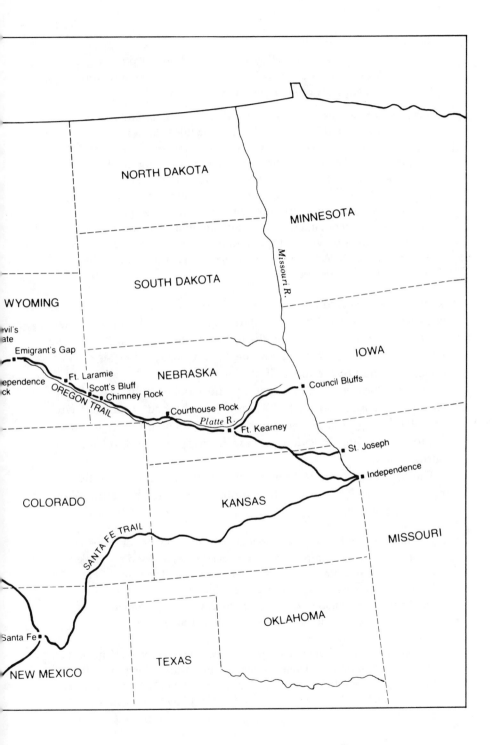

At the bottom of this valley are some very singular rocks. It appears
sublime to me to see these rocks towering one above the other &
lifting their majestick heads here in this solitary spot. Oh, beautifull is
the hand of nature.—*Lucena Parsons, 1850*

It is just four months today since we left our dear home and friends,
perhaps forever, and have since been leading this wild, wandering
gypsy life. Oh, when will the day arrive when we can say this long
journey is over? You may possibly infer from this remark that I am
becoming weary of this mode of life but indeed, my dear children,
were you all with us and our horses fresh it would notwithstanding all
its hardships be to me a perfect pleasure trip. There is so much variety
and excitement about it, and the scenery through which we are constantly passing is so wild and magnificently grand that it elevates the
soul from earth to heaven and causes such an elasticity of mind that
I forget I am old.—*Harriet Ward, 1853*

Despite the spectacular landscape, the journey to California was
exceedingly tiresome. On the western side of the Rockies the Cookes,
like many families, headed south to Salt Lake City. They were "so
tired of being in the crowd," wrote Lucy Cooke to her sister Marianne, "and had only come half our journey."

At the Mormons' wilderness city the Cookes split up. William
Cooke, Sr., continued on to California, for he had contracted with
several passengers and was bound to see them through to Sacramento. The others decided to stay until spring and resume the
journey then.

The Mormon community generally treated emigrants kindly, but
the visitors received an insistent indoctrination to the faith. Wrote
Lucy to her sister:

One day I was out riding with Sissy in an ox wagon with Mr. Roberts,
and he was trying to impress me with his religion, and soon he talked
of the sealing of women to Mormon husbands. . . . The man kept on
in this "convincing" strain as we jogged along the country road,
and finally he magnanimously offered to take me, baby and all, and
have me "sealed" to him and thus have my entrance secured in the
Celestial City. . . .

You can imagine how this proposition was received by me! The old
scamp! With his slipshod gait and lank figure; with his long, unkempt
hair, almost down to his shoulders—a rare prize, he! How William did
laugh when I got home and told him the offer I had from Sydney
Roberts.

Lucy added, "I assure you we hear Mormonism from morn till night." So did her mother-in-law. Sarah Cooke apparently liked what she heard, for in September she joined the church. Her son William refused to attend the ceremony, but Lucy and the rest of the family witnessed the river baptism. Lucy wrote Marianne that "Ma always was a fanatic on religion," and expressed relief that she and William lived outside the city and so were not expected to attend the Mormon meetings.

Meanwhile the elder William Cooke had reached California, writing that he'd obtained good employment as a farm superintendent at seventy-five dollars a month. He sent his wife some sheet music and she, having no piano, took it to Brigham Young's house to try it. Sarah Cooke so impressed the Mormon leader with her talent that he bought a fine English piano for her use in the music hall being built on church property. A theatre opened in December and Sarah Cooke was recruited as both musician and actress.

Lucy confessed that her feelings toward her mother-in-law were not the same "since Ma has joined the Mormons, and also become a stage actress." However, she and William attended the new theatre to see his mother perform in a production of the tragedy, *The Spaniards in Peru*. Lucy, spying her mother-in-law in the scene featuring a tribe of vestal virgins, collapsed in laughter.

For Lucy and William the winter in Salt Lake City otherwise held little humor. William worked at whatever odd jobs he could get, but their table held no luxuries. They rarely ate meat and went weeks without tea or sugar. They lived frugally, selling and trading many of their things for food. William exchanged his coat for four hundred pounds of flour, and Lucy traded her satin dress to get him another coat. At Christmas, when the senior William Cooke in California sent a dollar for each of the family, Lucy spent hers on meat.

The couple, eager to reach California, arranged an early spring start. On March 31, 1853, they departed Salt Lake City, Lucy writing to her sister, "We have met with much kindness among the Mormons, and shall always have reason to speak well of them."

Lucena Parsons did not share Lucy Cooke's opinion or intention. Lucena and her husband passed the winter of 1850–51 with the Mormons, paying five dollars a month, wrote Lucena, for a room "as good as a common hog pen." She apparently had unhappy experiences as a reluctant visitor in Salt Lake City, writing that "a meaner set lives not on this earth than those very people calling themselves

Latter day saints. And I am bold to say that an honest person can not live 6 months with them without saying the same."

She thought them an "unprincipled sect" for their polygamous practices:

> All the preaching & teaching that is heard in this valley is obedience to rulers, & womens rights are trampled under foot. They have not as much liberty as common slaves in the south.
>
> Brigham Young has some 70 women it is said. Heber C. Kimball has 50, Doctor Richards 13, Parley Pratt 30 or 40 . . . & in fact all the men who have but one are looking out for more. If when they have got them they would use them well it would be better but far from it. They fight & quarrel & the women leave one man & go to another. When a woman wishes to leave she goes to Brigham & gets a divorce & marries another & this is the way things are going all the time.

Lucena and her husband left the Mormon community in February 1851, their early start hampered by spring rains and muddy roads.

The Cookes, too, even though starting out near the first of April, forded swollen streams with difficulty. At one crossing the men were forced to wade back and forth in water to their shoulders, drawing emptied wagons to a midpoint where men on the opposite bank waded out to connect chains hitched to oxen on shore. All the goods from six wagons were taken across in a skiff, and the cattle prodded into swimming. The dangerous crossing consumed most of a day, and Lucy wrote Marianne: "Oh, surely we are seeing the elephant, from the tip of his trunk to the end of his tail!"

Not yet.

HUMBOLDT RIVER . . . your course is down its valley for three hundred miles . . . to the "sink." —GUIDEBOOK

> Away from the river, the soil is hard and dry, void of any vegetation except sage-brush. . . . Much of the level land of this valley is barren, from the salt and alkali in it. . . . The dust is intolerable. Many wear silk handkerchiefs over their faces; others wear goggles. It is a strange-looking army.—*Margaret Frink, 1850*

> Many women are on the road with families of children, who have lost their husbands by cholera, and who never will cross the mountains without aids. . . . there are yet twenty thousand [emigrants] back of the Desert. Fifteen thousand of this number are now destitute of all kinds of provisions. . . .
>
> —*William Waldo, relief party, Humboldt River, 1850*

1736 miles   SINK OF HUMBOLDT— . . . From this place to the [Truckee] river the distance is forty miles, and must be performed in one stretch, as there is no grass nor good water on the road. About twenty miles from the opposite edge of the waste, you reach several warm springs. . . .
—GUIDEBOOK

Laid at the sink, sick and weak, until noon, then started into the desert. About twelve at night came to the Boiling Springs, halfway . . . were so sick as to be hardly able to hold up our heads. I have no language to describe our sufferings through that long, tedious night.—*Mariett Cummings, 1852*

These springs boil up with great noise, emitting a very nauseous smell. . . . We hear that a woman and child have got scalded very badly by stepping into one of them.—*Eliza Ann McAuley, 1852*

. . . it was to be an all-night trek. It might well have been named "Death's trail," for as we followed the winding trail through the sage-brush, we saw white bones and carcasses of various animals. . . . About two o'clock in the morning, we came up to a very light cart-wagon drawn by two oxen, both of which were lying down while hitched to the wagon. On a quilt by the side of the cart lay a man, woman and two children. They had completely given out and were sick and starving.—*Henrietta Catherine McDaniel, 1853*

Stopped and cut grass for the cattle and supplied ourselves with water for the desert. Had a trying time crossing. Several of our cattle gave out, and we left one. Our journey through the desert was from Monday, three o'clock in the afternoon, until Thursday morning at sunrise, September 6. The weary journey last night, the mooing of the cattle for water, their exhausted condition, with the cry of "Another ox down," the stopping of the train to unyoke the poor dying brute, to let him follow at will or stop by the wayside and die, and the weary, weary tramp of men and beasts, worn out with heat and famished for water, will never be erased from my memory. Just at dawn, in the distance, we had a glimpse of the Truckee River, and with it the feeling: Saved at last!—*Sallie Hester, 1849*

Of the myriad possibilities for disaster, none surpassed the forty-mile desert. Unlike the surprise of accident or the randomness of disease, this life-threatening barrier loomed before every traveler. Guidebooks described it, and the emigrants dreaded it.

In addition to the Truckee route, another forty-mile desert

SCENE ON THE DESERT.

"We have heard of a great deal of suffering," wrote Mary Bailey, "people being thrown out on the desert to die. . . ."

stretched southwest from the Humboldt sink to the Carson River. The Carson River route provided a slightly easier trail over the mountains than the Truckee. But whether the choice was for the Truckee or the Carson, forty miles of desert intervened.

> It was a forced march over the alkali plain, lasting three days, and we carried with us the water that had to last, for both men and animals, till we reached the other side. The hot earth scorched our feet; the grayish dust hung about us like a cloud, making our eyes red, and tongues parched, and our thousand bruises and scratches smart like burns. The road was lined with the skeletons of the poor beasts who had died in the struggle. . . . Sometimes we found the bones of men bleaching beside their broken-down and abandoned wagons. The buzzards and coyotes, driven away by our presence from their horrible feasting, hovered just out of reach.—*Luzena Wilson, 1849*

Josiah and Sarah Royce, with their two-year-old daughter Mary, lagged among the last forty-niners crossing the desert. To avoid the heat, they traveled at night. In the dark they missed the fork to the meadows with its precious grass to be cut and carried for their animals. Far upon the desert, they realized the mistake. Sarah's recollection never faded:

> So there was nothing to be done but to turn back and try to find the meadows. Turn back! What a chill the words sent through one. *Turn back*, on a journey like that; in which every mile had been gained

by most earnest labor, growing more and more intense, until, of late, it had seemed that the certainty of *advance* with every step, was all that made the next step possible. And now for miles we were to *go back*. In all that long journey no steps ever seemed so heavy, so hard to take, as those with which I turned my back to the sun that afternoon of October 4th, 1849.

By the time overlanders approached these forty-mile deserts, they had plodded and slogged and climbed and descended nearly two thousand miles. Their animals not lost to Indians, thirst, starvation, sickness, accident, or killed to feed the poorly provisioned, were worn and thin.

Yoked oxen pull at about two miles an hour. On the desert, weakened from hunger and thirst, with wagons sinking deep in soft sand, even that slow pace slacked.

Whatever lost its necessity littered the trail's length as emigrants lightened loads too heavy to pull. Starving, thirst-crazed, and frightened for their very lives, emigrants dumped on the death-dealing desert possessions and treasures laboriously hauled for months.

For many weeks we had been accustomed to see property abandoned and animals dead or dying. But those scenes were here doubled and trebled. Horses, mules, and oxen, suffering from heat, thirst, and starvation, staggered along until they fell and died on every rod of the way. Both sides of the road for miles were lined with dead animals and abandoned wagons. Around them were strewed yokes, chains, harness, guns, tools, bedding, clothing, cooking-utensils, and many other articles, in utter confusion. The owners had left everything, except what provisions they could carry on their backs, and hurried on to save themselves. . . . But no one stopped to gaze or help. The living procession marched steadily onward, giving little heed to the destruction going on, in their own anxiety to reach a place of safety. In fact, the situation was so desperate that, in most cases, no one could help another. Each had all he could do to save himself and his animals.—*Margaret Frink, 1850*

Lucy and William Cooke had joined company with a Mr. and Mrs. Holly to cross the desert, with Holly providing three yoke of oxen to pull the heavy wagon William acquired at Salt Lake City. The ordeal of the desert crossing to the Carson River crushed even Lucy Cooke's ready cheerfulness:

We are now over the desert, the forty-mile desert of which we had heard much, consequently we dreaded it. . . . Every one filled their tin canteens with water at the last camping place, but the water was very poor (brackish); but there was no other well. Sis [daughter Sarah] and I went to bed [in the wagon] at dark, as usual, but the men folks were all walking, and expected so to do most of the night. The sand was very deep, and the wagons dragged along slowly. Toward midnight it began to rain, and the oxen showed signs of exhaustion, and what little water we carried was given to those most in need. Mr. Holly began to fear our wagon, which was the largest and heaviest in the crowd, could not be hauled any farther, and that some change must be made or he would get stuck on the desert. A consultation was held, and William came and awoke me, telling me that I would have to get out and go in one of the other wagons, as Holly would haul ours no farther. I was just all broken up at this bad news, for our roomy wagon had been our pride and comfort. But as we had given it to Holly in part payment for our passage, it was his, and he must do as suited him best. So I bundled up myself and baby, and the men gathered up the bedding and . . . I tumbled in anywhere. No more good bed for us, but just a chance to exist in among the pork barrels and all the dirt of men's old clothes. . . . Perhaps I did not cry, but I think I did.

1912 miles FOOT OF THE FIRST RIDGE OF THE SIERRA NEVADA.—
You now commence ascending the mountains . . . most of the way extremely
steep.—GUIDEBOOK

This is the way it was managed: A dozen yoke of oxen were hitched to one wagon, and with hard pulling they reached the top. After all the wagons were over, we took lunch on the top of the mountains, and then prepared to go down, which was more dangerous than going up, for in places the mountain was very steep. One yoke of oxen was hitched to a wagon, and one at a time went down. Heavy chains were fastened on behind the wagon and as many men as could catch hold of the chains did so, and when the wagon started they pulled back to keep the wagon from running down the mountain and killing the oxen. We were an exhausted community when we camped that night—the women and children as well as the men—for we had to walk all the way. I must pay tribute to our wheel oxen, Dick and Berry, who drew the family wagon all the way across the plains. They were gentle, kind, patient and reliable. I loved them and my heart often ached for them when they tried to hold back the wagon on a steep hill, and sometimes the wagon would strike them in spite of the driver's carefulness, and the dumb animals gave no signs of distress, although I knew they suffered.—*Mary Medley Ackley, 1852*

Most overland emigrants on the California Trail kept to the tried-and-true Carson and Truckee routes, but every rumor of a faster, easier way found an ear anxious to believe. At the Humboldt especially, with the dreaded prospect of the desert crossing ahead and the high mountains beyond, even wary travelers considered a convincingly proposed alternative.

In 1849 more than seven thousand of them succumbed to the temptation. Either through argument or the example of the wagon ahead, much of the tail end of that year's migration turned off for Peter Lassen's ranch. They succeeded only in exchanging one desert for another, while *adding* two hundred desperate and dangerous miles to their journey—traveling north nearly to the Oregon border.

Catherine Haun's party took that cutoff:

The alkali dust of this territory was suffocating, irritating our throats and clouds of it often blinded us. The mirages tantalized us; the water was unfit to drink or to use in any way; animals often perished or were so overcome by heat and exhaustion that they had to be abandoned, or in case of human hunger, the poor jaded creatures were killed and eaten. . . . One of our dogs was so emaciated and exhausted that we were obliged to leave him on this desert and it was said that the train following us used him for food.

Catherine Haun baked bread for their horses, giving "half a loaf each day to each horse until the flour gave out." J. Goldsborough Bruff, mistaking the family name as Horn, observed her:

Mrs Horn kindly gave me a slice of fried pork fat, and a cup of Coffee, so I made a very hearty meal: rested 15 minutes, and rode back, to the bluff, to see to the company; leaving Mrs Horn very busy baking a number of large loaves of bread, to serve out to the horses & oxen. . . .

Bruff, organizer and president of the Washington City and California Mining Association, had kept his company together as far as the rough going of the Lassen route. When the company's mules gave

out, Bruff volunteered to stay with the wagons while the men continued, packing on their backs what they could carry. By camping on
the trail, Bruff added, through his journal, sorrowful confirmation of
the hardship of the great rush of 1849.

One sad instance occurred near his camp on the Lassen road when
a storm-weakened oak tree fell on the tent of a man, his two grown
sons, and one of their friends, crushing them. The four died agonized
by their injuries, the distraught wife and mother and her daughters
"constantly going from one to the other, looking in their faces,
parting their hair, and sobbing."

Bruff also added to his voluminous journal the grim spectacle of
the remnant migration in its luckless trek past his camp. On October
25, 1849, he wrote:

> It is a queer sight now, to observe the straggling emigrants coming up
> and going in. Wagons of every kind, oxen, horses, mules, bulls,
> cows, and people—men, women, & children, all packed.

On the 26th a company with "about 16 women and 20–odd children"
camped nearby. In the following weeks he recorded the passing
before his camp of numerous emigrant families, specifically noting
about seventy women and ninety children, including ten infants.
Among them was the St. Louis Company, with twenty-five women
and children.

In three weeks on this route one government relief party rendered
aid to "not less than one hundred and fifty families."

To avoid the crowded California Trail, approximately nine thousand
forty-niners followed the southern road to California opened by the
Mormon Battalion for the war with Mexico.

Although shorter than the Oregon-California route, this trail
through present-day New Mexico and Arizona was considered more
perilous. It was Apache territory.

Nevertheless, Dr. John Strentzel and his family joined this road
from northwest Texas and followed it to California practically without
incident. Louisiana Strentzel, in a letter dated December 10, 1849,
wrote from San Diego that Apaches periodically raided a Mexican
village about a hundred miles east of Tucson, but she added no
mention of seeing them.

J. Goldsborough Bruff sketched these Lassen route stragglers of 1849.

Even without Apache harrassment, the trip was a hardship. For the Strentzels it consumed eight months because of the scanty feed for their animals and the frequent need to rest them:

> We found that the only way to get through was to travel slowly in the cool of the day, save the animals as much as possible and stop at every little grass we could find. . . . The dust was almost insufferable; it was generally from six to twelve inches deep. It was almost impossible for our wagons to travel nearer than fifty yards to another.

On this route, too, desert barred the way. Louisiana wrote that they crossed thirty-seven miles "without water or grass, the whole way a heavy bed of sand."

One advantage for travelers on this trail, though, was a general absence of disease. Louisiana reported:

> As far as I can learn the emigrants have been remarkably healthy on the road and comparatively few deaths. A great many would have suffered for provisions but the Government sent aid to them. We hear no certain account from those who went the Northern paths. . . . The doctor has [not] been sick a day since we left . . . and looks better than you have ever seen him. I have never enjoyed better health in my life than I have done since last May. Little Pussy [two-year-old daughter

Louise] and Johnny [an infant son] have not been sick an hour . . .
they both look red and rosey and have grown so they cannot wear a
garment that was made for them when we left home.

Less fortunate was the James M. White family. In the fall of 1849
Apaches attacked the Independence merchant at present-day New
Mexico's Point of Rocks. They killed White and his teamsters and
carried away his wife and young daughter. Kit Carson and a military
search party pursued the raiders, overtaking the Indians' camp only
to find Mrs. White's body.

The incident grimly presaged the famous Oatman massacre.

Royce Oatman and his family headed for California from Iowa on
May 8, 1850, in company with Ira Thompson and his family. At
Independence the Oatmans and Thompsons joined several other
families, forming a train of some thirty wagons and about a hundred
people.

Ira Thompson's daughter Susan enjoyed the first fun-filled weeks
of travel:

> We were a happy, carefree, lot of young people and the dangers and
> hardships found no resting place on our shoulders. It was a continu-
> ous picnic and excitement was plentiful . . .
>
> In the evenings we gathered about the campfires and played games
> or told stories or danced . . . so many evenings gave out the strains of
> 'Money Musk' and 'Zipp Coon' as the young folks danced in the light
> of the campfire and the lard-burning lanterns. Often during the day-
> time halts, we ran races or made swings. There was plenty of frolic. . . .

But the long months of travel soon depleted their animals' strength.
The train separated as families moved ahead or stayed behind to rest
and recruit their stock. Seven families, the Oatmans and Thompsons
among them, followed a new trail lightly blazed by soldiers from near
present-day Las Vegas, New Mexico. Susan Thompson Parrish recorded their misfortunes:

> From here to Tucson, Arizona, we suffered for bread. Captain Oatman
> allowed each person but a biscuit and a half per day. We tried to eat
> hawks and I recall how sick my mother was when she attempted to
> drink some soup made from coyote meat.

After more than seven months on the trail, the party reached Tucson.
The Thompsons and three other families halted several weeks to

replenish, but the Oatmans, Wilders, and Kelleys continued. At Pima Village, Mrs. Wilder bore a child and the Wilders and Kelleys decided to remain there a week. Ignoring advice to stay, Royce Oatman and his family started for Yuma alone.

Susan Thompson had the dreadful story from survivor Lorenzo Oatman:

> . . . near the Gila River, they reached a hill up which it was impossible to draw the loaded wagons.
> While the loads were being carried up the hill . . . Mrs. Oatman was seized with the pains of childbirth. During the anxiety for her comfort, no one noticed the approach of seventeen Apache braves who seated themselves in a circle about the frightened little family. From right to left each brave addressed the Chief, who in turn responded. So, on around the grim circle until the Chief himself was reached. Quick as thought came a terrible war-cry and the Chief struck Mrs. Oatman on the head. As Lorenzo, a boy of fourteen, sprang to his mother's assistance, it flashed through his mind like a ghastly joke, that the Indians were beating his sister Lucy with gigantic wooden potato mashers and then with the quick slash of a knife in his scalp and the spurting of hot blood, his mind went into darkness.

Consciousness returned the next morning and the boy walked three days back on the trail, finding Mr. Wilder and the Kelley brothers. Following Lorenzo's directions, the men discovered the tragic scene. They buried beneath a stone cairn the mutilated bodies of Royce Oatman, his wife, new-born infant, two daughters, and five-year-old son.

Two other daughters, Olive, twelve, and Mary Ann, seven, were missing. The captors later sold the girls to Mohaves, and Mary Ann died in their village. Americans ransomed Olive Oatman at Fort Yuma in 1856.

Another trail into southern California commenced from Salt Lake City. Hundreds of emigrants, to avoid the Sierra Nevada, headed south from the Mormon outpost, crossing the Mojave Desert to the village of Los Angeles.

The Pratt family took this trail and twenty-year-old Sarah noted in her diary the desert's beautiful flowers. The road's most notable travelers, however, left no record of pleasant observations. These people, among them four women and their children, suffered thirst, hunger, and despair in an environment unequaled for hostility to sojourners. These were the first non-native people to see the region.

They named it Death Valley.

In October 1849 more than a hundred wagons and three hundred people left a camp south of Salt Lake City. They formed the Sand Walking Company (possibly the "San Joaquin Company") under the leadership of Jefferson Hunt, a Mormon Battalion captain familiar with the Old Spanish Trail to Los Angeles.

When a passing pack train shared a map purportedly showing a cutoff from this trail, the specter of shortcut danced before emigrants' eyes. The temptation was too much for Methodist minister James Welsh Brier. A journal-keeper noted that Brier "took the opportunity to fire the minds of the people with a zeal for the cutoff." Several emigrants hounded Hunt to take it, but the guide refused, saying, prophetically, they would "get into the jaws of hell."

Wisely, most of the train stayed with him, but on November 4, 1849, some twenty-seven wagons, including those carrying four families, forged ahead into the unknown of the vast and desolate desert they would name Death Valley.

Thirty-four men, mostly young and mostly from Illinois, calling themselves Jayhawkers, entered the desert valley. Four died there. The Reverend James Brier, his wife Juliette, and their three young sons followed the Jayhawkers in a desperate search for a way out. When one young man suggested that Juliette and her children remain behind and let them send back for her, she adamantly refused:

> I knew what was in his mind. "No," I said, "I have never been a hindrance, I have never kept the company waiting, neither have my children, and every step I take will be toward California." Give up! I knew what that meant; a shallow grave in the sand.

Juliette, age thirty-five, earned the Jayhawkers' great respect and affection. One of them reported that in walking nearly a hundred miles through sand and sharp-edged rocks she frequently carried one of her children on her back, another in her arms, and held the third by the hand. Jayhawkers called her a heroine for caring for the sick among their company. Her own recollection was modest:

> Did I nurse the sick? Ah, there was little of that to do. I always did what I could for the poor fellows, but that wasn't much. When one

grew sick he just lay down, weary like, and his life went out. It was nature giving up. Poor souls!

Caring for her own family consumed most of Juliette's strength and determination. In a two-day period without water her oldest boy, Kirk, suffered terribly:

> The child would murmur occasionally, "Oh, father, where's the water." His pitiful, delerious wails were worse to hear than the killing thirst. It was terrible. I seem to see it all over again. I staggered and struggled wearily behind with the other two boys and the oxen. The little fellows bore up bravely and hardly complained, though they could barely talk, so dry and swollen were their lips and tongue. John would try to cheer up his brother Kirk by telling him of the wonderful water we would find and all the good things we could get to eat. Every step I expected to sink down and die.

Toward the end of the nightmare journey Juliette had to help her husband rise each morning. He reportedly lost a hundred pounds by the ordeal's end.

The Bennett, Arcan, and Wade families fared poorly, too. They banded together and finally camped at a spring, which they called Long Camp, fearing to continue.

Harry Wade was forty-eight, at one time a coachman to England's royal family. His wife, Mary, in royal service, too, had been a governess. They came to America in 1835 with their infant son Harry George and, in April of 1849, with three more children, left Missouri for California's goldfields.

The Arcans, Jean Baptiste and Abigail Harriett, had a three-year-old son. Asabel and Sarah Bennett had three children, ages eight, five, and one.

With the Bennetts were two young men hired as teamsters in Salt Lake City, John Rogers and William Lewis Manly. After weeks of scouting and wandering, Manly and Rogers told the families that the two of them would find a way out and return for the others.

The Wades, apparently believing the young men foolish to return if they could escape the desert, set out by themselves. Through extraordinary good fortune, nine-year-old Almira found water on the journey, crucial to their survival. They kept south out of the valley, eventually intersecting the Old Spanish Trail.

Amazingly, Manly and Rogers did return. Suffering that awful

Juliette Brier and family, forty-niner survivors of Death Valley.

journey once, with nothing to eat but fear, should have been enough for any man. They heroically endured it twice more, trudging back for the stranded families, not knowing whether they had stayed or died, and then leading them to safety.

The group walked out, 125 miles. After twenty-two days, eating six of their eleven emaciated oxen, they all reached safety. Concluding his story of the trek, Manly wrote:

Many accounts have been given to the world as to the origin of the name [Death Valley] and by whom it was thus first designated but ours were the first visible footsteps, and we the party which named it the saddest and most dreadful name that came to us first from its memories.

The Brier family, with much suffering, reached safety on February 12, 1850. The Wade family celebrated deliverance on February 10. The Bennett and Arcan families escaped the valley of death on March 7– more than *four* months after their fateful decision to take the cutoff.

The Wades settled in Alviso, at the southern edge of San Francisco Bay. The Briers eventually made a home in Marysville. The Bennett family went to the coast at Moss Landing, and the Arcans to Santa Cruz. Captivated by the beauty of the redwoods at Santa Cruz, Abigail Arcan announced to her husband:

You can go to the mines if you want to. I have seen all the God-forsaken country I am going to see, for I am going to stay right here as long as I live.

And she did.

TWO

ACROSS THE SEA

*I like my Voyage very much so
far and anticipate a great deal
of pleasure yet to come   i
have seen some things that i
never could at home.*
—MARY ANN ELLIOTT,
Rio de Janeiro, January 1850

Canvas sails, not canvas wagon covers, marked the path of the earliest gold rushers. Overlanders, forced to wait for the first spring grass for forage, rarely rolled out of Missouri's teeming trailhead towns before mid-April or the first of May. Ships, however, departed Atlantic ports almost daily from the moment President Polk confirmed that California's "mines are more extensive and valuable than was anticipated."

By January of 1849, gold rushers had sailed from New York, Baltimore, Boston, New Bedford, Philadelphia, New Orleans, and Galveston aboard no fewer than ninety vessels. By the end of the month, seventy more had posted sailing dates.

The traditional trading route around the Horn offered the tried-and-true passage to the Pacific, though no less dangerous or tiresome than the overland crossing. The voyage consumed from five to seven months, often with poor provisions, and faced the battering storms of Cape Horn.

Elizabeth Gunn was forty years old in 1851 when she and her four children sailed around the Horn aboard the *Bengal* to join forty-niner Lewis Gunn. They were six months upon the sea. Letters to her mother and sisters in Philadelphia detail the travails of the great stretch of time to fill and the distress of narrow confinements for four active young children. And then there were the storms:

A gale commenced on Tuesday at noon and lasted till Friday, and we were tossed about in fine order. We could neither stand nor sit and of course must lie down. . . . We could not go to the table. The children sat against the side of the cabin, and held their plates in their laps, and half the time one would spill his water or lose his spoon. . . . I went to the table once, and my tumbler turned over, and rolled down and upset the salt, and cavorted against a plate, and was at last caught by the steward. You can't keep hold of your things—they will move off. And you can no more walk . . . than you can fly. Down, down you slide till you land against the wall, and there you are fast at last and must try it over again.

Equally trying was the ship's slow progress up the Pacific side of South America. "I am quite downhearted at the slow way of getting on," wrote Mrs. Gunn. "The Captain says we shall be five years getting to California at this rate; it makes him cross."

When at long last the *Bengal* put in at Valparaiso, Chile, for wood and water, the captain brought a newspaper aboard. In it Elizabeth read about three ships carrying bituminous coal which had burned. "A lady writes the account," she wrote home, "she was on board each one of the vessels!"

Were it not for such corroboration, Mrs. D. B. Bates might be suspected of telling tall tales in the book in which she recorded her adventures.

She sailed from Baltimore on July 27, 1850, aboard the *Nonantum*, bound for San Francisco with a cargo of coal. Her husband was its captain.

The first storm hit the *Nonantum* with a ferocity that forced Mrs. Bates to keep to her berth "to prevent being dashed against the cabin walls." She remained there three days, ignorant of the real danger: the cargo of coal had caught fire. Sailors closed the hatches and caulked the seams to try to contain it, while Captain Bates set course for the nearest land, the Falkland Islands, eight hundred miles distant.

Mrs. Bates learned the "sad truth" when gas and smoke invaded her cabin. To avoid suffocating, she spent five drenching days and nights in a chair lashed to the deck:

If possible, the nights exceeded in anxiety the days; impenetrable darkness surrounded us, relieved only by sheets of white foam dashing over the bows, as the doomed ship madly plunged into the angry waters. When one sea more powerful than another would strike her, causing her to tremble in every timber, I would grasp my chair, shut my eyes, and think we were fast being engulfed in the sea. Oh, those nights of agony! Never, through all the vicissitudes of after life, will one thought, one feeling, then endured, fade from the volume of memory.

After scuttling the ship at the Falklands the Bateses accepted passage on the *Humayoon*, out of Dundee and bound for Valparaiso with a cargo of tar, liquors—and coal. Twelve days out found them "eighty miles from land, and, horror of horrors," recalled Mrs. Bates, "the ship on fire!"

Unlike the coal aboard the long-smoldering *Nonantum*, the *Humayoon*'s cargo burst into flames. Escaping in the ship's long-boat, crew and passengers watched her burn. Then, like something out of a dime novel, a passing ship, the *Symmetry*, rescued them. She was bound for Acapulco with a cargo of—coal. Her captain confessed himself too poorly provisioned to keep his unscheduled passengers and at the first opportunity saw them aboard another passing ship, the *Fanchon*, out of Baltimore and bound for San Francisco with *coal*.

Three days after Mrs. Bates insisted she smelled the gas of burning coal, the *Fanchon*'s captain discovered his cargo smoldering. Three frightening weeks later they made the coast of Peru where the scuttled ship burst into flames.

The thrice-rescued Bateses eventually reached San Francisco on a steamer they boarded in Panama.

Argonauts who took the direct route to Panama—across the Isthmus—endured travel adventures almost as harrowing as the Bateses'.

San Francisco customhouse reports by 1851, the year Mrs. Gunn and the Bateses arrived, revealed a steady favoring of the faster Isthmus route, despite its dangers. In 1851 San Francisco's sea arrivals totaled 27,202, with 15,464 via the Isthmus. Customhouse statistics for the previous year counted 11,770 arrivals via Cape Horn, with 13,809 choosing the Isthmus. Only in 1849 did those transiting the Horn outnumber Isthmus travelers, with 15,597 opting for the long sea voyage while 6,489 took the shortcut.

Seated behind a sawhorse equipped with reins, lady passengers on a voyage to California remedy seasickness by pretending the ship's motion is only the swaying of a horse carriage.

Among intrepid travelers crossing the Isthmus in 1849 was Mary Jane Megquier, Jennie to her friends.

Dr. and Mrs. Thomas Megquier, married eighteen years, had left with relatives in Maine their three children. Although Jennie suspected that it would be lain to her neglect should any thing come upon her children to "blast" their happiness, she nonetheless excitedly anticipated "some fine times crossing the Isthmus." Forty-niner Margaret De Witt echoed the expectations:

> I think if it is not too warm, it will be fine fun—sailing and riding the Donkeys—. Most of the conversation for the last few days has been about the Isthmus—and I really think some of the gentlemen dread it worse, than Mrs. Allen and myself.

The De Witts, Allens, and Megquiers were, like all passengers, unceremoniously discharged on the Atlantic side at Chagres, to get across the Isthmus to Panama City as best they could. Most travelers hurriedly engaged native transport and commenced the crossing at once.

Those passing a few hours or a night at Chagres found little to see. The only attraction was an old castle at the harbor's entrance, which Jennie Megquier admired for its moat, and "a high wall on which you can see the guns peeping at you. . . ." The Americans all rushed to see it, and she thought its one inhabitant, a Negro caretaker, would get rich charging sightseers admission.

Mrs. Megquier estimated Chagres village residents at about six hundred. She thought them a "simple inoffensive people" but believed that they "understand perfectly the getting of the dimes from Americans."

The villagers lived in bamboo huts. Travelers descending upon Chagres's Astor House and Crescent City Hotel discovered, despite the high-sounding names, bamboo huts with floors. Sojourners could get a meal of monkey or iguana at them, but most wayfarers, like Jennie Megquier, had not "appetite . . . quite sharp enough to relish those yet."

Accommodations were equally unattractive. Mary Ballou, who crossed the Isthmus late in 1851, wrote her sons Selden and Augustus, left behind in New Hampshire, an unhappy description of her Chagres "hotel." It was topped by a cloth "but no floor but the ground for my bed a valiece for my pillow a hard bed indeed. I wept biterly. there were twenty five in our company all Laid on the ground. the monkies were howling the Nighthawks were singing the Natives were watching."

Such accommodations at least compelled Lucilla Brown to some-what relax her sense of propriety.

Lucilla and Ezekiel Brown left New York late in 1849 on the *Empire City*. The ship, noted Mrs. Brown, carried seven "females." She intentionally did not call them "*ladies*," she wrote, "for all do not deserve the name."

Among those acceptable to her were pioneer John Sutter's family, journeying to join the husband and father after fifteen years' separa-tion. Since they were Swiss, Mrs. Brown could converse little with them, although she noted that daughter Eliza spoke a little English and was "a frank, warm-hearted girl. . . ."

To Lucilla Brown, the Sutter family's acceptability far exceeded that of most of the remaining women passengers:

> There is a Mrs. Brayner, an upholsterer by trade, going on to meet her husband in San Francisco. A Miss Scott, about fifty years old, going independent and alone, to speculate in California—of course, no very agreeable person. Then there is a Mrs. Taylor, whose husband left her some two years ago—is said to have a father in California, whither she purports to be bound. She is young and has some pretentions to beauty, and at first commanded sympathy and attention from the gentlemen; but they all left her except the keeper of the hotel at Chagres, a low fellow, who retains her at his lodgings there, and it is to be hoped she will proceed no further.

It was the lodgings at Chagres that lowered Lucilla Brown's standards of decorum. The discovery that men and women shared a room forced revisions on her sense of propriety. " 'Tis true," she wrote, "Mr. S., Gen. Henan, and some half dozen other gentlemen were to occupy the same apartment, but waiving delicacy on that point, we had a comfortable night's rest, felt refreshed and in good condition to commence our journey across the Isthmus."

That journey commenced with the Chagres River. Travelers' choices were native transportation aboard dugout canoes, *bungos*, single mohogany logs from fifteen to twenty-five feet long, or small, overcrowded steamboats that chugged a few miles upriver where passengers transferred to the mile-per-hour canoes. The trip between Chagres and the interior villages of Cruces and Gorgona, where travelers hired mules for the final distance to Panama City, usually consumed two to three days.

On the Megquiers' 1849 Isthmus crossing the small steamer *Orus* took them about sixteen miles upriver from Chagres, the extent of navigable river. There passengers transferred to canoes, the Megquiers obtaining transport in a two-foot-wide, twenty-foot bungo, seated on their carpet bags. Despite a broiling sun sending humid temperatures near a hundred degrees, Jennie Megquier drank in the exotic scene. The dense jungle foliage, the bright flowers, singing birds, "monkeys alligators and other animals" utterly captivated her.

At five o'clock the travelers stopped at a village where the Megquiers took supper cooked by natives. Jennie thought "it was rich to see us eating soup with our fingers, as knives, forks, spoons tables, chairs are among the things unknown. . . ." Crowding around her feet, waiting to catch the least crumb, were pigs, dogs, cats, ducks, and chickens.

Since Mrs. Megquier was the only woman in the party, the natives offered her their hut for the night. Jennie accepted, but because "a white lady was such a rare sight they were coming in to see me until we found we could get no sleep. . . ." Mrs. Megquier, who could endure almost anything and enjoy it, spent the remainder of the night in the open air.

Accommodations along the river rarely favored the self-indulgent. Lucilla Brown, on her first night crossing the Isthmus, slept in a canoe. The second night, halfway to Gorgona, the Browns shared a room with fellow passengers from the *Empire City*, an occasion that again offended Mrs. Brown's sense of decorum:

> We met with Mr. Stevens, General Henan, and many more of our
> fellow passengers, among them Miss Scott. The three named occupy a
> room with ourselves. We occupy our cots as usual; the others lie side
> by side on the ground, not a hand's breadth between Miss Scott and
> General H. It provoked me to see any female so devoid of modesty.
> Miss Scott ought to have placed her bed differently, but I am not the
> one to dictate.

Like Mrs. Brown, many gold-rushing journalists noted the presence of single women bound for California, but few observers detached themselves from societal expectations to remark the adventurous spirits such women possessed. The *Alta California,* however, in its issue of January 21, 1850, described one:

> *Metamorphose Extraordinary.*—The barque Eliza Ann, recently arrived here from Panama, landed an individual whose sex would certainly never have been satisfactorily ascertained from outward appearance. Presenting him or her, at Panama, our subject secured a passage hither and embarked. So completely was the lady (as she soon confessed herself to be) disguised, that discovery might have been easily evaded, but with the independence generally conceded the sex she boldly and *practically* proclaimed the right to "wear the breeches," by donning a pair of most unexceptionable ones, as also all the appropriate trimmings. "Charley," as our heroine was speedily christened, took up her quarters with the crew, with whom she speedily became quite a favorite, and displaying a formidable brace of pistols and dazzling bowie knife, defied insult, declaring it to be her "holy mission" to pursue and demolish a traitorous escort, who had robbed and deserted her at New Orleans. Charley's conduct on board was quite unexceptionable—to-day perusing her well-worn Bible, and to-morrow as aptly conducting a part in a game of old sledge. No sooner had the news of the barque's arrival reached the city, than a small boat might have been descried nearing her, and he who had sworn to preserve was locked in the embrace of her who had sworn to slay! The past was forgotten, and the boat conveyed the reunited pair to the shore, where doubtless ere this drafts have been made upon some of our merchants to enable the hero of the Eliza Ann to sail under true colors.

Also remarking a woman traveling the Isthmus alone was J. Goldsborough Bruff. Bruff, an overlander returning east via the Isthmus in 1851, was, like Lucilla Brown, taken aback both by Isthmian accommodations and women unperturbed by them:

> On awakening, and sitting up in my cot, I was astonished to see a young woman sitting up also in the next cot to me, and fastening the back of her dress; while all around were upwards of a hundred men perhaps, in every stage of rising and dressing. My evident astonishment compelled me to observe to her, that I thought it a very unpleasant predicament for a young lady to be placed in, and she replied that it was; but she had become accustomed to such inconveniences, having crossed the Isthmus several times!

Like Bruff's unnamed lady traveler, Annie Walton remained unruf-
fled by Isthmian accommodations. "We all slept in one room on
separate cots," she wrote breezily, "and we all *undressed*."

Mrs. Walton, crossing the Isthmus early in 1850 with her husband
and three young children, was another hardy female traveler having
the time of her life, even though their crossing was not without its
perils. Their boat got snagged in the rapids and started taking on
water. Mrs. Walton was frightened until she discovered the water
was not even three feet deep. Natives carried the women and children
to shore, the men hauled in the boat and mended it, and the party
was off in half an hour "good as new." Mrs. Walton wrote her sister
after the crossing that she never enjoyed anything better in her life.

Even oft-affronted Lucilla Brown thoroughly enjoyed the river trip.
The Browns' canoe was well covered and she sat comfortably without
a hat, able, she noted, to read, write, or do anything she chose.
Gliding up the Chagres River, which she thought beautiful, she
found the scenery "full of exciting interest." The luxuriant jungle,
with "flowers, birds of gay plumage flying hither and thither, the
chattering of monkeys, the scream of parrots," presented a novel and
fascinating scene. "I am," she wrote, "perfectly delighted."

Jennie Megquier was even more effusive: "Would to God I could
describe the scene. The birds singing monkeys screeching the Americans laughing and joking the natives grunting as they pushed us
along through the rapids was enough to drive one mad with delight."

While many women obviously enjoyed their travel adventure, men
frequently expressed surprise at the aplomb with which women met
the journey's discomforts. German-born Charles Grunsky, member
of a small, California-bound cooperative association, journeyed in the
same party as one Mrs. Angier, an uneducated woman never before
out of Alabama. She was with her husband and three small children,
the youngest just thirteen months.

Grunsky wrote admiringly to his wife Clotilde that he was greatly
astonished by Mrs. Angier's continuing fortitude: "She never seemed
afraid, although she never in her life had seen anything of the kind."

On the Chagres River the party had two small boats, which they
rowed themselves. The current was swift, they were constantly going
aground, and the work exhausted them. Stopping to rest on the
riverbank, one of the party crossed a narrow neck of land and
discovered the river flowing in the opposite direction. All agreed that
the river obviously formed a big bend just beyond them and came

Wrote Jennie Megquier of her Chagres River journey: "The birds singing monkeys screeching the Americans laughing and joking the natives grunting as they pushed us along through the rapids was enough to drive one mad with delight."

back on this other side. They decided to leave the heavy baggage with Mrs. Angier and her children while they negotiated the boats around the bend, which would ease her travel and their labor. They planned to pick up Mrs. Angier, the children, and the baggage, they presumed, in about an hour.

This plan severely tested Mrs. Angier's notable fortitude. The river did not form "a big bend" here at all. The men mistook the opposite bank for upriver when it was, in fact, a downriver point already passed.

Hours elapsed before the increasingly worried men discovered the true geography from an American familiar with the region. Grunsky remained with one boat while the rest immediately started back. Soon rain fell, then darkness. Grunsky, alone, imagined Mrs. Angier's feelings. He thought it almost unbelievable that a woman in the jungle with three children should not be frightened nearly to death. She had waited hour after hour for her husband, with not even bread for her children.

Fortunately, upriver travelers assisted Mrs. Angier. Good samaritans shared food with the worried woman and her children, and several people remained until her husband's return.

Despite this undoubtedly trying experience, Mrs. Angier and her children, Grunsky later discovered, were "all happy and feeling fine."

A far less happy Isthmus traveler was Jessie Benton Frémont. She was the wife of John C. Frémont, the famed Pathfinder, a national hero court-martialed for his role in California's conquest. She was also the daughter of Missouri Senator Thomas Hart Benton, an outspoken western expansionist.

Although Jessie Frémont was noted for her keen mind, love of learning, and spirited self-assertion, she had no heart for Panama's rigors. In fairness, she left the East not with the bright prospects of Jennie Megquier but exceedingly low spirits. She had recently lost a child; her beloved father had intended traveling with her and then could not; her favorite and familiar servant, Harriet, failed to accompany her at the last moment. Her husband, despite the president's pardon of the court martial, had resigned his position with the army and privately organized his latest expedition. He supposedly was crossing the Rockies when she departed the East, and she bore the added concern of not knowing how he fared.

The Frémonts planned to meet in California, where they expected to settle. It was to be a new beginning for the beleaguered couple. But even as Jessie sailed from New York on March 13, 1849, her husband lay weak at the Taos home of his friend Kit Carson, recuperating from his latest and worst disaster, his failed assault on the Rockies. Jessie would learn of it at Panama City.

Meanwhile, Mrs. Frémont, despite her reluctant journey, enjoyed the advantage of influential connections. William H. Aspinwall, co-owner of the Pacific Mail Steamship Company, whose steamers transported most argonauts from Panama to California, was a close family friend. Aspinwall had personally arranged for Mrs. Frémont's comfort and security on the crossing, putting the small company steamer at her disposal and securing a personal escort to accompany her.

Jessie Frémont, in the expression of the day was a "lady," and far more familiar with Washington parties than hardship. Panama's raw poverty and rough country appalled her. At Chagres, "if it had not been for pure shame and unwillingness that my father should think badly of me, I would have returned to New York on the steamer. . . ."

She persevered, acknowledging her advantages over other Isthmus travelers who "had to take the dugout canoes, with their crews of naked, screaming, barbarous negroes and Indians," while she had Aspinwall's company whale-boat and a responsible crew.

Other travelers slept on the ground or in Indian huts, but Jessie Frémont's entourage provided her a tent with "clean linen cots." At Gorgona she was guest of the village alcalde for breakfast. She was grateful for a caution that prevented her showing horror at the sight of the chief dish, a baked monkey. Even so, she thought it "looked like a little child that had been burned to death."

At this village of Gorgona, Jennie Megquier was less affronted by the sight of baked monkey than by the village church, which she thought "not as respectable as the meanest barn." It was overrun with domestic animals during services, and a mule, she wrote, took "the liberty to depart this life within its walls while we were there, which was looked upon by the natives of no consequence."

From the villages of Gorgona and Cruces, travelers commenced the most difficult part of the Isthmus crossing. The remaining distance to Panama City was traversed on foot, upon the back of a mule or clutching its tail, or carried in a hammock over what Jennie Megquier understandably described as "one of the roughest roads in the world, nothing but a path wide enough for the feet of the mule, which if he should make a misstep you would go to parts unknown. . . ."

Even the most adventurous women travelers quailed at the idea of clinging to a mule's back over the treacherous trail. And those with no liking for the journey cowered at the prospect.

When Mary Ballou, who had shed tears upon her ground-level bed at Chagres, encountered the mule path, she wept anew and wished for wings to fly home. A hot sun blazed down upon her as "part the way I walked Part the way I rode and part the way I Laught and part the way I wept."

Jessie Frémont met the challenge with misread bravado. She was provided by Aspinwall's influence with a fine mule and a solicitous guide. Her escort was delighted that she "was neither ill nor tired, nor in any way broken down by the unusualness of the whole thing." He judged, she wrote, by appearances: "As there were no complaints or tears or visible breakdown, he gave me credit for high courage, while the fact was that the whole thing was so like a nightmare that one took it as a bad dream—in helpless silence."

Lucilla Brown's concern with improprieties was quickly diverted by this infamous muleback route to Panama City. Twice, while descending the deep ravines cut into the rock hardly wide enough for a mule's foot, her mount fell. Both times her husband foresaw the danger and caught her.

In 1853, when Emeline Day crossed the Isthmus to join her husband in California's goldfields, the mule route remained without discernible improvement:

A description of the road bearing any resemblance to the reality is beyond any feeble powers to give. The road consists of a narrow trace, in many places only wide enough for one packed mule to pass at a time. . . . It has been traveled over by mules until they have worn a track in the earth so deep that the . . . level was far above our heads, and the track in the earth so narrow that we could touch each bank with our hands as we sat on our mules. In other places they had worn steps in the solid rock six inches deep in which they stepped as regularly and with as much ease apparently as they would pass over a level road. In places the track down the mountains look like regularly cut stairs and are as perpendicular. Up and down these mountains we rode our mules safely and with great ease. . . . For many miles together we traveled where one false step would have precipitated us down over steep and craggy rocks to a distance several hundred feet where no human being could hope to escape alive.

These hazards were known to Mallie Stafford's husband, who traveled from California to fetch her. He insisted she wear a pair of boys' calfskin boots for the mule journey. His experience also secured for her a "fine large gray mule" for the trip. Appreciating her own good mount, Mrs. Stafford's sympathies went to "a bulky lady, as she towered over her thin little donkey."

Thin donkey or stout, "there was nothing for it," Mallie wrote, "but to cling on with all the strength I possessed." Nearing the first descent, her mule paused briefly and then to her astonishment, "he carefully placed his feet together in a little niche worn in the rock and giving a spring like a dog, we were down altogether and safe. It gave us a terrible shaking up though. . . ."

She wondered how the timid ladies and the fat people on the thin little donkeys stood the fearful leap.

Mrs. Stafford's calfskin boots probably eased some of the journey's discomfort. For this rugged crossing women often donned men's clothing. Probably the first women to do so were the wives of the Rev. O. C. Wheeler, a Baptist missionary, and a Mr. Whitney. After natives murdered two men in their party, Wheeler urged haste and persuaded the women to wear trousers and "ride as I do." The two women, after entertaining the entire population of a Panamanian village with the novelty of their costumes, rode astride more than ten hours before arriving triumphantly at Panama City.

Another witness of women in men's clothes was newspaper correspondent Bayard Taylor. He noted that "some ladies, who had ridden over from Cruces in male attire . . . were obliged to sport their jackets and pantaloons several days before receiving their dresses."

The observant Taylor also reported that a "lady from Maine, who made the journey alone, was obliged to ford a torrent of water above her waist, with a native on each side, to prevent her from being carried away," and that a "French lady who crossed was washed from her mule, and only got over by the united exertions of seven men."

The obvious difficulty of the journey compelled suspension of normal reserve. Women did not then ride astride; modesty and fashion dictated the side-saddle. While some women were shocked by the expectation they assume the alternative position, others enjoyed the rarity of the experience and embraced this additional novelty with delight. One woman recalled there was "great frolicking and laughing with the ladies while fixing away on the mules. . . . I shall never forget *my* feelings when I found myself seated astride my mule, arrayed in boots and pants, with my feet firmly planted in the stirrups, ready for any emergency."

Echoing this woman's apparent pleasure in the experience was happy Annie Walton, who wrote of the Isthmus to her family, "Dear brother and sister, never dread the journey. It is only a pleasant excursion."

Annie Walton undoubtedly shared Jennie Megquier's appraisal of the experience. Wrote Jennie, "If we were rich, I should not grudge the expense at all if we did not make one cent, to see what we have seen. . . ."

The last stop on the Isthmus before continuing to California was Panama City. Most travelers found the walled city a colorful and interesting sight, despite decaying stone buildings and church bells lacking tongues. "It is all the same to them," wrote Jennie Megquier, "they take a stone and hammer away."

Like Mrs. Megquier and every other traveler descending upon Panama City in 1849, Jessie Frémont found herself amid a mad crush of gold rushers. They numbered some two thousand when she arrived, all waiting the return of the steamship *California* from San Francisco.

The *California*, one of four steamers owned by the Pacific Mail Steamship Company intended for mail service on the Pacific coast, was the first Aspinwall steamer to arrive at Panama City in 1849. Captain Cleaveland Forbes, who brought her around the Horn, had departed New York before Eastern newspapers predicted California's gold in the hundreds of millions of dollars. Consequently, the unsuspecting captain first encountered gold fever at Callao. There he only nominally stemmed a Peruvian rush for berths. His commitment was to take no passengers until Panama City.

When he arrived at Panama he found, to his dismay, an estimated fifteen hundred impatient gold rushers expecting passage to San Francisco aboard his ship. The frantic clamor for space on a vessel with accommodations for a hundred threatened violence. Forbes finally departed Panama with four hundred passengers wedged aboard, some paying a thousand dollars for the uncomfortable privilege.

Thirteen women made this historic maiden voyage initiating steamship service between Panama and San Francisco. Among them was Jane McDougal, wife of John McDougal, who would serve as California's governor from 1851 to 1852.

Mrs. McDougal was also among the women *returning* with Captain Forbes on the *California*'s first sailing *from* San Francisco. Her diary of that journey mentions other women passengers on the famed steamer's first return: Mrs. Bowdin, Mrs. Grimes, Mrs. Ogden, and Mrs. Smith. Possibly they were the women Jennie Megquier encountered in Panama when she wrote: "Some women that have gone [to

California] are coming home because they can get no servants to wait on them."

Jessie Frémont would also complain about the absence of servants when she reached California, but she arrived at Panama too late to be among the *California*'s first passengers. After reaching Panama City, she waited seven weeks for steamer passage. The delay, however, had its "very pleasant aspects."

This fine lady with influential connections was accorded the "reality of Spanish hospitality." She was not forced to camp in the hills or rent a room in a wretched hotel. She was an honored guest in the home of an elderly lady. She enjoyed the familiar ritual of visits received and returned. She took "delightful walks on the ramparts in the cool of the day just before sundown." She dined with the ladies of native or foreign consular families.

These pleasures abruptly ended with a letter from her husband. In it he detailed the disasters of his ill-starred fourth expedition. Jessie collapsed. She was "entirely unable to understand anything said" to her. From all her "uncertainties and discomforts, aided by the climate" she succumbed to a raging fever.

When she recovered, she seriously considered returning to the States. At the last moment she decided for California and departed aboard Aspinwall's *Panama* on May 18, 1849.

The Megquiers also waited long weeks for their steamer connection to San Francisco. To vary the dull routine the couple visited the nearby island of Taboga. There they boarded at what Jennie called "one of the best houses on the island," sleeping in hammocks or on the floor and killing two scorpions in their room. As usual, she met all her new experiences cheerfully:

> Another insect which is rather troublesome, gets into your feet and lays its eggs. The Dr. and I have them in our toes—did not find it out until they had deposited their eggs in large quantities; the natives dug them out and put on the ashes of tobacco—nothing unpleasant in it, only the idea of having jiggers in your toes.

Even a snake in a mango grove failed to alarm her:

> One of the party shot him; he measured nine feet, about as large as my arm a little above the wrist. In the course of the day, another came

down the tree very near us, but of a different species, not so large, which was very soon dispatched. The gentlemen took them to the village, to show what big things they had done.

On May 23, more than two months after their arrival at Chagres, the Megquiers finally left Panama aboard the *Oregon*, arriving in San Francisco on June 17, 1849.

Unlike the lengthy wait endured by Jessie Frémont and the Megquiers, later travelers often made the entire journey from the East to San Francisco in just thirty days. The completion of the Panama Railway considerably shortened the passage.

In 1854, when Mallie Stafford crossed the Isthmus, she found the railway crowded with "nine hundred passengers—more or less," and a picturesque assemblage it was:

> There was the Frenchwoman, with her poodle; . . . the old maid, with her bird-cage; the Dutch woman, with her four children, *and* her pair of twins in her arms. . . .

When Sarah Brooks crossed the Isthmus with her daughter Lena in 1852, the route already boasted an initial nine miles of railway from Chagres. Conditions remained rough, however, with no depot or waiting room yet constructed and seats frequently oversold. At the railway's terminus passengers transferred to a riverboat, a "flat-bottomed affair, with a seat which ran all round the inner edge" and a "wide board, which served as a sort of promenade . . . for the boatmen."

Mrs. Brooks could not know how much an improvement this "flat-bottomed affair" was over the bungos patronized by earlier adventurers, even though the boatmen still remained impassive to travelers' demands for speed, or even decorum:

> When our boatmen discarded their small amount of clothing the female portion of our company sought the seclusion of their umbrellas, whereupon the gentlemen commanded the boatmen to resume their garments. A stormy scene ensued. . . . They were an ugly set, and were constantly inventing excuses for tying up at every hut that promised a drink or a snooze. . . .

Whether by rail or bungo, once at Panama City, everyone encountered the final indignity of the boarding procedure for steamers.

Passengers, wrote Martha Morgan, "had to be lifted from the shore to the boats," since Panama had no wharves. Ships anchored in the harbor were reached by rowboats, and the rowboats were reached by wading. Those who didn't wade, were carried. Mrs. Morgan observed that "some of the ladies were very much opposed to being carried in this manner; they had to do it, however, and consequently submitted."

The absence of a wharf at Panama City had perplexed Sarah Brooks. She saw ships moored at a distance, but couldn't figure out how passengers reached them. The procedure took her by surprise:

> All at once, without a word of warning, I was grabbed from behind. One black arm was around my waist, another under my knees, and I was lifted up and carried straight out into the water. I wanted to scream. . . .

The adventure of crossing the Isthmus—river, mule, even the swoop from shore to ship—was matched on an alternate Central American crossing: the Nicaragua route.

Charles Grunsky, who had so admired the plucky Mrs. Angier when he crossed the Isthmus with her, returned eastward to fetch his wife Clotilde. Perhaps, despite Mrs. Angier's fortitude, he thought the Isthmus route too difficult. In any event, he chose Nicaragua for Clotilde.

By 1853 approximately three thousand travelers a month crossed Central America via Nicaragua. Despite the transit company's neglect of their customers' comfort and health, the route was popular because it was easier.

From the Atlantic side small steamboats carried passengers some seventy-five miles up the San Juan River to Lake Nicaragua. Larger steamboats crossed the lake, approximately another seventy-five miles. From there travelers rode mules the final thirteen miles or so to the Pacific. Although the distance from ocean to ocean was more than twice that of the Isthmus, the land portion via mule was shorter and less hazardous.

The Grunskys crossed in April 1852. Clotilde found river travel in a tropical country "extremely interesting," noting that she saw "crocodiles, monkeys and a great many parrots." She complained, however, of the crowded steamers and the inconvenience of transferring baggage from one steamer to the next. She especially disliked the portage past unnavigable rapids.

When the riverboat encountered rapids, passengers were put ashore to walk two miles through the dense forest. This inconvenient excursion took about two hours, as Mrs. Grunsky recalled, since the trail crossed several creeks, puddles, and other obstructions. It was, she wrote, a "great annoyance, particularly for a woman."

After the Grunskys crossed Lake Nicaragua, dusk fell by the time everyone had a horse or mule for the remaining overland journey to the Pacific. Wrote Clotilde Grunsky:

> The forest became dark, the trail more uneven, sometimes steep up and sometimes steep down. In the forest there appeared almost as many stars as in the heavens, because all about there were numerous fireflies. The humming of insects and the calling of the monkeys, although loud enough, were sometimes lost in the yelping of wolves. Even a tiger was heard.

A year after Clotilde Grunsky heard what may be presumed a jaguar, Mary Durant traveled the Nicaragua route to join her husband in California. In a letter to her cousins, personal pride tempered her complaint of the cramped and crowded river steamers:

> Two nights and two whole days we were in that pack in the small boat! No danger of any one's getting far out of proper place—we were a community too compactly put together for such mistakes. "How did you sleep those two nights?", I imagine you will inquire;—well—most of us took our rest more in the perpendicular than horizontal position. Miss Douglas and myself made out to keep our sitting on a hard board seat—not, however, without having to take many an upbraiding as well as a plenty of elbowings from envious and ill-humored bystanders—all of which we endured with becoming fortitude and equanimity.

The San Juan River, however, she thought one of the prettiest she'd ever seen, and with other passengers gathered "curiosities." Among these were "thick green leaves six feet in length" which some passengers used for umbrellas.

Although Mrs. Durant considered Lake Nicaragua beautiful beyond her ability to describe, she nonetheless tried. The sun was setting "gloriously in the West, the full moon rising in the East," she wrote, while "islands and distant mountains enriched the landscape. A more charming view of natural scenery could scarcely be imagined."

Her rapture suggests she was one of the women who enjoyed frontier travel. She found the crossing of Lake Nicaragua, with the full moon shining brightly, "delightful." Upon docking, her escort procured her a mule but, to her dismay, found no available side-saddle:

> Hereupon I ordered the very best man's saddle to be put upon the beast . . . the animal appeared decked with the most hideous-looking saddle, with two great wooden stirrups. . . . To demur at this style of equipage would be of no use. . . . So after requiring one stirrup to be made a comfortable degree shorter, I mounted my steed sideway, and in this way I went the whole distance (and carried an umbrella raised over my head to protect me from the hot sun) - in a little more than 3-½ hours. . . .

In this picturesque fashion Mrs. Durant arrived at the Pacific, not once toppling from her perch. Pleased with herself, she wrote that some of the "ladies fell from their mules—one more than once." But, she added, "the fun was not quite over yet."

The fun was in getting aboard the waiting ships. Like Panama, Nicaragua's port lacked a wharf. Natives carried passengers through the surf to rowboats which took them to steamers. Mary Durant accomplished this maneuver with philosophic composure:

> Each passenger was carried in the arms or on the back of a brawny Mexican . . . through water half a foot, I should think, higher than his hips! I had the honor to be borne by *two* such bearers, for I would not trust the strength of one alone.
>
> They made what the children call a *chair*, by crossing hands and wrists and then stooped down for me to be seated. I was afraid they would assume the prerogative of the Baptist Minister and give me *"immersion"* in the Pacific Ocean! But they were faithful to the trust committed to them, and I was borne in safety to the boat without even the skirts of my garments being dipped in water. It was a most amusing scene I do assure you—

Mary Durant arrived safely in San Francisco to commence a new life with husband Henry, founder of California's university at Berkeley.

Another gold rusher's wife crossing Nicaragua was Mary Crocker. Unlike Mrs. Durant, who traveled with a woman friend, Mary Crocker's husband escorted her. Even so, she complained about everything. The boats were "old & oh so dirty"; the weather so "*hot*, we could hardly breathe." She complained about insects: "The mosquitoes and flies and bugs biting, biting all the time. Some of the ladies looked as if they had the smallpox or some kind of spotted distemper."

And more:

> The water was *dreadful poor* too. I did not have a good drink from the time I left N.Y. until we reached San Francisco, nor did I relish a single meal. . . . The water . . . which we were obliged to drink all the time was the very poorest kind. We called it "Alligator Soup". . . .
>
> Everything I saw there was new & strange, particularly the *naked* natives, this we soon became accustomed to as also many other unpleasant things.

Given this multitude of endured inconveniences and indignities, Mrs. Crocker concluded—although others might have argued her vision—that she had "quite a near, if not a full view of the 'California Elephant.' "

At last arriving in San Francisco, however, she was pleased. Mary Crocker liked the city "very much":

> I saw a larger variety of the richest things of all kinds than I ever did before. Beautiful embroideries, silks & satins, carving in ivory, paintings by the Chinese, work boxes, fans in fact everything that is made by that ingenious people. I saw splendid jewelry, too, one Pin for $2,000, one for $800, another for $600, Diamond bracelets, pins & rings, that is a grand place for a person to go who does not know how to dispose of his money.

Mrs. Crocker unknowingly forecast her own gilded future. Her husband's name was Charles. He and three friends would build a railroad.

Meanwhile, the Megquiers, who had crossed the Isthmus to California in 1849 and eastward in 1851, returned to California via Nicaragua in 1852, Jennie complaining of her husband that the trip "has taken the jingle all out of him."

Mary Jane Megquier, second from right, Isthmus forty-niner, from a daguerreotype about 1833.

In 1854, amidst problems arising from illness, finances, and domestic incompatibility, the couple independently went east again. In 1855 Mrs. Megquier, who apparently left her heart in San Francisco, returned to California without her husband. She came again via Nicaragua.

More than the rigors of the Nicaragua route were needed to take the jingle out of her. As usual, this adventurous lady managed to have "any amount of fun," despite numerous discomforts. A woman who hadn't much minded "the idea of having jiggers in your toes" on Taboga, required more than the Nicaragua route could throw at her before flinching.

This fun-loving pioneer woman dined on wormy bread she spread generously with aplomb, and bedded down with rats and spiders beneath a large blanket of good humor. From Nicaragua she wrote with characteristic breeziness:

> We spent three days very pleasantly although all were nearly starved
> for the want of wholesome food but you know my stomach is not
> lined with pink satin, the bristles on the pork, the weavels in the rice
> and worms in the bread did not start me at all, but grew fat upon it
> all. Emily, Miss Bartlett and myself had a small room with scarce light
> enough to see the rats and spiders. . . .

The Isthmus and Nicaragua were good training grounds for keeping a sense of humor intact, an advantageous temperament in California.

THREE

HOME SWEET HOME

This place is not so different from home after all. The green
foothills are just as friendly, and the sky just as blue. . . . As
soon as we got into a house again, with our things around us, we
felt at home. . . . People all lived in tents . . . before there were
houses. I liked it, especially on warm nights when I could lie and
look at the stars. They seemed just above the treetops, and heaven
as near us here as at home. —ANNE SMITH, *Coulterville,*
California, 1853

Louisa Smith was thirty years old when marriage to Fayette Clapp, five years her junior, rescued her from the ranks of New England's spinsters. Small, fair, and frail, Mrs. Clapp attended as much to her headaches as to her literary inclinations. Studious as a child and self-consciously cultivated as an adult, she equaled, if not surpassed, the intellectual interests of her similarly well-educated husband.

Fayette Clapp studied theology two years at Princeton before enrolling at Brown University where he matriculated in 1848. Then young Clapp, perhaps because of a continuing attentiveness to his own health, turned to medicine, attending medical lectures and apprenticing with his physician brother-in-law.

Few couples seemed less suited to California's rigors than these upper-class New Englanders, ailing Louisa and inexperienced Fayette. That Louisa, in particular, might adapt to, and even prefer, the rough, rude West suggests how underestimated has been women's acceptance and enjoyment of frontier experiences.

But Louisa, despite her self-appraisal as "a shivering, frail, home-loving little thistle," had a passion for wandering and an impractical husband equally restless for adventure. It was 1849 and California's gold rush beckoned. No family or friends could dissuade them.

"When I make up my *mind* to it," wrote Mrs. Clapp, "I can be as wilful as the gentlest of my sex."

They sailed for California in 1849. When the ship *Manilla* deposited them in San Francisco, they must have been appalled.

In 1849 San Francisco, although California's largest and most favored city, boasted few comforts. Streets, far from being paved with gold, had, excepting litter and discards, no paving at all. Thoroughfares, winter-muddy and summer-dusty, swarmed with men of divers nations, conducting frantically their boomtown business in a cacophony of languages. Impeding the wayfarer's progress up harborside avenues were disgorged cargos of everything from fine wines and tinned oysters to flour barrels and tobacco bales. Many of these expensively transported goods of the world, for want of warehouse space, served as street paving.

Equally unattractive were travelers' accommodations. Expensive, makeshift lodging houses and hotels, hurriedly constructed from planks and canvas, offered uncomfortable, narrow bunks with more or less privacy, depending on rates. Guests typically supplied their own bedding.

No record survives of where the Clapps lodged, but they probably found their quarters both expensive and primitive. Even the best hotels provided only the rudest shelter, as Sarah Royce discovered.

In January 1850 the Royces took a room at San Francisco's Montgomery House. A single window lighted the hotel's small, uncarpeted sitting room furnished with one table and a few chairs. A length of calico partitioned it from the dining room. A saloon with a box-stove, Sarah discovered, was "the only place for a fire in the whole house, excepting the cook stove."

Upstairs, a hall extended the length of the building. On each side, cloth partitions framed narrow doorways to the hotel's "rooms." These rooms Sarah Royce described as "a space two and a half feet wide and six feet long, at the farther end of which was a shelf or stand, on which you could place a candlestick, while you had just room to stand and dress or undress. At the side of this space were two berths, one above the other; and these berths, so situated, were the only sleeping accommodations afforded by this hotel."

Mrs. Royce did not comment on the hotel's ceilings, but Sarah Walsworth, a missionary's wife arriving in 1851, wrote in astonishment: "Oh! you can have no conception of what a Cal. *"Hotel"* is . . .

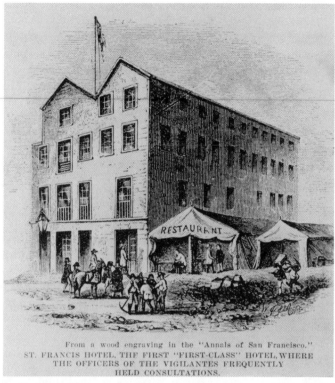

St. Francis Hotel, 1849–1853—despite paper walls and canvas restaurant, a luxurious hostelry acclaimed as San Francisco's first hotel providing sheets on its beds.

---

the cloth ceiling with the least breath of air goes capering & "skating" about, over your head & it is a mere chance if the rats do not too."

Even the finest accommodations had canvas ceilings and walls, as one female guest at the St. Francis Hotel discovered to her surprise. The hotel was grand, its elegant diningroom tables glittering with glass and silver and its epicurean menu featuring Charlotte Russe. The lady found her bed "delightful." With "two soft hair mattresses under, and a pile of snowy blankets over" her, she was soon asleep. But not for long.

> I was suddenly awakened by voices, as I thought, in my room; but which I soon discovered came from two gentlemen, one on each side of me, who were talking to each other from their own rooms *through*

mine; which, as the walls were only of canvas and paper, they could easily do. This was rather a startling discovery, and I at once began to cough, to give them notice of my *interposition*, lest I should become an unwilling auditor of matters not intended for my ear. The conversation ceased, but before I was able to compose myself to sleep again . . . a nasal serenade commenced, which, sometimes a duet and sometimes a solo, frightened sleep from my eyes. . . .

The price for this privilege fluctuated, with lodging-house bunks costing from six to twenty dollars a week and hotel rooms from twenty-five to two hundred and fifty dollars a week.

Given the limited comforts and high costs of rented sleeping space, many emigrants camped in tents on the city's hillsides. For women forced to such circumstances, good humor and a sporting sense of adventure was invaluable. On August 1, 1849, one such woman wrote a letter to a Mrs. Sophia Wiggins in New York. Signed simply Maria, its eighty-four rhyming lines appeared in the *Alta California* on January 9, 1850. Among them:

> My Dear Sophia—
>
> . . . .
> On tenter-hooks long I had been
> To see this dear, new, golden city,
> But after it came to be seen
> 'Twas a city of *tents*, what a pity!
>
> . . . .
> The houses were very few here,
> I know you'll wish to ask "why?"
> John says it's because *lumber's* dear,
> I myself know that *board* is quite high.
> Why a bed was *three dollars a night*,
> And neither of down nor of roses,
>
> . . . .
> John has just bought us a *tent*—
> It's the only thing, *now*, he can do;
> And on being *con-tent-ed* I'm bent—
> Tis the best way, I think, do not you?
> The prices of every thing here
> Are a hundred times dearer than home,
> And yet, pray believe me, my dear,
> We still are not sorry we come.
>
> . . . .

But John says for him it will do,
And in one year he'll make me a lady.

. . . .

He says he can buy some *lots* cheap,
Off of which he can make *lots of money;*
A rich harvest I hope he may reap.

. . . .

But Sophy, there's times when I so lonesome feel,
As I think of the dear friends behind me,
That sometimes an hour I'll steal
And *cry* till my tears almost blind me.

. . . .

Oh, dear—I'm—be—ginning to—cry,
Pray forget not your dear-friend Maria.
John tells me—my—tears—to—dry,
Or the people will think I'm *town crier*.
Farewell, then, dear Sophy, farewell—
(It seems as if I should expire)
Pray—write me and tell—me—you're well;
   And believe me your—faith—ful

MARIA

Despite occasional "squatting," emigrants were not free to pitch their tents where they chose. San Francisco's land was not free for the taking. In 1847 Jasper O'Farrell surveyed lots for the city, and most of them had sold by the middle of 1849. Speculation and demand kept prices high even for property remote from the business section; even prior to the rush of 1849, San Francisco lots on good corners brought ten thousand dollars.

Inadequate and overpriced housing must have confronted Louisa and Fayette Clapp, as it did every emigrant. Possibly the Clapps stayed aboard the *Manilla* for some time, for few ships left San Francisco after anchoring. Since owners and crews often abandoned their ships to pursue new opportunities, some emigrants arriving by sea continued to sleep aboard.

Many women remained weeks and months aboard the ships in which they came, often quite comfortably. John McCrackan, an observant young lawyer from New Haven, Connecticut, believed "more than half the ladies of San Francisco live upon the water." On a day when McCrackan dined aboard the *Balance*, the ship on which

"More than half the ladies of San Francisco live upon the water," observed lawyer John McCrackan. This 1851 forest of masts was captured in the earliest known photograph of the city.

---

he'd sailed round the Horn, a Mrs. Smith, who lived aboard a nearby vessel, sent over "a lump of nice fresh butter made but a few hours and that too by her own hands, from the cream of pure milk furnished by her cow, which she still retains having brought her from the states, and I assure you a good cow, for a Lady living in the Bay, is one of the most expensive & greatest luxuries one could ask."

Mrs. Smith also enjoyed the luxury of a servant girl she'd brought with her, as well as a "beautifully fitted up" ship. Her cabin, McCrackan wrote, was "inlaid with—rose wood, her state room large and convenient and indeed the whole vessel in perfect order."

Another shipboard resident was Anne Booth. She arrived with her husband at San Francisco on September 21, 1849, "to dig gold." Learning the unhappy news that "a very small room brings $100 a month," Anne remained aboard the *Andalusia*, her uncle's merchant ship, while her husband sought a suitable alternative. Buying a lot and building a house was so costly that she was unwilling for her husband "to incur the expense, unless we can have one or two spare rooms for the purpose of accommodating a few boarders; so that I can contribute my quota towards accumulating something."

After more than a month of residing upon the water she was "ready and anxious to embark in almost anything that may be profitable." Yet, like rhyming Maria, she was not sorry she came. Her diary entries suggest no regrets for her decision to join California's gold rush:

> I have not for a single moment . . . felt the slightest wavering in my resolution to remain here a few years; and by active exertion, try what kind Fortune may do for us . . . it is true, there are many disadvantages and privations attending life in California; but these I came prepared to encounter, and by no means expected to find the comforts and refinements of home. . . .

Like many redoubtable women emigrants, Anne Booth willingly accommodated discomfort and inconvenience. Expressing her determined adaptability, she wrote: "I know of no single circumstance calculated to annoy or trouble us with which we were not already acquainted; while on the other hand, there are many causes to encourage and induce us still to persevere in this undertaking. . . ."

The Booths eventually paid three hundred dollars for a lot on which they built a house with lumber scavenged from the *Andalusia*'s staterooms. For a roof they used the ship's "mizzen top gallant sail stretched over the boards and painted," making the canvas "impervious to rain." After two months' residence on the bay, Anne Booth closed her journal and moved into her new California home.

No description survives of Louisa Clapp's first California home, although it is known that she and her husband lived more than a year in San Francisco after arriving. The city's often damp and windy weather apparently disagreed with Fayette, for he ailed "an entire year," wrote his irritated wife, "with fever and ague, bilious, remittant, and intermittent fevers—this delightful list, varied by an occasional attack of jaundice."

In June of 1851, seeking a climate more favorable, Fayette departed San Francisco for the interior. He chose the mining settlement of Rich Bar after hearing it had but one physician for the thousand residents intent on extracting riches from the Feather River's north fork.

There Fayette Clapp's health almost miraculously improved, and he soon wrote for Louisa to join him.

The prospect "perfectly enchanted" her. Her San Francisco friends, however, undoubtedly as cultivated and refined as she, were horrified. Despite a "universal shout of disapprobation," she decided to go. She was, after all, as she described herself, "an obstinate little personage, who has always been haunted with a passionate desire to do every thing which people said she could *not* do."

Among protestants was one lady who "declared in a burst of outraged modesty," wrote Louisa to her sister, "that it was absolutely indelicate, to think of living in such a large population of men; where at the most there were but two or three women. I laughed merrily at their mournful prognostications, and started gaily for . . . Rich Bar."

That letter, the first of twenty-three written to her sister from the mines, she signed "Dame Shirley."

Sarah Royce's son, California-born philosopher and historian Josiah Royce, declared those letters "the best account of an early mining camp that is known to me." First published serially in 1854 and as a collection in 1933, the Shirley letters are acknowledged by enthusiasts and authorities alike as among the most important contributions to gold rush literature.

A vibrancy and spontaneity fill the letters with the vitality of life in the mines. Exuberance for her experience overwhelmed Mrs. Clapp's penchant for the stilted and literary phrase; she uncharacteristically wrote charmingly direct and wonderfully detailed descriptions of all she saw—scenery, people, events—and her own home.

It was a log cabin, and the first women in the mining districts would have envied her for it.

The earliest women at a mining camp rarely encountered comfortable accommodations even as rough as Mrs. Clapp's. For these women the cramped conditions of life in tents and wagons often overshadowed any pleasures afforded by novelty.

Mrs. John Berry's residence in the northern mines preceded Louisa Clapp's by two years. She, her husband, and children arrived there October 10, 1849, and camped the entire winter. For companionship Mrs. Berry had "one female . . . she happens to be located next tent to me."

With no snug cabin for shelter, Mrs. Berry endured a "very disagreeable" winter:

The rains set in early in November, and continued with little interruption until the latter part of March and here were we poor souls living almost out of doors. Sometimes of a morning I would come out of the wagon (that is & has been our bedroom ever since we left the States) & find the tent blown down the shed under which I cooked blown over & my utensils lying in all directions, fire out & it pouring down as tho' the clouds had burst. Sometimes I would scold & fret, other times endure it in mute agony and again amid all the war of the elements feel a consolation in thinking I had all my family around me. Comfortless as it was they were bearing it with me—better that by far than luxury with one member of it missing.

Louisa Clapp believed, as did Mrs. Berry and thousands of other wives, that accompanying her husband to the mines was preferable to being left behind, whatever the discomfort. And like most emigrant women, Mrs. Clapp readily adapted to her rustic log cabin. As Harriet Ward, a fifty-year-old grandmother, observed of her log home: "Living in such a house does not make half the difference with one's happiness you would imagine."

Even so, Louisa Clapp's home at Indian Bar, near Rich Bar, was a far departure from her New England, or even her San Francisco, experience. Dame Shirley's cabin still enchants those who tour it with her:

Enter my dear; you are perfectly welcome; besides, we could not keep you out if we would, as there is not even a latch on the canvas door. . . .

The room into which we have just entered is about twenty feet square. It is lined over the top with white cotton cloth, the breadths of which being sewed together only in spots, stretch apart in many places, giving one a birds-eye view of the shingles above. The sides are hung with a gaudy chintz, which I consider a perfect marvel of calico printing. The artist seems to have exhausted himself on *roses*; from the largest cabbage, down to the tiniest Burgundy, he has arranged them in every possible variety of wreath, garland, bouquet, and single flower. . . .

A curtain of the above-described chintz, (I shall hem it at the first opportunity), divides off a portion of the room. . . .

The fireplace is built of stones and mud. . . . The mantle-piece—remember that on this portion of a great building, some artists, by their exquisite workmanship, have become world renowned—is formed of a beam of wood, covered with strips of tin procured from cans, upon which still remain in black hieroglyphics, the names of the different eatables which they formerly contained. Two smooth stones—how delightfully primitive—do duty as fire-dogs. I suppose that it would be no more than civil to call a hole two feet square in one side of the room, a window, although it is as yet guiltless of glass.

Most cabins, like the Clapps', typically were "guiltless of glass." Harriet Ward lamented of her otherwise roomy and comfortable cabin at Indian Valley, on the north fork of the Yuba River in remote Sierra County: "All the sunlight we are blessed with comes peeking through holes cut in the logs."

Susanna Townsend's cabin at Amador County's Jackson Creek also lacked windows. She concluded, sagely, that since miners were only home at night "a window is of no consequence to them." It was, however, of consequence to her. And although, like Louisa Clapp and Harriet Ward, Susanna Townsend liked her rustic habitat, she wanted a window.

It was her responsibility, as a miner's wife, to "take charge of the company purse and clean the gold and weigh it" when her husband Emory brought the day's take home in a tin cup. Some of that gold she splurged on the luxury of glass, as she wrote her sister Fanny on January 19, 1852:

> I have a *window* in my house. It is a fine thing to have a tight roof and a floor but you have no idea how delightful it is to have a window. It was so gloomy before inside to be burning a candle (when it was too cold to have the door open) and know that the bright sun was shining outside. It did not seem practicable for us to have one before as it would have been necessary to have ordered it just one from Sacramento, and taken the risk of its being broken on the road up but Emory fell in with a man who was building a house a few miles from us and learned from him that he was about to order a set of windows, and so got him to order one additional for us.
>
> All the passers by stare and gaze at the wonderful phenomenon, a glass window! in a log cabin! I don't think there is another in all the county round.

Some cabin dwellers with no chance at window glass devised creative alternatives. Louisa Clapp visited "the best built log cabin on the river," owned by several young men, and wrote her sister: "This cabin is lighted in a manner truly ingenious. Three feet in length of a log on one side of the room is removed and glass jars inserted in its place; the space around the necks of said jars being filled with clay. This novel idea is really an excellent substitute for window glass. . . ."

Equal creativity characterized cabin furnishings. Mrs. Clapp wrote of her own:

> My toilet table is formed of a trunk elevated upon two claret cases. . . .
>
> The looking-glass is one of those which come in paper cases for doll's houses. . . .
>
> The wash-stand is another trunk covered with a towel, upon which you will see for bowl, a large vegetable dish, for ewer, a common sized dining pitcher. . . . I brought with me from Marysville a handsome carpet, a hair mattress, pillows, a profusion of bed linen . . . I am in reality as thoroughly comfortable here as I could be in the most elegant palace.
>
> We have four chairs. . . . I seriously proposed having three-legged stools; with my usual desire for symmetry I thought that they would be more in keeping. . . . I must mention that the floor is so uneven that no article of furniture gifted with four legs pretends to stand upon but three at once, so that the chairs, tables, etc., remind you constantly of a dog with a sore foot.

Women furnished their homes with whatever opportunity provided. At Indian Valley, Harriet Ward's furniture was "manufactured from the pine trees, our tables are pine boards, and can boast of four good legs. For seats we use little stools, except for three small barrel chairs and one large one, made from a pine tree and covered with a coyote skin."

No pine tree upholstered in coyote skin adorned Jessie Benton Frémont's first California home. Always enjoying the best available, Mrs. Frémont, after her husband fetched her from San Francisco and escorted her to Monterey, settled into one wing of a large adobe residence. Her furnishings were equally fine. Wrote Jessie:

> For furniture we had what could be gathered in San Francisco and shipped down by steamer. Beautiful Chinese matting of varied colors, whole pieces of French and Chinese furniture damask, and Chinese bamboo furniture. An exquisite circular table of carved and inlaid work made a dining table, and we had beautiful Chinese, French, and English china. There was no toilet china, but a punch bowl makes a good basin. . . .

Emigrants, whether forced to rusticity or enjoying elegance, cheer-fully made do—a punch bowl for a basin, jars for a window, a trunk for a table. But for one household object, most newcomers found no suitable substitute.

How they yearned for a comfortable bed. Mrs. John Berry, the forty-niner camped in the northern mines, wrote:

> Oh! you who lounge on your divans & sofas, sleep on your fine, luxurious beds and partake of your rich viands at every meal know nothing of the life of a California emigrant. Here are we sitting, on a pine block, a log or a bunk; sleeping in beds with either a quilt or a blanket as substitute for sheets, (I can tell you it is very aristocratic to have a bed at all), & calico pillow-cases on our pillows.

For those accustomed to feather beds, California's beds, however "aristocratic" Mrs. Berry thought it was to have one, usually were sorry stopgaps. Harriet Ward, who happily described her barrel and pine-stump furniture, ignored what passed for beds in her cabin, except to write: ". . . oh, such beds! I will say nothing about them!"

Mary Staples, however, a New Englander who reached Stockton on January 8, 1851, described her California bed "for the benefit of other pioneers in future time." It was constructed from "four posts cut from young willow trees, with four long poles for side and end pieces, drawn together with strips of rawhide instead of the old fashion bed cord.—a few days drying brings the rawhide very tight, forming a very firm bedstead." For a mattress Mrs. Staples cut "the green grass in the bottom land (a couple of days of January sun dried it enough)," and "improvised ticks . . . from sheets we fortunately had with us."

The most impressive of hand-fashioned beds may have been those seen by Louisa Clapp in Rich Bar's Empire Hotel. They were "so heavy that nothing short of a giant's strength could move them," she wrote. "Indeed, I am convinced that they were built, piece by piece, on the spot where they now stand."

The spot were they stood, the Empire Hotel, Mrs. Clapp thought amazing in many respects. It was, she wrote, "*the* hotel of the place; not but that nearly every other shanty on the Bar claims the same grandiloquent title." The only two-story building in town, the Empire boasted a barroom of "dazzling splendor," completely draped in "that eternal crimson calico . . . in the centre of a fluted mass of which, gleams a really elegant mirror. . . ." The saloon's furnishings consisted of "several uncomfortable looking benches" and a table covered with a green cloth topped by a pack of monte cards and a backgammon board. A "hopeless confusion" of goods, everything from flannel shirts to preserved meats, constituted the shop occupying the remainder of the room.

Four steps up was the parlor, its floor covered with a straw carpet and furnished with "quite a decent looking glass" and a fourteen-foot-long sofa "painfully suggestive of an aching back." The sofa was "of course covered in red calico." A round table with a green cover, six cane-seat chairs, a cooking stove, a rocking chair, and red calico curtains completed the decor.

Up another four stairs were four rooms measuring approximately eight by ten feet, and containing the weighty bedsteads. By their lavish spaciousness the rooms betrayed the building's intended purpose: "It was built by a company of gamblers, as a residence for two of those unfortunates, who make a trade—a thing of barter—of the holiest passion. . . ."

The gamblers' speculation, "to the lasting honor of *miners*," wrote Louisa, proved a failure. They sold their building for a few hundred dollars, although it had cost them more than eight thousand dollars to erect. Inflating the high cost of construction was the need to pack building materials from Marysville at a cost of forty cents a pound.

Despite the Empire's expense, "nothing was ever more awkward and unworkmanlike than the whole tenement," concluded Mrs. Clapp. "It is just such a piece of carpentering as a child two years old, gifted with the strength of a man, would produce, if it wanted to play at making grown-up houses."

This "impertinent apology for a house," as Mrs. Clapp termed it, typified California construction, as Sarah Walsworth confirmed. After observing the building of a house in Oakland, the missionary's wife who had stayed briefly beneath "skating" ceilings in a San Francisco hotel, wrote:

> Only a slight underpinning is laid on the ground, upon which rest the joists of the floor which is carefully laid down the *first thing*. This looked so odd to me at first, that I could but laugh Give a carpenter a few feet of *lumber*, a few doors, & windows, a few pounds of nails & screws a few hinges: to a paper-hanger, a few yards of cloth & a

few rolls of paper—to them *both* a *good deal* of *gold* & you may have a house in 6 days—perhaps in less time. You will have no trouble with "digging cellars," laying wall, "having a *"raising"* nor with dirty "masons"—but after it is all done it is but an improved speaking-trumpet We have learned to speak in *whispers. . . .*

Mrs. Bates, of the fated coal-carrying ships, also found California construction memorable. Her estimated time for building a house was not Sarah Walsworth's six days, but two:

> It may not be amiss to state here the manner of building frame-houses, when the time occupied in building was two days for a private dwelling, four days for a hotel, and six days for a church. The last mentioned, however, was not often raised. A building would boast of a very slight frame [with] split clapboard nailed on [it], and the outside was finished. Upon the inside . . . bleached or unbleached cotton cloth is stretched smoothly and tightly, and fastened to the frame. This cloth is then papered over, and it looks as nice as paper upon plastering. The ceiling overhead is nice bleached cloth. . . . For partitions a frame is raised, and each side of this frame is cloth and paper, leaving a hollow space between the two partitions of three or four inches in width. These partitions look as firm and solid as they do made the usual way [with lath and plaster]; but they afford but a slight hindrance to the passage of sounds.

Rich Bar undoubtedly contained some of these canvas houses along its street, which was, according to Louisa Clapp, "thickly planted with about forty tenements; among which figure round tents, square tents, plank hovels, log cabins, &c.—the residences, varying in elegance and convenience from the palatial splendor of 'The Empire,' down to a 'local habitation,' formed of pine boughs, and covered with old calico shirts."

These "local habitations" of pine boughs enclosed with calico shirts suggest poor imitations inspired by the Spanish *ramada.* These colorful shelters erected at Sonora, a mining settlement established by emigrant families from the Mexican state of Sonora, delighted a Canadian forty-niner named William Perkins:

> The habitations were constructed of . . . upright unhewn sticks with green branches and leaves and vines interwoven, and decorated with gaudy hangings of silks, fancy cottons, flags, brilliant goods of every

description; the many-tinted Mexican *Zarape*, the rich *manga*, with its gold embroidery, chinese scarfs and shawls of the most costly quality. . . . The scene irresistibly reminded one of the descriptions we have read of the brilliant bazaars of oriental countries.

Perkins was at Sonora when Elizabeth Gunn arrived with her children. By then, however, the colorful ramadas had been supplanted by buildings typically constructed of "thin wood," as Elizabeth Gunn observed, "one story, and there is not a chimney to be seen."

The Gunn house was undoubtedly the finest construction in town. The well-built, two-story adobe had a full garret, with a large window at one end, used as a bedroom by the three young men employed in Lewis Gunn's printing office. The house was solid and comfortable.

Elizabeth's one complaint was the constantly open printing office doors that let in the dust. She was "cleaning all the time." She looked forward to the wet season in hopes rain would settle the dust, but that proved no solace. "In the house mud turns to dust," she wrote, "and it is still dirt. Mud and dust, wet and dry, all dirt, though I sweep over and over."

At nearby Columbia, Clementine Brainard also complained of dirt. She had joined her husband Marcellus to make a home in the "gem of the southern mines" and liked her new life, despite her husband's frequent absence.

She was, not atypically, a woman adapting well to frontier life. She even surprised herself. "I would not have believed before I came here," she wrote in her diary, "if any one had told me that I ever should enjoy myself so well. . . ."

Although she had few domestic skills, she made curtains and a carpet for her parlor and decided "it would be very convenient now if I had a knowledge of cooking; but it is all my own fault, for I never would learn though my Mother tried to talk to me about learning: I always told her there would be time enough when I was obliged to do it: so according to my decision there is time enough now, and I am resolved to improve it, though learning to cook is rather a bitter pill to me."

Socially inclined, Mrs. Brainard visited with the other ladies of Columbia, calling October 27, 1853, upon a Mrs. Houlton, where she "had a pleasant time with the exception of the walk a part of the way, which was rather wet and difficult to get along, got so muddy could make no more calls. . . ." Like Elizabeth Gunn, she was dismayed by the dirt: "When I got home was completely covered with mud and dust, one cannot enjoy going out here very much, for it is so much work to put their clothing in order, after going out, for it is almost impossible to get the dust out of them."

But Clementine Brainard's dusty clothes and Mrs. Gunn's muddy floors were as nothing compared to Emily Rolfe's dirty discoveries.

In 1854 Emily Rolfe and her husband Ianthis bought a house in Nevada City. The view from the Rolfes' five-room home on Spring Street included the back of the National Hotel on Broad Street, its rear clump of pines thoughtfully preserved for the sheltering of saloon customers unable to sustain sitting positions.

Emily Rolfe, who knew nothing of brush shelters or tents, failed to appreciate the luxury of a bat-and-board house, at least the one on Spring Street:

> Some of the boards and strips just reached to the sills, some covered them and others of all lengths below making the house at the back look like an old broken tooth comb. . . . .
>
> As we drove to the house I could see under the house through to the back yard. It was not enclosed in anyway. The view was not artistic.

Emily Rolfe slept little her first night in her new house, principally because of the pigs and fleas. The pigs slept under the house, and the fleas kept the pigs company, or at least those that didn't keep company with the Rolfes. Next day Emily insisted the pigs must go. Ianthis thought the pigs a good idea, since they ate the refuse thrown under the house. Emily insisted the refuse must go, so Ianthis hired a man to clean out from under the house. Wrote a disbelieving Emily:

> The miscellaneous things that came to light were astonishing to a person just from civilization. There were gum boots, old coats, pants, and vest, red shirts, blue shirts, and white ones, any number of old socks, bottles of all sizes and description, tin cans of every shape and size, bones that the dogs had carried under there and I cannot describe the odor. . . .

Mrs. Rolfe found the inside of her house equally amazing:

> The house had been papered and painted inside and looked clean, but after a fire had been built in the cook stove, the paper soon showed

grease spots and I noticed two little pyramids shaped like blocks on top of the paste boards below the grease spots on the paper. I investigated and found the cold grease that had piled up from fry pans that had evidently been hung up by the miners without having been washed. The grease had drained from the pans and the painter had painted over them. On the sides of the front doors I noticed a great deal of sticky stuff where the miners had cleaned their knives after scraping the remains of the table to the pigs. . . .

As remarkable as the Rolfe house was, it was a house. And in mining camps that survived to become boomtowns like Nevada City, Jackson, Sonora, and Columbia, houses soon supplanted cabins.

Where the gold gave out, however, as it did at Indian Bar on the Feather River's north fork, miners moved on, deserting settlements and abandoning cabins.

With the "failure of the golden harvest," wrote Louisa Clapp on November 21, 1852, men "left the river in crowds." With the gold and its seekers gone, and winter upon their unrepaired and now-dilapidated cabin, she painted a sad picture of stained ceiling, worn carpeting, and faded rose-garlanded hangings. Rain poured down the inside of her stone-and-mud chimney, splashing mud spots "all over the splendid tin mantle piece."

Even so, the prospect of leaving the log cabin saddened her. She had once wondered how she should ever be contented "to live in a decent, proper, well-behaved house, where toilet tables are toilet tables, and not an ingenious combination of trunk and claret cases, where lanterns are not broken bottles, book cases not candle boxes, and trunks not washstands . . . I am sure I do not know. . . ."

And now it was time to know.

The Clapps lingered long among the last to depart. As Louisa packed their few belongings, she marveled. "Really," she wrote, "everybody ought to go to the mines, just to see how little it takes to make people comfortable in the world."

With sadness she wrote her sister of the forlorn and abandoned community of "calico hovels, shingle palaces, *ramaras*, (pretty, arbor-like places, composed of green boughs, and baptized with that sweet name). . . ." The nearly deserted settlement lay snow-dusted as Mrs. Clapp composed her final Shirley letter from the mines.

While the expressman collected her bundles, the "frail, home-loving little thistle," the *"now* perfectly healthy sister," penned her parting. Her farewell expressed sentiments not hers alone. More than one leavetaking echoed that of the sophisticated New Englander, of the Dame Shirley who mourned, "My heart is heavy at the thought of departing forever from this place. I *like* this wild and barbarous life; I leave it with regret."

FOUR

ASHES TO ASHES

*Some of the men lay sick in their bunks, some lay asleep, and out
from another bunk, upon this curious mingling of merriment and
sadness stared the white face of a corpse. They had forgotten even
to cover the still features with the edge of a blanket, and he lay
there, in his rigid calmness, a silent unheeded witness to the
acquired insensibility of the early settlers. What was one dead
man, more or less! Nobody missed him. They would bury
him tomorrow to make room for a new applicant for his bunk.
The music and the dancing, the card-playing, drinking, and
swearing went on unchecked by the hideous presence of Death.
His face grew too familiar in those days to be a terror.*
—LUZENA STANLEY WILSON, *Sacramento, 1849*

Mary Lee was still in bed the morning Ida Vanard came looking for
her. If she had known that Ida had paced all night and drunk a
brandy cocktail for breakfast, perhaps Mary would have left Sacramento—and perhaps she would have lived.

It was early on October 21, 1853, a Friday, when Ida left the house
she shared with Rosanna Hughes and the other girls, dragging her
friend Gus—Augusta Dennison—along with her to Anne Woods's
house on Second Street where Mary Lee lived.

Ida found Mary in Miss Anne's room and confronted her with
what she had heard. Was it true that Mary had gone out riding with
Ida's man and slept with him? Mary confessed she had and apolo-
gized. She'd been drinking, she told Ida, and was sorry for it.

Even though it wasn't yet ten in the morning, Bill Cameron, a
painter and paperhanger visiting from San Francisco, was in Anne
Woods's saloon. He overheard "hard language"; Ida called Mary a
"bitch" and challenged her to fight.

Anne Woods, also hearing the commotion, came and told Ida she wanted no fuss in her house. Ida then dared Mary to go outside with her. Mary refused, saying she wouldn't make herself a blackguard by fighting over any man. Ida called Mary a coward and slapped her.

Cameron and a couple of other men heard the girls scrapping and hurried to the doorway to watch the scene. "Let me look and see," said William Revere, the barkeeper, elbowing others aside in eager curiosity.

From the next room Mary Ferguson heard the quarreling and pushed open the adjoining door just as Ida slapped Mary. She saw the two girls pull hair and tussle with each other.

And then Mary Ferguson saw Ida draw a knife and stab Mary Lee.

Revere saw Ida Vanard with a knife in her hand, and so did Bill Cameron. Cameron rushed to Mary, too late. "Oh God I am going to die—I am cut," she cried out to him. Cameron carried her to the bed, with Mary pointing at Ida. "There, Billy," she said, "is the woman who cut me."

Anne Woods grabbed Ida's hands, pried the eight-inch bowie knife from her grip, and hollered at Revere to get a policeman. Another man went for the police, and Revere ran for a doctor.

Dr. Bell and Dr. Harkness arrived as Mary was fast failing. They found a cut on her thigh a little above the knee, and then another, deeper, in her abdomen, left and below her navel. She died within a few minutes of their examination. Both doctors judged her death the consequence of the stabbing.

Next day, the Sacramento *Union* published an account of the killing—on page two. Death wasn't front-page news. Not even violent death. Not even a woman's violent death.

Death in gold rush California wasn't noteworthy. Death was, as Luzena Wilson observed, too commonplace, too familiar. The pioneers had an "acquired insensibility" to it.

How lightly pioneers regarded death is indicated in a coroner's jury verdict on a man found dead from inebriation: "Death by hanging—round a rum-shop."

For most emigrants death lost much of its sting long before they reached California, for few arrived without frequent witness of the fearful spectre en route. It was a rare voyager around the Horn who didn't see at least one companion rendered to the deep, with little ceremony. On the Isthmus hundreds fell from fever, and thousands from illness and accident on the overland trails. No route west escaped death's commonplace accompaniment, and few journalists failed to record one or more firsthand observations.

Death, the great leveler, respecting neither age, gender, or station, assured women's full participation as observers, victims, and bereaved in this too-familiar gold rush experience.

Mr. and Mrs. William Ferguson and their six children, for example, saw twenty-eight shipmates succumb to cholera. On the Isthmus, the Ferguson family camped a month when William became ill. Mrs. Ferguson buried her husband under a mahogany tree at a place called the American Burying Grounds, one son carving his father's name on the tree. Continuing to California from Panama City aboard an old Peruvian whaler, the widowed woman saw all her children taken ill and the youngest die.

So routine had death become for travelers that Emeline Day, aboard a steamer heading from Panama to San Francisco, noted that when two men were found dead on the ship they were "throwed over, with little ceremony. . . . Appears to have no effect on the passengers. Card playing & swearing all the time within a very short distance of the place where men's bodies were committed to the great deep."

Women, as vulnerable as men to accident and illness, risked the added danger of childbirth. Few diarists wrote of pregnancy, and deaths at childbirth usually are revealed only by mention of an infant, as in forty-niner Catherine Haun's account of a Canadian woman named Mrs. Lamore, who "suddenly sickened and died" on the desert trail, leaving two little daughters and a grief-stricken husband:

> We halted a day to bury her and the infant that had lived but an hour, in this weird, lonely spot on God's footstool away apparently from everywhere and everybody.
>
> The bodies were wrapped together in a bedcomforter and wound, quite mummyfied with a few yards of string that we made by tying together torn strips of a cotton dress skirt. A passage of the Bible (my own) was read; a prayer offered and "Nearer, My God to Thee" sung. . . . Every heart was touched and eyes full of tears as we lowered the body, coffinless, into the grave. There was no tombstone—why should there be—the poor husband and orphans could never hope to revisit the grave and to the world it was just one of the many hundreds that marked the trail of the argonaut.

The Lamore infant's life was almost too brief for grief, and the death of newborns common. Yet Susanna Townsend's sorrow for her baby probably was not atypical.

Susanna was nearly thirty when she married Emory Townsend in 1846; a few years later she had "much fun" crossing the Isthmus when Emory decided to try his luck in the mines. From a log cabin on Jackson Creek Susanna wrote her sisters Shotty and Lizzy in excitement about her glass window, which she believed the first in an Amador County cabin.

At the time she wrote that letter, Susanna Townsend was pregnant. Since women rarely mentioned pregnancy in their letters and journals, Susanna made no announcement until surprised by her brother's visit in December 1851. Since he had seen her condition, she wrote her sisters: "I did not mean to let any of you know a word about it till the tea party was over. . . . Next March a little after the middle I shall look for an arrival of the young miner."

Childbirth for Susanna Townsend, marrying late and now in her mid-thirties, living in a remote mining camp, was an event of mixed anticipations. "I can't help being pleased," she wrote, "in spite of the adverse circumstances in which it must take place." Then, recalling the stillborn birth of her first child, she added, "but I dare not anticipate . . . having a living child, owing to my disappointment before. . . . "

Having shared her secret, Susanna wrote fully of her concerns. She was anxious to have a woman help her through the birth, but although several women lived in the area none could stay with her. One young woman had a new infant of her own, and another woman, Mrs. McKenzie, who lived about a mile beyond the Townsends, was unable to assist, as Susanna wrote her sisters:

> Her husband is mining and they live in a little bit of a cabin with a canvas roof. I called on her when she had been here about two weeks, and when I saw her house, if house it could be called, I felt that mine was a spacious mansion, and she has two children too. I am sure the poor things in bad weather must stay on the bed, or under it for there was only room for the table and two chairs between that and the fireplace. I saw at once by her dress and manners that she was a *lady* not a low-bred woman used to a rough life. . . .

Susanna admired Mrs. McKenzie's "slender white hands with rings on them," observing that "they would not look so delicate long." Yet the woman was cheerful, telling Susanna that living with her husband under any circumstances was preferable to the two-year separation they had endured. "Such is woman," wrote Susanna.

Also nearby were two Irish families, "quite the better sort of Irish," Susanna added. The women were sisters, both young, one with an infant and three-year-old daughter. Neither could stay with her.

Eventually the Townsends engaged a Mrs. Carroll, who, for twenty-five dollars a week, arrived four days before Ellen Beulah Townsend's birth and stayed three weeks. The doctor also stayed several days, Susanna providing herself semi-privacy by hanging a length of calico around her bed. Emory and the doctor slept on the floor, Mrs. Carroll with Susanna. When Susanna's pains started at two in the morning, Mrs. Carroll gave what comfort she could, but "Emory and the Dr. lay and cracked their jokes," wrote Susanna, "as people will in the beginning of such affairs." With detail unusual to letters of the time, on April 6, 1852, Susanna wrote:

> I had no idea from my former experience that a Dr. could render so much assistance to a woman in that fearful hour. I believe that with no better aid than I had before my little one would have shared the fate of her brother. As it was her life was doubtful for a few minutes. There was no pulsation except in the umbilical cord, and the Dr. instead of severing that immediately as is customary allowed her to remain in connection with me in hopes that circulation would be renewed through that, and it was so after a few very anxious minutes. I was so prostrated that I could scarcely think or feel, but poor Emory when he saw as he supposed the second dead child bowed down his head like a bulrush and went out of the room.

On April 13, the proud mother wrote:

> No doubt you are prepared to hear that she is a wonderful child in all respects when you remember that my hen used to lay two eggs a day and my cat that was addicted to blushing when reproved for her misdemeanors.

How great was the sadness of heart, however, on November 23, 1852, when Susanna informed her sisters of the baby's death:

> & if I were near you I could tell you so many of her little winning ways, and how very pretty and cunning she was—Of course being

only four months when she died her faculties were not greatly developed, but I talked to her so much she came already to understand a good deal, and she talked to me with her countenance. When she was a month old she began to notice the singing of birds around our house, and did sing last spring as I never heard them, perhaps I never rose so early before of spring mornings. every tree seemed a fount of song. She would lie and listen to them delighted and when a single bird would sometimes pour forth a sweet strain she would look at me and say as plain as any words ever expressed it, 'Isn't that pretty.' . . . You ought to have seen Emory, delight when he saw her first intelligent smile bestowed upon him. . . . Bless her little heart he exclaimed she is smiling at me. It did please me so much to hear him.—

These are little things to write perhaps you think who have had so many babies, but I think we must be excused if we were a little extra delighted with our baby being you know rather *old folks* to have the first one. At any rate we did feel very happy with her all the time she was with us and it was hard to part with her—

Such expressive sorrow as Susanna Townsend shared with her sisters was atypical of the usual experience. So familiar did death become both on the journey and in the mines that its dominating presence in California inspired little notice. Readers of the Sacramento *Union* probably would have been surprised had Mary Lee's death been reported on page one. What was noteworthy about death? It was too commonplace to be remarkable, although many pioneers considered that in itself worth remarking.

Luzena Wilson, for example, who beheld the unblanketed face of death in a Sacramento tent filled with merrymakers, forever chastised herself for an equal disregard:

It has been a life-long source of regret to me that I grew hard-hearted like the rest. I was hard-worked, hurried all day, and tired out, but I might have stopped sometimes for a minute to heed the moans which caught my ears from the canvas house next to me. I knew a young man lived there, for he had often stopped to say "Good morning", but I thought he had friends in the town; and when I heard his weak calls for water I never thought but some one gave it. One day the moans ceased, and, on looking in, I found him lying dead with not even a friendly hand to close his eyes. Many a time since, when my own boys have been wandering in new countries I have wept for the sore heart of that poor boy's mother, and I have prayed that if ever want and sickness come to mine, some other woman would be more tender than I had been, and give them at least a glass of cold water.

Fever, scurvy, or possibly cholera extinguished the life that haunted Mrs. Wilson's remembrance of Sacramento in the winter of 1849–50. Illness was the commonest of California's multiple opportunities for departing earthly existence. Thousands of California's newcomers succumbed. One goldfield physician, Dr. Joseph D. B. Stillman, estimated that as many as 20 percent of the forty-niners died from illness within six months of arrival.

Sacramento City was too well acquainted with death to be stunned by Mary Lee's. J. Goldsborough Bruff, the meticulous journalkeeper who recorded the many women and families passing his camp on the Lassen route, reached Sacramento on November 29, 1850. He and a friend, while strolling through the back part of town, discovered a burial ground, "long parallel lines of graves," of cholera victims. "These mournful heaps of sand," wrote Bruff, "were the resting places of upwards of 1700 persons, who had fallen in 15 months; 900 of them were placed there in 3 weeks."

The Sacramento *Transcript* of November 29, 1850, placed the number of graves at 1,966, with 850 of them freshly made. According to the *Transcript*, cholera raged in the three weeks between October 20 and November 12. Sixty Sacramentans were buried on November 1. Deaths from the epidemic in that city were estimated as high as 15 percent.

The Pratts, a seafaring family from Maine, anchored at Sacramento in their ship, the *Abby Baker*, in the midst of the scourge. Timothy Pratt, head of the family and captain, had died near San Francisco from an unspecified illness, but at Sacramento cholera soon extinguished the lives of his wife, Jane, and three sons, leaving only the youngest boy, nine years old, as survivor.

The epidemic haunted mining camps, Indian villages, and communities large and small throughout California. Cholera reportedly killed 5 percent of San Francisco's population. Nearly 10 percent of San Jose's citizens died of the disease, including two pioneers of the first wagons over the Sierra, genial and enthusiastic Dr. John Townsend and his wife. Mrs. Townsend had been in her mid-thirties and childless when the couple crossed the plains in 1844. The neighbor who discovered the couple dead in their farmhouse bunks on January 1, 1850, found their infant son playing on the floor nearby.

Dysentery was another common killer; on the Trinity River it killed ten of a party of nineteen. On the journey west, seafaring emigrants endured unwholesome food, bad water, and crowded surroundings, conditions ideal for the disease. When they reached San Francisco hundreds were hospitalized for it.

Within a few months of arrival, one of the thirteen women aboard the steamer *California*'s maiden voyage, Mrs. Frank Ward, died of dysentery. Margaret De Witt, also a passenger on that historic journey, wrote sympathetically:

> It seems a mysterious providence she only came out this spring—had just got settled at housekeeping—handsome house, furnished with every comfort and luxury that money could procure—and if any one had prospects of happiness here, it was her—It seems hard to die so far from all her friends—but more trying to leave her husband. She suffered very much—but was sensible—and said she was not afraid to die. . . .

Another dying woman expressed little fear but much sorrow at leaving her husband. Several months after her death he found a letter she had written to him as she lay dying. The *Alta* printed a "touching fragment" of it on July 20, 1851, observing that many "will return to desolate hearths to weep over the graves of the loved and lost":

> When this shall reach your eye, dear G—, . . . I shall have passed away for ever, and the cold white stone will be keeping watch over the lips you have so often pressed, and the sod will be growing green that shall hide forever from your sight the dust of one who has so often nestled close to your warm heart. . . . Many weary hours have I passed in the endeavor to reconcile myself to leaving you, whom I love so well, and this bright world of sunshine and beauty. . . .
>
> I could have wished to live, if only to be at your side when your time shall come. . . . But it is not to be so—and I submit. Yours is the privilege of watching, through long and dreary nights, for the spirit's final flight. . . .

The "spirit's final flight" was observed in every community of every size. At Rich Bar, Louisa Clapp wrote in her "Shirley letter" on September 22, 1851, of the death from "peritonitis (a common disease in this place)" of "Mrs. B.," one of the four women at Rich Bar:

Last night we were startled by the frightful news of her decease. Confess, that without being egotistical, the death of one out of a community of four women, might well alarm the remainder.

Her funeral took place at ten this morning. . . . On a board, supported by two butter-tubs, was extended the body of the dead woman, covered with a sheet; by its side stood the coffin of unstained pine, lined with white cambric. . . . About twenty men, with the three women of the place, had assembled for the funeral. An *extempore* prayer was made, filled with all the peculiarities usual to that style of petition. Ah! how different from the soothing verses of the glorious burial service of the church.

As the procession started for the hill-side graveyard—a dark cloth cover, borrowed from a neighboring monte table, was flung over the coffin. Do not think that I mention any of these circumstances in a spirit of mockery; far from it. Every observance, usual on such occasions, that was *procurable*, surrounded this funeral. All the gold on Rich Bar could do no more; and should I die to-morrow, I should be marshaled to my mountain grave beneath the same monte-table cover pall, which shrouded the coffin of poor Mrs. B.

Equally somber were the final rites of a young Spanish woman. A Belgian gold rusher named Perlot discovered her corpse unattended in a tent, with a single candle burning nearby. A note in Spanish identified the woman as Mrs. Pedro de Alquijo, dead at the age of twenty-three, and asked passersby to pray for her, respect her tomb, and relight the taper if found extinguished.

No such gentle considerations attended young Mary Lee to her grave. Whatever observances were hers went unreported, excepting only the court documents approving payment from her estate of fourteen dollars for a winding sheet and seven dollars for a shroud.

Although newspapers dutifully followed Ida Vanard's legal enmeshment, none noted anything about the life she had taken. A life cut short was too ordinary an occurrence, whether by violence, illness, or accident.

Journalists noted numerous deaths by accident in the mines, typically, as forty-niner Charles Ferguson observed, to men unknown. Ferguson saw a man trip on a stone, fall into a stream, and drown. No one knew who he was or where he came from. "So it has been with hundreds of men," wrote Ferguson, "who have gone to California, met with some accident, and, being unknown, their

Sallie Hester's teacher, Miss Winlack, died in the explosion of the *Jenny Lind*, one of many steamer disasters.
CALIFORNIA STATE LIBRARY

friends could not be written to; they died among strangers and were soon forgotten."

While women were less likely victims of accidents than were miners, they were not immune. Steamboat explosions, for example, killed both men and women indiscriminately and frequently. Sallie Hester recorded in her diary the explosion of the *Jenny Lind*, "killing most of the passengers, my friend and teacher Miss Winlack among the number."

Steamer service for California's freight and passenger trade commenced in 1849. Increased competition spurred faster and faster runs, with steamers racing rivers and bay in frantic pursuit of one another. So common were accidents that the *Alta* editorialized a chastisement to both passengers and steamboat captains: "It is a tacit agreement that if they [the passengers] will travel on his boat, he shall blow them into eternity sooner than see his boat left behind. They understand it, and he understands it; in accordance with the implied contract, he ties down the safety valve and they all go into eternity together."

While aboard the steamer *Sophie*, Sam Ward, erudite brother of Julia Ward Howe, explained to a befriended Indian how the vessel was propelled. Ward took the Potoyensee Indian with him from

Mariposa to San Francisco to give the native a peek at civilization, and aboard the *Sophie* he illustrated his lesson on steam propulsion in the ship's galley, showing the effects of steam on the cook's saucepan lids. The principle and potential of steam apparently was not lost on the Indian, for he ran away in San Francisco to avoid returning on the "tea-kettle."

Would that immigrants had had his understanding.

Explosion was not the only danger aboard ships. In 1854 an estimated 150 people died when the *Yankee Blade* went up on the rocks in rough seas and heavy fog encountered north of Santa Barbara. Jane Elwell, a passenger who "distinguished herself . . . heroically" in rescuing others, told reporters that "the captain ought to be hung" and she herself would like to kill the chief mate. In one overcrowded lifeboat fifteen of twenty passengers died, including four women and seven children. Some passengers believed others had been murdered by ruffians aboard the ship who robbed them, and even that the ship was lost by contrivance with these "shoulder strikers." Among several bodies floating ashore after the wreck was that of a man with deep cuts on his head and his pockets turned inside out, suggesting he had been murdered and plundered by villains after the *Yankee Blade* went ashore.

So common was death by violence and so overrun was California by lawlessness that the formation of vigilance committees was almost inevitable. Yet, old-timers, those who participated in California's olden, golden days of 1848 and even 1849, recalled an Arcadian era free of crime. Miners testified to leaving unguarded their cabins, tools, and even pounds of gold without thought or risk.

Perhaps exaggeration or wishful thinking purchased such memories on behalf of the past. Certainly not everyone suffered encounters with the lawless element that increasingly threatened the average good citizen's pursuit of golden happiness. If one's mining camp was crime-free and rich with good fellowship, California was utopian. Conversely, if it was your gold stolen, your life threatened, California was a godless, lawless wasteland.

Evidence supports California's reputation for lawlessness. Although laws were quickly enacted, there was no one to enforce them; hence, vigilance committees. And violent death, like accident and illness, was democratic: women were not slighted.

One of the earliest reports of women murdered was recorded by Monterey's alcalde, the Rev. Walter Colton. He wrote in his diary early in the rush, which some men swore was crime-free, that "the emigrants to California are composed of two classes—those who come to live by their wits, and those who come to accumulate by their work."

While in the mines, Colton met two men he described only as "a Hessian and Irishman," men obviously intending to live by their wits. According to Colton these men, on their way to Stockton, murdered and robbed two miners of their gold. Then, falling in with "three deserters from the Pacific squadron," the party imposed on the hospitality of "Mr. Reade, an English Ranchero of respectability and wealth." Colton wrote that during the night the men "rose on the household, consisting of Mr. Reade, his wife, and three children, a kinswoman with four children, and two Indian domestics, and murdered the whole!"

Because citizens quickly caught and killed the guilty five, Colton used the story to illustrate how speedily retribution followed crime in California. H. H. Bancroft noted numerous incidents similar to Colton's record, with similarly swift reprisal.

In Yuba City, for example, on the evening of June 10, 1852, a man named John Jackson knocked on the door of a Swiss couple named Baker to ask for food and a bed. Having business the next morning at Sutter's nearby Hock Farm, Mr. Baker left his house, returning at noon to find his wife missing. Surprised by Baker's return, Jackson rode off, with Baker and a neighbor in pursuit. Bancroft tells the story in his *Popular Tribunals*, a two-volume account of gold rush lawlessness and vigilance committees compiled from court records and newspapers:

> Jackson was soon caught, and on him were found thirty dollars and Baker's pistol. The body of the woman was discovered, with marks on the throat and three bullet-holes under the left breast. A law jury sat upon the case; but without waiting for its verdict, the enraged people threw a lasso round Jackson's neck and hanged him to the nearest tree.

In 1850 an Australian woman living in Georgetown, in the hills just north of Placerville, was shot and killed by her husband, John Williams, in a fit of jealousy. Mr. Williams reportedly provided Georgetown its first hanging, the miners storming the jail with a battering ram to have at the man who had killed his wife. The citizens placed a rope about his neck and led him to a big pine tree. They threw the rope over a convenient limb, hoisted Williams upon a mule's back, told him to kneel on the saddle and make his peace with God. When he had finished his prayer, the murderer was ordered to stand up. Then someone hit the mule a sharp cut with a whip and the animal gave a bound, leaving Williams dangling in the air. "He fell about the regulation distance," wrote an unsympathetic chronicler, "and in four or five minutes life was extinct."

This may have been the same incident related by William Manly, the rescuer of the forty-niners lost in Death Valley, who was mining near Georgetown in 1850. In Manly's version, the wife, from laundering miners' shirts at a dollar apiece, was making more money than her miner husband:

> As she began to make considerable money the bigger, if not better, half of this couple began to feel quite rich and went off on a drunk, and when his own money was spent he went to his wife for more, but she refused him, and he, in his drunken rage, picked up a gun near by and shot her dead.

Manly described the lynch mob as "a pack of reckless, back-woods Missourians who seemed to smell something bloody . . . . They said justice must be done if there was no law, and that no man could kill a woman and live in California."

Another story of a woman murdered by her husband is related by John Steele, a minister of the Methodist Episcopal Church, who in 1851 was at Onion Valley, where the murder occurred. The husband is identified only as "Doctor Y,—" a West Point graduate who had been a surgeon in the army and discharged for drunkenness. Doctor Y, presumably from shame, drifted to California and ceased correspondence with his wife, left behind in Kentucky. She, in Steele's words, "resolved to save him if possible," and followed to Sacramento. Reunited, she pried him from unsavory associates and they established a home, happy for a time, at Yankee Jim's, a mining camp in Placer County. But her husband could not forsake alcohol. "Gambling was added to drunkenness," wrote Steele, "his earnings were soon gone, and he was reduced to want. His wife was neglected, sometimes abused. God only knew the burden of that devoted heart; away from congenial society, all her efforts vain. . . ." One night after he was thrown out of a saloon for being troublesome, the doctor went home and there shot and killed his wife.

Women were both intended and incidental victims of violence. During one of California's frequent stage robberies, the Tom Bell gang shot and killed Mrs. Tilghman, a black woman then living in Marysville with her husband, a barber. She had been riding on an outside seat with the Chinese passengers, several of whom were wounded in the holdup.

In addition to such murderous danger, women were also at risk from sexual violence, although chroniclers generally masked rape with euphemism or vague and veiled references. In Victorian but nonetheless unmistakable language, historian H. H. Bancroft reported an instance occurring on January 17, 1853:

> One Conrad Sacksin . . . was caught in the commission of an act too infamous for record; and the description of his punishment is scarcely more fit for perusal. He was taken to the levee, tried, and convicted. The question then arose what the punishment should be. Rev. O. C. Wheeler presented the case to the people and put the question to vote. Some were for hanging and others for mutilation. At last whipping was decided on, one hundred lashes to be the infliction. Six respectable citizens were chosen for the execution of the sentence. Then with sickening detail the matter is discussed and the punishment described in the account before me, which I will gladly spare the reader.

A presumed rape accompanies the legend of Joaquin Murieta. One hypothesis has the notorious bandit adopting violence in retaliation for the rape of his wife. This version has Joaquin Murieta mining in Stanislaus County in 1849, and there evicted from his claim by Americans who beat him and raped his wife. She is identified as Rosita Felix in one account, and in another Antonia Molinera, who, clipping her hair short, rode with the band attired in men's clothing.

Scholarly detective work mostly abolished credence for the Murieta story, and the probability of establishing a woman's rape as motivation for gang violence seems unlikely. What is likely, however, is that many Mexican women were raped, as were Indian women. The low regard of many men for dark-skinned women, both Indian and Spanish-speaking, was tragically illustrated at Downieville on July 5,

1851. "Their majesties the mob," as Louisa Clapp had it, hanged a woman.

Her name was Josefa.

The first that San Franciscans had of the news was the July 9 *Alta*. "We can hardly credit the report. . . ." added the *Alta*'s editor to the story reprinted from the Marysville *Herald*:

> We are informed . . . that on Saturday afternoon a Spanish woman was hung for stabbing to the heart a man by the name of Cannan, killing him instantly. . . . The deceased . . . had the night previously entered the house of the woman and created a riot and disturbance, which so outraged her, that when he presented himself the next morning to apologize for his behavior, he was met at the door by the female, who had in her hand a large bowie knife, which she instantly drove into his heart.
>
> She was immediately arrested, tried, sentenced, and hung at 4 o'clock in the afternoon of the same day. She did not exhibit the least fear, walking up a small ladder to the scaffold, and placing the rope round her neck with her own hands, first gracefully removing two plaits of raven black hair from her shoulders to make room for the fatal cord. Some five or six hundred witnessed the execution. On being asked if she had any thing to say, she replied, "Nothing; but I would do the same again if I was so provoked"—and that she wished her remains to be decently taken care of.

On July 15 the *Alta*'s editor confirmed the story, confessing that in its July 9 telling he "expressed some doubt as to the genuineness of the statement." Forecasting the stain that attached to Downieville's reputation for years after, the *Alta* continued:

> Now will not [the Marysville *Herald*] so far accommodate the wants of its readers as to collect and present the particulars of the crime committed and the testimony by which a woman was convicted and hung, within the circuit of its home or district affairs? Unless the hanging of a woman is a matter not unusual in its province, it would be well worthy a place in its columns, if so much room might be set aside from its ordinary requirements as a California newspaper.

Actually, the *Herald* had the story fairly correct. An issue too subtle to address, not part of the account, quite probably influenced the incident. It was the attitude most men had toward Spanish-speaking women. Richard Henry Dana revealed it years earlier, writing of the Californio women in *Two Years Before the Mast*, that they "have but little virtue." Such prejudice as Americans expressed against Mexicans over the late war with Mexico and the conquest of California did not encompass the full scope of their feelings regarding Mexican women. The nature of that prejudice is evident in a verse from a folksong popular during the war with Mexico:

> *Already the senoritas*
> *Speak English with finesse.*
> *Kiss me! say the Yankees*
> *The girls all answer "Yes."*

In keeping with that implied attitude, most Downieville miners thought nothing of hanging Josefa; she was, after all, from Mexico, not Ohio or Iowa.

Josefa lived in Downieville with a man named Jose, and possibly worked in Craycroft's saloon where Jose dealt monte. No evidence supports any conjecture, beyond that proposed by prejudice, that she was a prostitute.

Contemporaries described her as an attractive woman in her mid-twenties, one saying, "She might be called pretty, so far as the style of swarthy Mexican beauty is so considered. She . . . dressed with considerable attention to taste."

Given the scarcity of women and the prevailing opinion about Spanish-speaking women, it would be surprising if Josefa did not frequently resist unwelcome advances. In fact, during her trial she testified:

> I had been told that some of the boys wanted to get into my room and sleep with me; a young Mexican boy told me so and it frightened me so that I used to fasten the door and take a knife with me to bed. . . .

Cannon may have been among the men she feared. He was certainly among the wild celebrants of Downieville's Independence Day festivities.

Downieville, like every California community, observed the state's first Independence Day with bands, bunting, parades, and speeches—all accompanied by prodigious drinking.

Fred Cannon, on the night of the glorious Fourth, was as drunk as any miner in town. He also was well liked, and fun. The night of the Fourth he delighted his friends with hilarious entertainment, one recalling that Cannon sang and enacted Chinese love songs "using different tones of voice, alto, tenor and base, taking in turn the parts of the maid, the lover, and the excited old opposing father who is totally averse to giving up his daughter. Cannon enacted it all in first class style."

Sometime after midnight, in company with a friend named Lawson and another miner named Charley Getzler, while staggering down the street, Cannon either fell against or kicked Josefa's door. The door, connected only by thin leather hinges, collapsed, with Cannon sprawling on the cabin floor.

Some people said Cannon intentionally broke in on Josefa because she had spurned his advances. Getzler, however, testified that as soon as they saw Josefa they stood the door in place and, laughing, left.

Very early the next morning, according to witnesses' testimony, Cannon, while purchasing medicine from the doctor who lived next door to the Mexican couple, was approached by Jose for payment for the broken door. Cannon refused and the two argued. Hearing their voices, Josefa joined them and she and Cannon argued in Spanish.

Although Cannon's friends agreed that his part of the dispute was good humored, Jose testified that during the exchange Cannon called Josefa a whore. Everyone agreed that Josefa was enraged. Before jury and spectators, she testified, "I told deceased that was no place to call me bad names, come in and call me so and as he was coming in I stabbed him."

A few lone voices tried to defend Josefa, Dr. Cyrus Aiken even attesting she was three months' pregnant and that hanging her would take two lives. Three doctors retired with the defendant for examination and determined she was not pregnant.

As the day wore on, miners along the river got word of the popular Cannon's stabbing and the trial. The crowd that had numbered some five hundred in the morning was estimated at two thousand by the afternoon, growing into what one eyewitness called "the hungriest, craziest, wildest mob standing around that ever I saw anywhere."

To background cries of "Bring her out!" and "Hang her!" the verdict was read: "The jury find that the woman, Josefa, is guilty of the murder of Frederick Alexander Augustus Cannon, and that she suffer death in two hours."

A correspondent for the *Pacific Star*, who was in Downieville to cover the community's Independence Day festivities, witnessed the proceedings. He wrote that she approached the gallows without the least trepidation and there admitted that she had killed Cannon, and expected to suffer for it. Her only request was that her body be given to her friends for decent interment. She extended her hand to the bystanders immediately around her, bid each an "adios, señor," and voluntarily ascended the scaffold. All reports agree that Josepha adjusted the rope around her neck with her own hand. In the final moments her arms were pinioned, wrote the *Pacific Star*'s reporter, to which "she strongly objected, her clothes tied down, the cap adjusted over her face, and in a moment more the cords which supported the scaffolding had been cut, and she hung suspended between the heavens and the earth."

Downieville's infamy for having hanged a woman lingered for years. It was still fresh in people's minds when, on December 26, 1853, twelve Sacramento jurors sat in judgment on Ida Vanard.

Judge Monson's courtroom overflowed with curious onlookers at ten o'clock on the morning after Christmas, 1853, when the Sixth District Court convened.

The first order of business, empaneling a jury acceptable to both the prosecution and the defense, consumed more than two hours.

It was twenty minutes past noon when the deputy clerk read the indictment in the case of the People of the State of California vs. Ida Vanard. The charge was murder, and the indictment's archaic language must have temporarily revived memories of Salem, Massachusetts, and an earlier day.

"The said Ida Vanard on the 21st day of October A.D. 1853 at the county of Sacramento and state of California aforesaid," intoned the clerk, "not having the fear of God upon her eyes but being moved and seduced by the instigation of the Devil with force and aims in and upon Mary Lee in the peace of God and the said People . . . did make an assault . . . of which said mortal wound she the said Mary Lee then and there immediately died. . . . "

Upon hearing the indictment Ida wept and seemed greatly affected. She was dressed somberly in black silk and a straw bonnet, a gauze veil drawn back to reveal her rosy complexion and deep blue eyes. The pretty girl, not more than twenty years old, wore an expression at least as winning as remorseful.

The crowd's sympathies seemed to embrace her, despite District Attorney J. H. Hardy's forceful and eloquent opening argument delineating the magnitude of the accused's crime. Hardy contended that justice demanded her life on the gallows, but the prospect of hanging the pretty girl was not welcomed by those watching her weep as each witness testified to her guilt.

More damning than the words of the doctors or of Anne Woods, William Revere, or even Bill Cameron was the testimony of Police Officer Cady, who had arrested Ida. Cady, upon questioning, revealed that Ida had said to him that she "cut the woman," that "her man had slept with Mary Lee the night before, and she was going to have revenge out of her."

Judge Monson inquired and Cady confirmed that no enducements were offered the prisoner to make acknowledgments of her act.

As if her confession and the number of eyewitnesses to the crime were not enough, those appearing for the defense offered little in Ida's favor. Rosanna Hughes testified that she thought at times that Ida was out of her mind, and had often remarked to the other ladies in her house that Ida was "flighty." "She did not seem to have good sense, or know what she was doing," Rosanna added. Both Anne Matthews, with whom Ida boarded, and a man named Parkinson who knew her at Pine Grove, confirmed they had previously seen Ida carry a knife.

Yet, in closing for the defense in a summation occupying two and a half hours, Ida's attorney captivated the spectators, after which Judge Monson added his own not unsympathetic charge to the jury: "I know that it is impossible for either you or I to regard the condition and situation of the prisoner at the bar without deep feelings of sympathy and commiseration. Her sex, alone, is sufficient to excite our sympathies . . . the expression of her face bespeaks mildness and amiability. It appears hardly creditable that she can be so abandoned; so lost, so profligate, so depraved in heart, as to be guilty of the highest crime known to the laws—that of wilful, deliberate and premeditated murder."

Even so, the judge declared they must not consult "feelings of sympathy . . . inconsistent with the strict performance of our duty." To District Attorney Hardy, at least, it seemed the jurors must have done just that.

The jury returned in about two hours with an ink-blotted scrap of paper bearing the scratchily penned words, "The Jury find for the defendant Not Guilty."

At the announcement, wrote one reporter, "the Court House rang with applause."

FIVE

WORKING WOMEN

*A smart woman can do very well in this country—true there are
not many comforts and one must work all the time and work hard
but [there] is plenty to do and good pay If I was in Boston now
and know what I now know of California I would come out here If
I had to hire the money to bring me out. It is the only country
that I ever was in where a woman received anything like a
just compensation for work.*
                                    —Unsigned letter, San Francisco, 1850

Luzena Wilson tugged her worn and faded sunbonnet over her
sunburned face and stared, embarrassed, at the sleeves fringing
tatters at her elbows. The cotton square tied around her neck must
look like what it was: a scrap torn from a discarded dress. A ragged
hem of skirt circling her ankles showcased shoes so worn that their
soles had long ago, she noted wryly, "parted company with the
uppers."

The arduous overland journey, the life-threatening crossing of the
forty-mile desert, and the difficult ascent over Carson Pass erased all
concerns but survival. The tidiness of one's dress counted for nothing
when the urge was hunger or thirst. With those basic necessities
satisfied, however, vanity soon rekindled. When Luzena Wilson, fifty
miles east of Sacramento, met a man wearing an honest-to-goodness
white shirt, she shrunk from being observed in her threadbare
shabbiness.

In the mining region the Wilson family encountered many men
and, despite her scruffy appearance, one evening a miner approached
Luzena as she cooked biscuit for her family over a campfire. "I'll give
you five dollars, ma'am," he said, "for them biscuit." Stunned at
what sounded like a fortune, Luzena stared at him speechless.

Taking her hesitation for reluctance, the miner doubled his offer.

He wanted bread made by a woman, he said, and put a shiny ten-dollar goldpiece in her hand.

Luzena marveled at her first California gold, and the apparent ease by which she came by it. That September night in 1849, she dreamt that crowds of bearded miners struck gold and each gave a share to her. Luzena Wilson had caught the fever.

Margaret Frink contracted the fever long before she and her husband even reached Sacramento. In 1850, traveling into St. Joseph, the Frinks took lodging with a Mr. and Mrs. McKinney, and Margaret wrote in her diary:

> Mrs. McKinney had a nephew who went to California in 1849, and she told me of the wonderful tales of the abundance of gold that she had heard; 'that they kept flour-scoops to scoop the gold out of the barrels that they kept it in, and that you could soon get all you needed for the rest of your life. And as for a woman, if she could cook at all, she could get $16.00 per week for each man that she cooked for, and the only cooking required to be done was just to boil meat and potatoes and serve them on a big chip of wood, instead of a plate, and the boarder furnished the provisions.' I began at once to figure up in my mind how many men I could cook for, if there should be no better way of making money.

California's gold seduced thousands of women. They could and did cook for it, sew for it, clean, iron, wash, dance, pour drinks, or do whatever was required and returned the most.

With a little initiative and minimal equipment, women often were in business for themselves and earning as much, and often more, than the average miner. As Luzena Wilson discovered, baking biscuits could be profitable.

In fact, as soon as Luzena reached Sacramento, a goldpiece traded for biscuit fresh in her memory, she set herself to cooking. Among the first customers at her campfire was a town official who ordered a breakfast of two onions, two eggs, a steak, and coffee. He paid five dollars. Given the exorbitant cost of groceries, Luzena disappointedly realized her price "was not much above cost." Mrs. Wilson, a quick study, tucked away the economics lesson by concluding, "If I had asked ten dollars he would have paid it."

Men did pay well for women's cooking. As Margaret Frink heard, if "a woman could cook at all" she could make a living. Some women came west with just that intention. Margaret saw one such woman

In November 1849, Luzena Wilson cooked breakfast over her Sacramento campfire for a man who paid her five dollars, not much above the cost of the groceries.

while crossing the desert, noting in her journal for August 12, 1850, that "among the crowds on foot, a negro woman came tramping along through the heat and dust, carrying a cast-iron bake oven on her head, with her provisions and blanket piled on top—all she possessed in the world—bravely pushing on for California."

That determined woman's aspirations were realized at Sonora by another black cook. "Aunt Maria," as the former slave freed in California was known in the town of Sonora, earned a hundred dollars a week cooking for the Gunn household. She also managed her own boardinghouse and was acknowledged "an excellent cook . . . always well paid for her services, especially at weddings and banquets."

Wages varied with time and place. At distant Weaverville, Sarah Royce met a woman exultant over an offer of a hundred dollars a month to cook three meals a day for a hotelman's boarders. The enticements were multiple: she had an assistant and did no dishwashing. "She had been filling the place some days, and evidently felt that her prospect of making money was very enviable," recalled Mrs. Royce. "Her husband, also, was highly pleased that his wife could earn so much."

In March 1850, at equally remote Downieville, Mrs. Galloway, wife of the justice of the peace, opened a restaurant in the couple's log cabin. William Downie admired this "most estimable wife," observing that for a woman "to brave the difficulties, not to say dangers, of traveling up the mountains in those days, was enough to arouse the admiration of us all, and the arrival in our midst, of Mrs. Galloway, was hailed with much enthusiasm."

No record survives of Mrs. Galloway's success, but women who cooked often earned substantial sums. A fiercely independent California woman so testified in an anonymous letter published in the *Merchant's Magazine and Commercial Review* in 1852:

> I have made about $18,000 worth of pies—about one third of this has been clear profit. One year I dragged my own wood off the mountains and chopped it, and I have never had so much as a child to take a step for me in this country. $11,000 I baked in one little iron skillet, a considerable portion by a campfire. . . . I bake about 1,200 pies per month and clear $200. . . .

Given their numbers, these pies must have been simple, single-serving tarts or English "pasty" equivalents, not fancy double-crust or lattice-decorated confections serving six.

Whatever the style of preparation, the pie business in California was a good one. Forty-niner Mary Jane Caples, when her miner husband, James, fell ill "concluded to make some pies and see if I could sell them to the miners for their lunches. . . . " Dried apples were plentiful and there were "dried pealed peaches from Chili, pressed in the shape of cheese, to be had, so I bought fat salt pork and made lard, and my venture was a success." Mary Jane sold fruit pies for $1.25 each and mince pies for $1.50.

So profitable was her pie business that Mrs. Caples soon bought a stove to replace her two small dutch ovens. The following spring, however, the couple left the creek and moved to town. Mary Jane, enjoying success, left with regret: "Sorry I was to lose my customers."

Another industrious piemaker was Mrs. Phelps, who had brought a cooking stove over the plains to Nevada City. There, in 1850, she commenced making dried apple pies, which sold readily at one dollar a pie, and coffee at ten cents a cup. "She drove a wonderful trade," reported one customer, "especially on Sundays when the miners came to town, they having played euchre every evening of the week to determine who should pay for the pies when they went to the 'city.' "

Mrs. Phelps, to satisfy the increasing demand, bought a second stove as well as two cows, a great attraction. Their milk, a rare commodity, Mrs. Phelps readily sold at a dollar a pint, "and one-half water at that," testified a young miner.

From cooking to keeping boarders was a natural progression for women with the initiative to seek fortunes in California. In 1850 nine out of every thousand persons gainfully employed in California ran boardinghouses or hotels.

One of them, a woman from Maine who started a boardinghouse in the mines in 1849, wrote her children that she worked "mighty hard—I have to do all my cooking by a very small fire place, no oven, bake all my pies and bread in a dutch oven. . . . "

From her ten boarders she earned $189 per week, expecting to clear $75 after expenses. She shared with them accommodations decidedly modest, or at least minimal. They had one small room about fourteen feet square, "and a little back room we use for a store room about as large as a piece of chalk," she wrote. "Then we have an open chamber over the whole, divided off by a cloth. The gentlemen occupy the one end, Mrs. H—and daughter, your father and myself, the other. We have a curtain hung between our beds, but we do not take pains to draw it, as it is of no use to be particular here. . . . "

Mary Ballou, who had wept so much while crossing the Isthmus, also kept a boardinghouse in the mines. The letter she wrote her son Selden from Negro Bar on October 30, 1852, must have been tear-stained:

> Now I will try to tell you what my work is in this Boarding House.
> well somtimes I am washing and Ironing sometimes I am making mince
> pie and Apple pie and squash pies. Somtimes frying mince turnovers
> and Donuts. I make Buiscuit and now and then Indian jonny cake and
> then again I am making minute puding filled with rasons and Indian
> Bake pudings and then again a nice Plum Puding and then again I am
> Stuffing a Ham of pork that cost forty cents a pound . . . sometimes I
> am making gruel for the sick now and then cooking oisters sometimes

making coffee for the French people strong enough for any man to walk on that has Faith as Peter had. three times a day I set my Table which is about thirty feet in length and do all the little fixings about it such as filling pepper boxes and vinegar cruits and mustard pots and Butter cups.

As though the Herculean labor of filling that thirty-foot table three times a day was not sufficiently taxing, Mrs. Ballou also contended with wandering animals. In her house, she explained, "anything can walk into the kitchen that chooses to walk in and there being no door to shut from the kitchen into the Dining room you see that anything can walk into the kitchen and then from kitchen into the Dining room so you see the Hogs and mules can walk in any time day or night if they choose to do so." In exasperation she complained, "Somtimes I am up all times a night scaring the Hogs and mules out of the House." Whatever the golden reward, it seemed unworthy the effort:

Somtimes I am making soups and cranberry tarts and Baking chicken that cost four Dollars a head and cooking Eggs at three Dollars a Dozen. Somtimes boiling cabbage and Turnips and frying fritters and Broiling stake and cooking codfish and potatoes . . . somtimes I am taking care of Babies and nursing at the rate of Fifty Dollars a week but I would not advise any Lady to come out here and suffer the toil and fatigue that I have suffered for the sake of a little gold. . . .

The name Negro Bar attached to four mining camps, one each in Placer, Sacramento, Sierra, and Yuba counties. Since Mary Ballou mentions other women and babies she was probably near Sacramento; the diggings there were rich and in 1851 the camp by that name numbered seven hundred.

Regardless of location, the work of running a boardinghouse or hotel was daunting, as Mary Ballou, despite her orthography, so eloquently attested.

It was also unpredictable, especially in the mining districts. At news of a richer strike miners packed up at the drop of a pick, leaving stores and boardinghouses to wither at the deserted camp.

Birds Valley, a remote mining camp in Placer County, in 1850 counted a population of three thousand. In 1853 declining mine productivity began affecting Maria Tuttle's business. "I have about twelve regular boarders in our family besides transient custom, which is quite irregular," she wrote on February 16. "Sometimes we have ten and then again none at all." Two years later, the gold depleted, only three houses remained in Birds Valley.

City boardinghouses also proved unreliable moneymakers, as Mrs. D. B. Bates discovered.

The Bateses were gold rushers by circumstance—after a series of disastrous coal fires while sailing 'round the Horn—rather than intention. Nonetheless, the couple doggedly joined in. They were in San Francisco in May of 1851 and witnessed one of the great conflagrations that periodically destroyed that city. Another couple, identified only as Mr. and Mrs. B—, suggested that with the city in ruins they should "go to housekeeping" together and take boarders. Seizing the moment, Mrs. Bates agreed: "No time was to be lost: after a fire in California was the time for immediate action."

They found a house that very day. Its owner had gone back to the States and his agent was gone to the mines. Noting that "our husbands had the audacity to take quiet possession," Mrs. Bates and her friend proceeded to furnish the kitchen:

> Dishes, knives and forks, and spoons, we had picked up from the
> heterogeneous mass of half-consumed rubbish upon the former site of
> Mr. B—'s store. But, at such a time as that, if one could get anything
> to eat, he never stopped to see if his fork was blessed with one prong
> or three; and, if the knife was minus a handle, it was just as well,
> provided the blade was good. And then, too, a person was not
> particular about enjoying both cup and saucer, if at any time there
> were more people than dishes.

Next day their husbands rounded up boarders and the women were in business. Mrs. Bates soon concluded, in apparent agreement with her three partners, that "the proceeds derived from keeping this boardinghouse was decidedly insufficient remuneration for the amount of physical labor expended."

Abandoning their San Francisco boardinghouse, the four set off for Marysville and the mines to seek their fortunes.

The short-lived San Francisco venture prepared Mrs. Bates for her next foray into the boardinghouse business. Marysville "perfectly delighted" Mrs. Bates, but board at the United States Hotel, where they took a room, cost four dollars a day. Their limited means required Mrs. Bates to find work while her husband looked about for a business to engage in. She applied to the newly erected Tremont Hotel for a position superintending the "domestic department" for $125 a month. After five weeks she and her husband rented the Atlantic Hotel to operate themselves.

The labor of running a hotel was considerable, as others had discovered before her. Mrs. Bates's boardinghouse, always filled to capacity, offered good prospects of future success, "provided I had strength given me to sustain the weight of care and labor necessarily devolving upon me," she wrote. "Often, on account of exorbitant demands from servants,—demands which could not reasonably be granted,—I would be compelled to work early and late, for days and weeks in succession."

No cataloging of boardinghouse labor is more complete than that recounted by Mary Jane Megquier, the intrepid traveler who so enjoyed her Isthmus trip. From San Francisco, on June 30, 1850, she wrote her daughter:

> I should like to give you an account of my work if I could do it justice
> . . . . I get up and make the coffee, then I make the biscuit, then I
> fry the potatoes then broil three pounds of steak, and as much liver,
> while the [hired] woman is sweeping, and setting the table, at eight
> the bell rings and they are eating until nine. I do not sit until they are
> nearly all done...after breakfast I bake six loaves of bread (not very
> big) then four pies, or a pudding then we have lamb, for which we
> have paid nine dollars a quarter, beef, pork, baked, turnips, beets,
> potatoes, radishes, sallad, and that everlasting soup, every day, dine
> at two, for tea we have hash, cold meat bread and butter sauce and
> some kind of cake and I have cooked every mouthful that has been
> eaten excepting one day and a half that we were on a steamboat
> excursion. I make six beds every day and do the washing and ironing
> you must think that I am very busy and when I dance all night I am
> obliged to trot all day and if I had not the constitution of six horses I
> should [have] been dead long ago but I am going to give up in the fall
> whether or no, as I am sick and tired of work. . . .

Whether "sick and tired" of it or not, most California women worked, as Luzena Wilson adamantly attested: "Yes, we worked; we did things that our high-toned servants would now look at aghast, and say it was impossible for a woman to do. But the one who did not work in

'49 went to the wall. It was a hand-to-hand fight with starvation at the first."

To stave off starvation, Luzena Wilson and her husband, after only three days in Sacramento, sold their oxen for six hundred dollars and bought an interest in the local Trumbow House hotel, its kitchen Luzena's "special province." At once, gold gravitated to the woman who'd dreamed every miner would share with her.

Also successful in the Sacramento boardinghouse business was Margaret Frink, the woman who had once figured up in her mind how many men she could cook for, "if there should be no better way of making money."

In September 1850 she and her husband Ledyard reached Sacramento, by then a thriving community with steamer connections to San Francisco and stage service to mines north and south. The rough-looking tent town encountered by the Wilsons the previous year had, by Margaret's arrival, blossomed into a full-fledged city with a post office, courthouse, hotels, stores, houses, and churches.

The Frinks plunged into the hotel business in Sacramento, renting a two-story house on K Street for $175 a month. Like many, the house had been shipped in pieces around the Horn. It consisted of one roughly made large room below and one above, with stairs on the outside. Margaret could put her hand through the cracks between the boards. Ledyard paid eighteen dollars for lumber to make a dining table and benches. For fifty dollars he bought a stove and installed it in a tent at the rear, Margaret's kitchen. With a sign over the front door reading "Frink's Hotel," they were in business.

The Frinks cleared two hundred dollars the first month, but a cholera epidemic sweeping the community felled both of them by the end of October. They recovered, but business on K Street didn't. They moved to a similar house on J Street, paying three hundred dollars a month for a one-year lease to continue in the hotel business, adding cows to their assets. Despite the prevailing price of two dollars a gallon for milk, Margaret offered free to her hotel guests all their herd produced. "This was a great attraction to men, many of whom had not tasted milk for one or two years," she noted. "No other hotel in the city set it free on the table for their guests to drink. People would come from distant parts of the city to get meals on account of the fresh milk."

Luzena Wilson and her husband succeeded in the Sacramento

hotel business, too. They, however, decided they could make more money by speculating on commodities. After two months the Wilsons sold for one thousand dollars the hotel interest purchased for six hundred. They moved into a canvas house, and invested their small fortune in barley.

The Wilsons' decision was not fortuitous, although commodity speculation often proved quickly enriching. San Francisco lawyer John McCrackan met a Mrs. Smith who did very well on onions. She and her husband had come around the Horn and stopped briefly at a Pacific island, where Mrs. Smith heard about California's vegetable shortage. In a letter dated October 13, 1850, McCrackan reminded his sister:

> I have before spoken of her. . . . Her husband would give her no money to speculate with, so she sold some pieces of jewelry, which she didn't value particularly, & which cost her about twenty dollars at home, with this jewelry she purchased onions which she sold on arriving here for eighteen hundred dollars, quite a handsome sum, was it not? . . . She also brought some quinces & made quite a nice little profit on them.

The Wilsons' investment in barley, however, was catastrophic. The Sacramento flood of the winter of 1849–50 trapped them seventeen days on the second story of a hotel. Upon emerging they discovered their sacks of barley had burst and sprouted. Wrote Mrs. Wilson, "Ruin stared us again in the face."

The flood so frightened Luzena that she insisted on higher ground for her next home. Hearing that miners had struck it rich at Nevada City, she persuaded an idle teamster to transport her, her children, and her stove there. He wanted seven hundred dollars and she had nothing, but on her promise to pay him if she lived and "made the money," he took her.

At the Nevada City mining camp on Deer Creek, with her stove installed beneath a pine tree, Luzena set herself to repairing the family's fortune: "As always occurs to the mind of a woman, I thought of taking boarders. There was already a thriving establishment of the kind just down the road, under the shelter of a canvas roof, as was set forth by its sign in lamp-black on a piece of cloth: 'Wamac's Hotel. Meals $1.00.' "

"Ruin stared us again in the face," wrote Luzena Wilson after Sacramento's disastrous flood of 1850. She moved her family to higher ground in Nevada City.

Nevada County's 1850 census records reveal that four of the thirteen women counted in the community that was to become Grass Valley kept boarders. In nearby Nevada City, twelve of the twenty-three women counted by the census took in boarders or ran hotels with their husbands, and another three women worked in family-run taverns that accepted boarders.

Mrs. Stamps must have been one of them. An early history of Nevada County names the C. F. Stamps family from Tennessee as the first to settle in the area. C. F. kept a trading post and, in time, his wife kept a boardinghouse.

Hers was not the first boardinghouse there, however. That distinction is Martha Womack's. Using canvas for the walls and roof, she and her husband, Peyton, opened the first boardinghouse at Deer Creek, site of what was to become Nevada City. The community's first wooden hostelry, the Nevada Hotel, built by Harriet and Joshua Turner, opened on May 1, 1850. And in the summer of 1850, twenty-three-year-old Phoebe Ann Kidd managed the Missouri Boarding House while her husband traded goods.

By 1851, wrote miner Charles Ferguson, "Nevada City was graced by the presence of the fair sex numerously, who lent a charm to the place we had never anticipated."

No history of the genesis of these establishments has yet surfaced. The beginnings of Nevada City's El Dorado Hotel, however, survive in the reminiscence of its proprietor, Luzena Stanley Wilson:

> I determined to set up a rival hotel. So I bought two boards from a precious pile belonging to a man who was building the second wooden house in town. With my own hands I chopped stakes, drove them into the ground, and set up my table. I bought provisions at a neighboring store, and when my husband came back at night he found, mid the weird light of the pine torches, twenty miners eating at my table. Each man as he rose put a dollar in my hand and said I might count him as a permanent customer. I called my hotel "El Dorado."
>
> From the first day it was well patronized, and I shortly after took my husband into partnership.

In six weeks Mrs. Wilson saved enough to pay the teamster his seven hundred dollars. Before long she enclosed her cook stove, and the family's brush house gave way to a frame one. This she gradually enlarged "room by room, to afford accommodation for our increasing business." Success crowned her labors: "We had then from seventy-five to two hundred boarders at twenty-five dollars a week. I became luxurious and hired a cook and waiters. Maintaining only my position as managing housekeeper, I retired from active business in the kitchen."

The Wilsons started a store during these flush times and made money fast. Within six months they had ten thousand dollars invested in the hotel and store and owned a stock of goods worth perhaps ten thousand more.

Men on their own so disliked cooking that they made Luzena Wilson rich. Washing clothes was an equally onerous task, and men paid handsomely for the service.

In the earliest days of the gold rush, washing could cost twenty dollars a dozen because no one wanted to do it. Men often sent their dirty shirts to the Sandwich Islands and even China to be laundered, their garments sometimes three to six months upon the sea. Development of the washing industry in San Francisco was a great convenience, although the quality of the work, like the cost, often proved uneven, as Mary Jane Megquier observed in 1849: "Uncle had some washing done for which they charged six dollars a dozen, they looked so bad, he gave them two dollars to keep them. . . . "

The first washerwomen in San Francisco were Mexicans and Indians. They established themselves at a pond that came to be known as Washerwomen's Bay. Because the pay was good, a number of men took up the business too. By 1850, as Bayard Taylor observed, the men, their fluted washboards at the water's edge, had set up tents for ironing, with large kettles for boiling the clothes. "It was an amusing sight to see a great, burly long-bearded fellow, kneeling on the ground, with sleeves rolled up to the elbows, and rubbing a shirt on the board with such violence that the suds flew and the buttons, if there were any, must soon snap off," wrote Taylor. "Their clear-starching and ironing were still more ludicrous; but, notwithstanding, they succeeded fully as well as the women, and were rapidly growing rich from the profits of their business. Where $8 a dozen is paid for washing clothes, it is very easy to earn double the wages of a Member of Congress."

At Washerwomen's Bay, in March of 1850, convened a "highly respectable meeting of the laundresses and washerwomen of San

Francisco" to discuss fees. The *Alta California*'s reporter covering the event apparently enjoyed himself:

> The meeting was called to order by a lady in a very rich shawl and a shirred hat with a feather in it who was chosen to preside. . . . This lady, whose name was said to be Spriggins, stated to her fellow-women that "this was Californy!" which announcement was received with a burst of enthusiasm. "They had not come to Californy for nothing—they hadn't! They had come to Californy to make money. (cries of "hear! hear!") They were useful members of society, and without their aid mankind would be as dirty as pigs, and the world one vast stye. . . . The object of the meeting was to take into consider-ation the expediency of reducing the price of washing from six dollars to four dollars per dozen! . . . Who, she would ask, of all that well dressed assemblage which, she was bound to say, wouldn't disgrace the court of Queen Victory . . . had ever wore such fine clo's afore? . . . Let us then," she continued with great warmth, "plunge all our hands into our tubs and not strip them as has put all these fine clo's upon our backs . . ." A very sloppy looking lady, with a red face and dishevelled hair, flimsy cap, and a slab-sided, soiled calico dress, with her arms bare and red, rose and addressed the meeting as follows:
>
> "Och m'a'am, its mighty fine for the likes of ye's wid all your fine silks and yer satins to be talkin' about the reduction of prices; but its not for the likes of we to be consintin' to wash for divil a hap'porth less nor six dollars the dozen. What for'ud we do it! . . . Sure if the gintlemen wants to have clane shirts let 'em pay for 'em, and if not why divil the bit do we care! . . ."

The washerwomen's meeting was less remarkable for the mocking reportage than for its outcome: the women formed a society. Among other resolutions adopted, the society agreed to a reduction in the "price of washing in exact ratio to the fall of soap."

For many years Washerwomen's Bay was a familiar San Francisco sight. It lay west of Clark's Point a few miles, between the city and the presidio, bounded by what today are Franklin, Octavia, Filbert, and Lombard streets. On February 14, 1851, the *Alta California* re-ported some two to three hundred people there, with "not flags flying but pillow cases, shirts, sheets, and unmentionables. Women of every clime and color engaged in pious work."

As Bayard Taylor observed, men willing to endure ridicule com-peted with the washerwomen. Practical considerations of competition undoubtedly influenced the washerwomen's decision to reduce rates. But the competition that eventually defeated the women came from China.

By 1853 Chinese men had captured the trade and established themselves at Washerwomen's Bay. Mrs. Bates, an indefatigable observer of the California scene, described the excellence of their work:

> After the articles are dry, they take them to their houses to iron. They starch every article, even to sheets and pillow-slips. Their mode of ironing is entirely different from anything I ever before saw. They have a copper vessel, shaped like a sauce-pan, and large enough to hold about two quarts of coal. The bottom of this vessel is very thick, and highly polished. They fill it with burning coal; then take hold of the handle, and shove it back and forth over the articles.
>
> They have a dish of water standing beside them, to which they put their mouths, and draw up such a quantity of the water, that their cheeks are inflated to their utmost capacity. All the while they are shoving this vessel back and forth, they are blowing the water out of their mouths, which falls like spray upon the garment, and renders it of an equal dampness. They iron very smoothly, and the clothes have a beautiful polish.

Although in San Francisco men quickly competed in the laundry business, and Chinese men eventually monopolized it, women in the mines had little competition.

Miners laboring with pick and pan under a summer sun enjoyed an occasional clean shirt, and willingly paid women for the luxury.

One was Charity Hathaway Hayward. She and her husband settled at Sutter Creek but fortune didn't smile on them early. The high cost of food quickly diminished the meager store of dust and nuggets Alvinza Hayward uncovered.

Charity frugally saved every drop of bacon grease, and not a single bean was thrown out. Eager to help earn money without letting her sensitive husband know he wasn't supporting them, Charity decided to wash clothes. After Alvinza left for his claim each day, she took an old wooden washboard, cracked but better than none, to the creek to launder other miners' shirts. So many badly needed mending that she soon had all the sewing she could do, and fondly recalled the miners' loyalty to her.

Alvinza Hayward, in storybook fashion, beat the odds and struck it rich. The Sutter Creek washerwoman forever after lived a life of fabled wealth.

In recalling the days she scrubbed miners' shirts to buy food, Charity Hayward mentioned nothing about how backbreaking was the labor required to wash clothes in a stream or pond, or kneeling over a tub, scrubbing against a washboard, wringing out clothes by hand.

Louisa Clapp, who avoided the chore of washing, much admired "Mrs. R.," Rich Bar's washerwoman. Mrs. Clapp thought it wonderful "what femininity is capable of," for looking at Mrs. R.'s "tiny hands . . . you would not think it possible, that they could wring out anything larger than a doll's nightcap."

Rich Bar's Mrs. R. earned a hundred dollars a week washing clothes, and Louisa Clapp heard one unnamed man heap praises on the woman for her industry:

> "Magnificent woman that, sir," he said, addressing my husband; "a wife of the right sort, *she* is. Why," he added, absolutely rising into eloquence as he spoke, "she earnt her *old man*," (said individual twenty-one years of age, perhaps) "nine hundred dollars in nine weeks, clear of all expenses, by washing! Such women ain't common, I tell *you*; if they were, a man might marry and make money by the operation."

Abby Mansur's neighbor at Horseshoe Bar also earned a good income from washing clothes. The woman's husband and a partner farmed, Abby noted, and she "has them to wait on and her work to do and she makes from 15 to 20 dollars a week washing when she has all she wants to do so you can see that women stand as good chance as men. . . ."

Few women appear to have stood a better chance than Luzena Wilson. Not only was the Nevada City hotel and store successful but, unwilling to be idle when gold beckoned, Luzena "did little pieces of sewing for the men." She accumulated about five hundred dollars this way, and decided to lend the money out, to earn more: "I loaned the money, but at such an extravagant rate of interest that I might have foreseen that my man must fail and run away, which he finally did. I believe the rate of interest at which I loaned it was ten per cent a month."

Despite such initiative, California vicissitudes continually tested her fortitude. Barely more than a year after establishing their lucrative Nevada City enterprises the Wilsons were again homeless.

The Nevada City fire of March 1851 destroyed every building in the main part of town. Gone was the Wilsons' store, the hotel, all their stocked goods and belongings. Their vast fortune was reduced to the five hundred dollars Luzena's husband had in his pocket.

The Wilsons left Nevada City and eventually settled in a verdant valley profuse with wild oats. With hay selling for $150 a ton in San Francisco, Mason Wilson commenced cutting and baling on land purchased from Manuel Vaca. Mrs. Wilson once again set up her stove and camp-kettle. Once again she hung up her sign, this time a piece of board scratched with a burnt stick to read "Wilson's Hotel." The boards from a wagon bed became her table, its canvas cover her shelter, stumps and logs her chairs. Guests retired to a haystack.

For a woman accustomed to looking for the bright side, such primitive conditions had advantages. "Housekeeping was not difficult then," Luzena recalled, "no fussing with servants or house-cleaning, no windows to wash or carpets to take up." Cooking utensils hung from nails driven into a tree trunk, and neither "crystal or French decorated eggshell china added care to my labors."

Despite absent amenities, Luzena's hotel prospered. It was long the only hostelry on the road between Sacramento and Benicia. But, years passed and others bought property nearby. Eventually towns-people clustered around the Wilson Hotel in sufficient numbers to justify naming the place. When a post office opened, a town name at last adorned the spot on the Sacramento-Benicia road where Luzena Wilson opened her last hotel.

Add to Luzena Wilson's achievements, this one: she founded the town of Vacaville.

SIX

FREE TO BE

it is all the same whether you go to church or play monte,
that is why I like [California], you very well know that I am a
worshipper at the shrine of liberty. —MARY JANE MEGQUIER,
San Francisco, November 11, 1849

Freedom was in the very air Californians breathed, for the country offered a unique and seductive draught of liberty. People here were free from censure, from Eastern restrictions, from societal expectations.

In California nearly everyone's principal concern was grabbing a share of gold. Consequently, what you could accomplish and whether you behaved yourself was just about all that mattered. Almost no one cared whether you or your family was distinguished or disgraced, rich or poor, aristocratic or humble.

Lawyer John McCrackan, who appreciated the importance of family connection at home in Connecticut, observed to his family there:

> You cannot know the perfect freedom and independence that charac-
> terizes all our relations. Society if it exists at all is freed from the
> multitude of prejudices and embarrassments and exactions that
> control the Eastern cities.

A gold rush trader, Franklin Buck, also from New England, agreed: "We come and go and nobody wonders and no Mrs. Grundy talks about it. We are free from all fashions and conventionalities of Society. . . . I like this."

Within this vast freedom a man could presume to be whoever he wished to be. With none to say nay, a person might aspire to heights elsewhere impossible. Many achieved ambition simply by claiming it. Eliza Farnham wryly discerned this tendency among Californians to exaggerate status and ability: "If he could blow a fife on training days, he will be a professor of music here; if he have built a pigsty or kennel at home, he will be a master-builder in California."

One nearly illiterate Missourian, flushed with sudden success in California, exchanged his homespun for a fine suit of clothes. Looking so smart, he decided to be a doctor. Encountering a surprised acquaintance from Missouri who asked him what he knew about the practice of medicine, the man replied: "Well, not much; but I get all I can do, and I kill just as few as any of them."

In San Jose Mary Jones met a man named Stokes who confessed that when he came to California he didn't know what to do for a living, for he had no trade:

> He knew a little about carpenter work and a little about surgery and he could not decide what to call himself, so he flipped a half dollar and said "Heads, doctor - tails, carpenter". And it was heads and that was why he was a doctor, and he was the only one in the place for a year, and he had a good practice, and never lost a patient that I ever heard of.

In the general spirit of advance, Californians readily elevated others as well as themselves. Englishman Frank Marryat, finding himself addressed as "captain," noted: "I rank as Captain in California, being *nothing*; if I was a real Captain I should of course be a General there."

Although women were less likely to assume unearned status, they were equally taken with the freedom that permitted such presumption. By 1855 Mary Jane Megquier confessed: "The very air I breathe seems so very free that I have not the least desire to return [to Maine]."

One of the freedoms women enjoyed was grubbing in the dirt for gold. The most immediate source of the glittering mineral was, after all, direct withdrawal from what Walter Colton called "Nature's great bank."

A chronicler of Tuolomne County claimed that the camp of Martinez, between Sawmill Flat and Yankee Hill, was named after Señora Martinez who brought several peons from Mexico to work for her. Colton reported, too, that a woman from Mexico's Sonora did well in the mines. She worked, he wrote, in the "dry diggings forty-six days, and brought back two thousand one hundred and twenty-five dollars."

Among American emigrant women miners was Lucena Parsons, who wrote in her journal of her great desire to see the gold diggings. After watching the process, she "washed a little & got a little gold."

Subsequent journal entries record her fever's progression:

> May 31. This morning the gold fever raged so high that I went again to dig with the rest but got very little gold. . . . Came home tired to night. Still in good spirits.
> June 2. We again went to the canion to find that bewitching ore that is called gold. We had better luck in finding it to day, my husband & I making 16 dollars in fine dust.
> June 3. This morning there was a general turn out to the mines. . . . We made 10 dollars to day.
> June 4. We went to the canion again and did very well, made some 8 dollars to day. It is very hard work to dig & wash sand.

Unlike Lucena, many women visiting the mines in curiosity remained immune to the fever. Eliza Farnham, wearing a riding-habit, washed but one panful of paydirt under a burning noonday sun. The small particle of gold she found did not compensate the labor and discomfort nor "in the least excite the desire to continue the search."

Louisa Clapp, the Dame Shirley of Rich Bar, likewise found the prize unworthy the labor:

> I have become a *mineress*; that is, if the having washed a pan of dirt with my own hands, and procured therefrom three dollars and twenty-five cents in gold dust . . . will entitle me to the name. I can truly say, with the blacksmith's apprentice at the close of his first day's work at the anvil, that "I am sorry I learned the trade;" for I wet my feet, tore my dress, spoilt a pair of new gloves, nearly froze my fingers, got an awful headache, took cold and lost a valuable breast-pin, in this my labor of love.

Mrs. Clapp further noted, "*Apropos*, of lady gold-washers in general," that women often made up pleasure parties to the mines. The miners, she said, to flatter their female visitors often "salted" the earth "before the dainty fingers touch it; and the dear creatures go home with their treasures, firmly believing that mining is the prettiest pastime in the world."

The alluring metal aroused even staid Elizabeth Gunn. After hearing that a Sonora man walking in the rain had stubbed his toe against

Some women mined with their husbands, while others, like this woman pictured in a rare daguerreotype of 1852, only visited the diggings.
CALIFORNIA STATE LIBRARY

a quartz stone that yielded eight hundred dollars in gold, she wrote: "I tell Lewis if it rains so hard again, I would go out walking, mud or no mud, if I could walk to such good purpose. He once, before I came, picked up a lump with eleven dollars in it, but I want one with a thousand!"

Real mining meant digging and washing dirt. It was hard work, demanding muscle and stamina. But women were strong enough to use a goldpan or a simple contraption like the rocker. Later, when the mineral became scarcer, modified techniques favored group efforts. Shaft mining ("coyoting"), riverbed damming and diversion, flume construction, hydraulic and quartz mining generally required not only the labor of several men but organized capital as well.

Until such methods supplanted the goldpan and rocker, women often mined with their husbands. James Delavan, in the spring of

1850, saw two such women at Volcano Bar. As "good wives should," Delavan observed, they followed the fortunes and shared the hardships of their husbands. The women "assist at the rocker and the pan," he wrote, "and undoubtedly, by the conjoint labors of all, they will realize large fortunes, as they have been a long time at the Bar."

From Sonora, in August 1851, Elizabeth Gunn wrote that a "Frenchman and his wife live in the nearest tent, and they dig gold together. She dresses exactly like her husband—red shirt and pants and hat."

A San Francisco newspaper editor made a similar observation in 1850:

> We saw last April, a French woman, standing in Angel's Creek, dipping and pouring water into the washer, which her husband was rocking. She wore short boots, white duck pantaloons, a red flannel shirt, with a black leather belt and a Panama hat. Day after day she could be seen working quietly and steadily, performing her share of the gold digging labor. . . .

The same newspaper, interestingly, earlier denied the likelihood of two independent women miners reported near Sacramento. A young man told the editor that he and friends found "two intelligent and beautiful young ladies" from Florida mining in remote diggings, with only an "old grey headed negro" servant with them. The girls' imaginations had become excited by gold stories they had heard and they had determined to try their hands at making a fortune, the young man said. The old negro, past work, looked after the household affairs and kept watch while the girls pursued their mining operation. Apparently unafraid of being molested or robbed, they intended to return to Florida when they had accumulated ten thousand dollars, and had already gathered seven thousand of it.

"This is a most melancholy untruth," the editor concluded. "The idea of a lady 'young, intelligent and beautiful' digging gold on the slopes of the Sierra Nevada is supereminently preposterous."

Whether the story was true or the editor merely doubtful is unknown. But at least one attractive unmarried female mined, because forty-niner Charles Peters met her. At Forman's Gulch, about ten miles from Mokelumne Hill, Peters found a man with his wife and sister-in-law working a placer claim. The man shoveled the paydirt into a bucket which his wife carried to her sister, who rocked the rocker.

The unmarried sister, "a comely maiden," according to Peters, prevailed upon him for assistance. "I have always been susceptible . . . to the flattery of the female sex," wrote Peters, "and when this young maiden expressed a wish that she had my physical strength, in order to perform her task easily, I took her place and rocked for about four hours. . . ." Peters eventually concluded that the young lady was "more interested in the result of the clean ups than basking in the sunshine of love," so, disappointed, he resumed his journey toward Jackson.

According to Peters a Mrs. H. H. Smith, in French Ravine, who worked with her husband a few hours daily in mining, discovered a lump weighing ninety-seven and a half pounds. "It was two-thirds gold," Peters affirmed, "and was estimated by Langton and Company, bankers, at Downieville, by whom it was exhibited in January, 1855, to be of nearly $13,000 in value."

An inadvertant miner was Harriet Behrins, who accompanied her husband in 1851 to the mining camp of Quartzburg, in Calaveras County. "Almost the first day, as I sat in the doorway of my cabin, I saw something moving and shining," she wrote. "I ran to investigate, and found that it was a 'pocket,' as the miners call it, broken loose from the dirt on the bank of the ravine. . . . I took a horn spoon and extracted from the lump what proved to be an ounce of coarse gold."

Mrs. Bates heard a similar story from a woman who daily, after finishing her housework, took her "crevicing-spoon" out among the rocks and searched for gold. In one year, she told Mrs. Bates, "she collected five hundred dollars in that way."

While in Marysville Mrs. Bates heard many such stories and occasionally met their subjects. One woman, unnamed but described as "fine-looking" and about thirty years of age, upon arrival in Marysville told the proprietor of the Tremont Hotel that she was destitute, the trip from New York having exhausted her funds. He loaned her twenty dollars to continue her journey to Downieville, where she expected to find a friend and relative.

At Downieville this woman started a boardinghouse, receiving twelve dollars a week each from the thirty to forty miners she cooked for. But it was not cooking that made her rich. Mrs. Bates, who was present at the woman's triumphant return to Marysville to pay her twenty-dollar debt, recounted the story:

> One day, as she was sweeping her floor,—which, by the way, was nothing but the earth,—she saw something glitter. Upon examination, it proved to be a lump of gold. She searched farther, and found the earth was full of particles of gold. She instantly summoned to her presence the friend who had assisted her in locating herself in such rich diggings. They removed the table, benches, and stove. Upon the last-named utensil a dinner was in progress; but who would think of preparing dinner . . . should they suddenly find themselves in possession of such rich diggings. . . .
>
> That day they two took from the kitchen floor, as she termed it, five hundred dollars, mostly in lumps. Every day witnessed similar success. As soon as she could think of leaving her treasures for two days, she hastened to Marysville to cancel her debts. . . . She acquired a fortune. . . .

Entrepreneurs like the Downieville mineress, and what one might call mavericks or "free spirits," responded to California's freedom and gold as moths to a porchlight. Most were men, but not a few were women.

One of them was Sophia Eastman. The California bug bit the dark-eyed eighteen-year-old Massachusetts teacher in 1849. The resultant infection propelled her into a story that might best begin, "Once upon a time . . ."

That time was the summer of 1849, and Sophia wrote of nothing but California to Maria, her married sister living in Boston. Boston ships frequently advertised California passage, and Maria must have tired of Sophia's constant pleas to investigate first one rumor of California sailings and then another.

"Impress it upon the minds of all who are interested in the California mission," wrote Sophia to her sister, "that I wish to go in the capacity of a teacher; that I can perform all kinds of labor, but teaching would be preferable to any other kind."

"Answer all my California questions," she wrote insistently, followed quickly by, "I was disappointed not to hear more from the California line." When Maria wrote she was planning to visit, Sophia replied, "Come well loaded with news from that [California] quarter."

Practical arrangements for such a long journey to a rough frontier imposed considerable impediments to an unmarried young woman, educated and of good family. During the summer of 1849, hearing that the Boston shipping firm of Baxter & Howe was arranging passage to California for an emigration company, Sophia requested a booking for herself. A representative politely replied that "the Franklin Co will be composed of 100 men and no ladies and therefore presume it would not be such an opportunity as you desire."

In August Sophia heard about a vessel providing a separate cabin for "five or six ladies" and the captain promised to make arrangements for a female companion for her. "It seems to be the best chance that has been offered; though I imagine the company is not of the first order," Sophia told her sister. This plan, too, collapsed, but not before Sophia, who apparently didn't have the fare anyway, requested Maria to "consult Mother, & the rest, & tell me if you are willing to loan me the money now."

When Sophia's brother-in-law, Isaac Child, observed that she had "accomplished nothing material toward her intended emigration," Sophia pressed him for assistance. His inquiries led to a Mrs. Wright, a widow who was thinking of going to California. Sophia confessed that the "California fever rages so high, it seems as though I could not wait," and visited Mrs. Wright herself.

At last Sophia had a ship and a companion, although the circumstances suggest a compromise of practicality over preference. Mrs. Wright's arrangements were to accompany a portable tavern house that she would manage in California.

Whether Sophia was to have some responsibility for the tavern is unclear. Wrote Isaac Child, "Mr Doane who we saw day before yest. about Sophia's going out, appears to be a very fair man, and says, it could not be expected of them to take females out—and then leave them in the lurch with their tavern on their hands & none to take care of it—He says a a black woman and a first-rate Irish girl well recommended have offered to go for $4 per week, who will do the hardest part of the work, except the cooking, which is all to be done by *men*—Mrs Wright is fully capable of the full charge of any house."

As Sophia's departure drew near, her Aunt Harriet wrote Maria that she wanted to give Sophia "a lecture as long as the Mississippi River."

"Sophia has indulged in some silly fastidiousness which was well enough in a timid girl," wrote Harriet, "but will be hardly in character with a *woman* who has the courage to venture a voyage to California. . . . Her silly squeamishness about *men must* be thrown aside or she will be accused of affectation. A woman who dare go to California, virtually avows that she is not afraid of men. Tell her to meet them as *fellow beings*—not merely as masculine bipeds. . . . And tell her to engrave on her heart's core that *all* men, even vicious and depraved men, always respect a true woman, who respects herself. Monsters there may be in men's forms, but I can not think that we often meet them. Tell Sophia that she must rid herself of that shyness, which invites suspicion of affectation. . . . There is a vast difference between boldness, and a just confidence in ourselves and others."

In October 1849, weighed with advice and baggage, Sophia Eastman, hardly more than a schoolgirl, sailed at last for the California that consumed her imagination.

Eight long months later the *Colorado* anchored in San Francisco Bay. Sophia Eastman, girl adventurer, had at last achieved her heart's desire.

On June 30, 1850, Sophia wrote Maria and Isaac of her safe arrival—and that she had already refused her first marriage offer: "[He] proposed having me marry him, & going to the mines; but this I think I shall never do. If he is not able to build a house, & give me a good comfortable home then I had better not marry him."

Marriage, for the time being, held few attractions for the independent-minded New Englander. Neither was she bound by any responsibilities to Mrs. Wright and the tavern house. Mrs. Wright unexpectedly died, claimed by California's fearsomely high mortality. Sophia attended her funeral, visited the grave, and wrote an obituary notice for the local newspaper.

Keeping her accommodations aboard the *Colorado*, Sophia, armed with a sheaf of letters of introduction, commenced calls on Californians numbered among her family's and friends' influential acquaintances. Dr. May, formerly of Boston, she reported, "seemed to manifest an uncommon interest . . . introducing me to many influential citizens who all very kindly encouraged me with a hope that I should immediately obtain a school."

It was to Miss Winlack's school on Vallejo that interested friends directed the newly arrived young teacher from New England. Sophia Eastman found Miss Winlack "in a two story house, living in splendid style; keeping a few genteel boarders; her school consisting of a few young misses, & some small children."

Receiving permission to visit the school, Sophia met Miss Winlack's assistant, Mrs. Shore, and pronounced her a "simple, innocent woman of perhaps 25 years of age; unfit for this station, especially with such an energetic woman as Miss Winlack."

Sophia also discovered upon closer examination of Miss Winlack's school "much gentillity combined with poverty; a struggling to keep up appearances. . . ."

Miss Winlack offered Sophia the position as her assistant at forty dollars per month, including board and laundry. Sophia's duties would include teaching the children and, after school hours, "entertaining the young misses." Also, for every scholar Sophia might obtain for the school, Miss Winlack would pay one dollar.

Although Sophia wanted the position, the compensation was too small. She worried also that she might not be paid at all because of the school's precarious finances. When Miss Winlack confessed that she was obliged to close the school during the rainy season, Sophia regretfully declined the offer.

Most of Sophia's newly met influential friends frowned on her decision to accept the hospital attendant's job offered her by Dr. Peter Smith. One feared she should lose her "caste in society by going to the Hospital." Yet, one friend, after speaking with Dr. Smith, told Sophia that if she succeeded in pleasing Dr. Smith and his wife she might well become matron of the establishment and earn a large salary.

Shortly before Sophia's arrival in San Francisco, the Board of Aldermen had provided for the creation of a city hospital. On June 15, upon petition of local physicians, they appointed Dr. Peter Smith the City Physician, promising compensation at "$4 per diem for board, lodging and medical attendance for each patient."

In turn, that month Smith offered Sophia the position of hospital attendant. Her work would not be laborious and she was to do no washing of linens or floors. When Dr. Smith asked Sophia what price she would work for, she replied, "nothing short of the current prices of the city." Smith answered that times were hard, that he could not afford to give but $75 per month. He did promise to raise her wages after three months, and intimated she should "never go home poor."

Sophia accepted the position, though fearing she might "lose every cent." Smith struck her as sincere, but a man of poor judgment. He might, she thought, make her independent; but she also suspected she was "very apt to lose in such a place as this."

And what a place it was. Dr. Smith's hospital was not such a place as good society might expect to find a well-educated young woman. Sophia herself described the hospital as "in a deplorable state, filled with the offscourings of creation; inmates of the most loathsome diseases; the deaf, lame, blind, & maimed."

The only female attendant at the hospital when Sophia took up residence there was eighteen-year-old Sarah Mahon. During the voyage to California with her husband Mrs. Mahon had borne a child. She failed to recover from the birth and her husband took her to Dr. Smith's hospital. Apparently, there she tried to care for other patients. Shortly after Sophia's arrival, both the infant and the young woman died.

"I believe she had too much medicine given her," observed Sophia, "& the fact was she suffered for the want of care. . . . When I went there she was almost struck with death; too far gone to be saved."

Sophia arranged for the funeral when the young woman's husband proved reluctant. "I had a great trial with the husband to get this young lady buried in a decent manner. He declared he had no money, but I knew where he worked; & told him he must collect it. Then I ordered that the coffin might be made different . . . a mahogany one was sent very neatly lined."

Sophia assumed management of the funeral, writing to her sister: "I had a great deal of respect shown her. More than I ever care to receive myself, should I choose to die in this strange land. It was one of the sweetest sights I ever witnessed to see the Mother & Child laying together; & then that heavenly smile & angelic look!"

Sophia wrote long letters home from her room at the hospital. From its three large windows she enjoyed a delightful view of the harbor, watching ships come in. But invariably some tragedy interrupted her rare leisure. "Been called to the bedside to close the eyes of the dying," she wrote in explanation of having been interrupted in writing "no less than twenty times. . . . & then a feeling of humanity and sympathy obliges me to write many letters for these poor unfortunate beings, who are brought here to die," she added in explanation of her infrequent correspondence home.

"You have no idea how hard it is for some to die in this place," she wrote. One "beautiful young man," however, she described poignantly: "While his spirit is passing from earth to heaven there is a sweet smile of resignation & trust in God which leads one to the beautiful reflection that death will have no terrors if the life be pure."

More often Dr. Smith's patients distressed Sophia with their suffering: "Since I have been writing there has been a great variety of new patients in. One who has been stabbed; another with his face almost destroyed & made blind by having rum poured on the face & being set on fire. These two are the most wretched looking objects my eyes ever beheld."

On July 6, 1851, Dr. Smith dashed Sophia's hopes for promotion to matron and increased pay. He hired a Mrs. Basley to officiate in that position. Wrote Sophia: "She calls herself a widow lady, has a child 9 years of age & is about 45. There is a certain something which is not right though. She is quite smart but very irritable & is not very companionable."

Sophia's judgment proved keen. Mrs. Basley remained six weeks before being discharged. She was "too immoral & coarse a character to remain in such an institution," Sophia told her sister, adding, "the trials and troubles which I had to encounter from this female were too numerous to mention."

After Mrs. Basley's departure, Smith appointed Sophia matron, increasing her pay to $150 a month. Two months later, however, he reduced her wages to $75 a month and hired another matron. At this point Sophia described herself as "sort of company keeper to Mrs. Smith, who came to the hospital to live. She was simple & amiable, but I was obliged to neglect the patients to wait on her ladyship, & this galled me exceedingly. . . . "

Although Sophia tried seeking new employment she found nothing suitable. She was the more anxious to leave because Smith owed her four hundred dollars in unpaid wages and she feared the hospital was so poorly managed that she would never collect it.

She was still at the hospital on October 29, 1850, when the steamer *Sagamore* exploded. She wrote Maria:

> This was the most melancholy accident which ever occurred, for among the 85 persons on board not one escaped uninjured. The few which escaped with their lives were scattered all over the city, & many were brought in the Hospital, some dead others dying & multitudes crowding in to learn the fate of their friends. I have not time to give you a full description of the awful scene which offered so much gloom, & sadness over those who witnessed the scene.

Two days later a more terrible incident overwhelmed the young woman. Flames from a fire originating in a neighboring house of ill fame spread to the hospital and engulfed it. All 150 patients were rescued and Sophia's friends rushed to her aid. They saved most of her wardrobe and books, "& the small sum of $75, which is all that I have received for my hard & faithful labors."

Among those who hastened to assist Sophia was Harrison Eastman, also from New England and possibly a distant relation, who worked nights at the post office. He offered a man that night the handsome sum of thirty dollars to take his place so that he might aid the woman he loved.

And he was not alone in his adoration of the dark-eyed, independent New Englander. By October of 1850 Sophia had already rejected two more marriage proposals, including Col. Paige, a forty-year-old lawyer and former army officer. Although Sophia described him as "very gallant," fluent in French and Spanish, she told him she "did not love him well enough to marry him." To her sister she added, "there is nothing particularly objectionable in his character . . . but I have not roamed long enough; have not accomplished my object."

Harry Eastman, however, she had yet to refuse. Of him she wrote, "Perhaps I may marry him if he has a mind to wait my time."

It was Harrison Eastman who wrote Maria what could not have been news to her: "Your black eyed sister does just as she has a mind to, and always will." He added his dismay that after the fire at Peter Smith's hospital she "migrated to the City Hospital, and occupied a small 10 by 12 room; the apartments over this Room were unfinished; the Roof leaked like a Basket, and it usually rained in Sophia's Room 3 days after it was fair weather out doors; the hospital was wet and the whole room so damp and dirty that I often wondered how she lived. A history of her activities in California would be very interesting."

Indeed it would.

By April 1851, still unmarried and still unpaid by Dr. Smith, Sophia Eastman was earning one hundred dollars a month working for the Binghams, a theatrical family who left in her care two young children while they traveled. "You need not tell people what I am doing," she wrote Maria.

What she was doing was merely earning her living, as women did in California however they could, often encouraged by the West's free and open society to pursue nontraditional employments.

Julia Shannon, for example, advertised in a San Francisco business directory of 1850 that she was both a midwife and a daguerrean artist. The *Alta* of January 29, 1850, announced her photography business by noting: "Those wishing to have a good likeness are informed that they can have them taken in a very superior manner, and by a real live lady, in Clay Street, opposite the St. Francis Hotel, at a very moderate charge. Give her a call, gents."

The *Alta* also boosted the business of a lady barber in its issue of April 3, 1851:

> Stepping into a barber's shop, yesterday, in Commercial street, we
> saw a huge Frenchman, with an awful pair of mustacios and grizzly
> beard, undergoing the operation of shaving from a delicate little
> French *demoisell*. This may be customary in France, but it is certainly a
> new idea among Yankees. It is not an unpleasant operation, however,
> to take a clean shave at the hands of a lady fair.

Men generally admired such women, although an occasional jibe undoubtedly found its mark. The *Alta California* was not above a cheerfully delivered deprecation, such as in 1852 when it announced that a female doctor was on her way to San Francisco: "So few ladies in San Francisco that the new M.D. may attend them all. . . . No circumlocutions necessary. . . . Simply, as woman to woman: 'Saw my leg off!' "

The female Dr. Kammel opened offices at 300 Dupont street and advertised, with the same absence of timidity required to obtain her skills, that she had "cures for all female diseases, scrofula, cancer, dropsy, etc."

Mrs. E. S. Sleeper, M.D., "from the Boston Medical School," advertised in San Francisco during 1852 that she received female patients at her Fremont street residence at San Francisco's Rincon Point.

In that year, too, Madame St. Dennis advised that she could be consulted "on matters of love, law and business, from 8 a.m. to 8 p.m. Office second brown cottage on Union street, between Stockton and Dupont."

Madame De Cassins advertised herself as "the celebrated diviner," and offered to explain the past and predict the future in English, French, Italian, Greek, Arabic, and Russian, from 8 a.m. to 5 p.m. at No. 69 Dupont street.

In a less exotic pursuit, Mary Ann Dunleavy, in the remote mining camp of Rough and Ready, near Nevada City, was, as early as 1850, helping her husband, a Methodist minister, operate a ten-pin bowling alley. This attraction boosted business at their saloon, which they'd opened the first of the year. Either operation undoubtedly was expected to prove more profitable than evangelism.

Other women profiting in California included two known to lawyer John McCrackan. He wrote his sister that one of his lady friends had made large sums in real estate and another had "set her husband up in business here, manufacturing Soda and they are making money fast. She doesn't trust him with the profits 'nary time' but keeps the stuff in her own hands."

Franklin Buck, a trader living in Weaverville, was smitten by an entrepreneurial young Spanish woman:

> She is genuine Castillian, owns a train of mules and buys and loads them. We bought the flour she sent to Weaverville. I had a strong idea of offering myself . . . but Angelita told me she had a husband somewhere in the mines and she has a boy about five years old. So I didn't ask her.

Even more unusual was Enos Christman's discovery of a woman bullfighter, whom he saw perform in Sonora. He wrote in his diary for September 11, 1851:

> A dusky Mexican senorita, magnificently dressed, entered the arena, sword in hand. For a time she parried with the bull, pricking him slightly and stepping quickly to one side whenever he ran toward her. He soon became furious, roaring and tossing his horns high into the air and making the most formidable plunges at the lady until, at a favorable opportunity, she plunged the sword to the hilt into the breast of the animal. She was sprinkled with crimson dye, and in a moment the beast lay dead at her feet. The lady was greeted with a shower of silver dollars. . . .

Among equally unusual occupations was one briefly held by a young woman whose given name has not survived with her story. Seeking employment, she called on a friend of her father's, recalling later, "I guess I was one of the first career girls, because I told him I wanted to work."

Her father's friend was Leland Stanford, then a Sacramento merchant. Stanford gave the girl a letter of introduction to Wells, Fargo &

Company, whose manager hired her for one of the oddest jobs ever undertaken by any career girl.

Bandits had robbed the company's stage three consecutive times on its run to Sonora, and the manager thought an unobtrusive but observant girl might help identify them. She rode the stage, which was duly robbed. Other passengers described the thieves simply as masked, with nothing unusual about them. But the future Mrs. Lee Whipple-Haslam specified their height, size, and clothing. Although the men wore gloves, she described one as having a sore on his hand because she had noticed blood seeping through. Another she judged to be about forty-five, based on his hair, and added that a cataract filmed one eye. Her testimony convicted bandits named Benson, Parks, and Bryan.

Wells, Fargo & Company employed another woman, but didn't know it. Until death exposed her secret, she successfully masqueraded as a man and lived as a man.

Charley Parkhurst is believed to have arrived in San Francisco in 1851, when she was nearly forty years of age. She was from Providence, Rhode Island, where, as a youngster, she had first worn boys' clothing while working in a stable. Acquiring exceptional skill with horses, she disguised herself as a man to earn a living as a stage driver.

In California, where she drove for Wells, Fargo & Company, she continued to wear gloves that hid her small hands and a pleated shirt to conceal her figure. She drove stages until her retirement to a cattle ranch she purchased near Watsonville. The San Francisco *Morning Call* reported on Charley Parkhurst's death on December 28, 1879:

> He was in his day one of the most dexterous and celebrated of the
> famous California drivers ranking with Foss, Hank Monk and George
> Gordon, and it was an honor to be striven for to occupy the spare end
> of the driver's seat when the fearless Charley Parkhurst held the
> reins of a four- or six-in-hand. . . .

When the news of Charley Parkhurst's death, and the subsequent discovery of her sex, reached Rhode Island, the Providence *Journal* reported:

> Now that it is known that Charlie was a woman there are plenty of
> people to say they always thought he was. . . . His hands were small
> and smooth, and so far from being proud of the fact it disgusted him

and he wore gloves Summer and Winter. He was thought to be putting on style, but as he always dressed well, the gloves were looked upon only as a part of his high-toned ideas. He was beardless and his voice was a little thin . . . but . . . Charley weighed 175 pounds, could handle almost any one that ever took hold of him, smoked with the placidity of an Oriental, would take one or two glasses of whiskey punch without winking.

George F. Harmon, as a young boy, knew Charley Parkhurst well. He wrote:

What caused Parkhurst to adopt male attire and follow a man's work will never be known, as the secret died with her. My father and mother were her most intimate friends. . . . A short time before her death, she said that she had something to tell him, but there was no hurry about it. She kept postponing telling him, and he was not present when the end came. I have no doubt that she intended to tell him the secret of her life, what caused her to dress and live in the way she did.

Perhaps the maverick woman lived the lie simply because she loved horses, was an expert driver, and earned a fine wage for her skills.

Sophia Eastman, on the other hand, earned little and had difficulty collecting even that. Months after she'd left his employ, Dr. Peter Smith still owed her four hundred dollars. And California costs were so high that she despaired of paying her debts. An express order for $15 she mailed to her brother-in-law, in partial repayment of money he'd loaned her, cost $6.30 to send.

In June 1851 she was working for her board at the house of a Mrs. Wimmer. "Wages are becoming low," she wrote her sister, "& it is quite difficult to obtain a place. As soon as I can get my pay, I think I shall leave for Sacramento, or some other place. . . . I have rejected all my old lovers excepting Mr. Eastman. Had one more offer of marriage. . . . Mr. E's love is too pure and devoted to reject."

For several weeks that summer she was out of employment. "Am still engaged in trying to collect that debt due me from Dr. Smith, & there has been so many perplexities attending it that it has quite unfitted me for any other business & made me sick of San Francisco & money though I well know I cannot live without it. . . ."

Sophia believed her apparent "intelligence & refinement" prevented people from employing her. A woman who wanted child care refused to take Sophia as a servant. "She said she knew I was not accustomed to that kind of life, & it would be too great a condescension. On telling her that necessity obliged me to do something . . . she replied I must tell you frankly that we people who hire servants want those who always have been servants."

Meanwhile, the Binghams owed her $125 "and are now too poor to pay me."

Smith she considered suing but feared "this would cost me more than half the sum." After failing to obtain a sheriff's assistance in collecting the money due her, however, she consulted several lawyers. When Smith learned she intended a lawsuit he asked her to take a note for $250 given him by someone else and payable in three months. This she did, and quickly exchanged the note for two lots of land valued at three hundred dollars. "So you see I am a land holder in Cal, & fifty dollars in debt to a speculator! But he told me he would trust me as long as I wanted to be trusted, & I think I shall not trouble myself about paying him at present, as he made a pretty good bargain out of me."

With the distressing debt finally squared, Sophia turned her attentions elsewhere. And they settled on Harrison Eastman.

Through all her trials and tribulations, Harrison Eastman was her constant support. Harry, she had written Maria, "loves me to distraction & almost worships me."

She wrote Maria that before the year expired she might be Mrs. Eastman, "But don't spread it widely about, for he may go to the mines, & I shall not be married for a year, as he may die & I never marry him."

But on November 1, 1851, the *Alta California* published this announcement: "Married—In this city, on Thursday evening, October 30th, Mr. Harrison Eastman to Miss Sophia A. Eastman, both of New Hampshire."

And they lived happily ever after.

SEVEN

ALL THE WORLD'S A STAGE

*The population of San Francisco has been more liberally provided
with dramatic and musical entertainments than that of any
other city of its size in America. Notwithstanding its remoteness
from the old states, and its isolation from any thickly-peopled
country, it has had, since the city was a year old, from one
to three theatres open continually, and however their performances may be marred by the occasional appearance of a stick
where a living man or woman should be, there are generally
clever persons enough on the boards to keep the entertainments,
at the worst, up to decent mediocrity.*
   —ELIZA FARNHAM, *California, In-Doors and Out, 1856*

On May 22, 1853, *The Golden Era*, a San Francisco newspaper, advised
its readers: "The world-renowned Lola Montez, Countess of Lands-
feldt, arrived in this city on the *Northerner.*"

None other than the celebrated Lola—legendary beauty, mistress
of kings—had come to California.

And why not? The renowned Lola Montez danced, and was well
rewarded for her performances. Quite possibly the world around
there could be found no more appreciative audiences than those
entertainment-starved Californians who eagerly paid exorbitant
prices for their pleasures.

Gold rush California was a plum ripe for plucking by women with
any musical or theatrical talent. Here was an audience eager for
entertainment, and with gold-heavy pokes to pay for it. Rarely having
more than an empty tent to go home to, men naturally sought
amusement, avidly supporting the performing arts with stomps,
whistles, tossed nuggets and, occasionally, expensive jewelry.

Lola Montez, flamboyant beauty of international repute, undoubtedly anticipated garnering a fair share of California gold.

Her checkered career had commenced in Spain, where she adopted a vaguely romantic accent and a new name, finding none suitable among the long list given her at birth. Marie Dolores Eliza Rosanna Gilbert, born in Limerick, Ireland, became Lola, the Spanish dancer.

Lola's greater skill, however, lay in delighting men with her charms. On the continent, she took a series of lovers, among them Franz Liszt. Her coup was Ludwig I, King of Bavaria, who bestowed upon the dazzling beauty the title of Countess of Landsfeld.

When political events forced her to flee Europe, she sailed for America. She arrived in New York in 1851 to commence a tour throughout the East, Midwest, and South.

In the spring of 1853, sailing from New Orleans, she crossed the Isthmus to extend her tour to far-off California. She was preceded by her notoriety as a king's mistress, a stunning beauty, a political revolutionary, and as a performer of a near-scandalous dance. Jennie Megquier, one of the thousands intrigued by Lola's risque reputation, on May 31, 1853, wrote:

> Lola Montes is making quite a stir here now but many say that her
> playing is of that character that it is not proper for respectable ladies to
> attend but I do want to see her very much. Mr Clark said in dancing
> the spider dance a favorite play of hers where she performs the antics
> of one with a tarantula upon their person and some thought she was
> obliged to look rather higher than was proper in so public a place. . . .

Montez had adopted the *Tarantella*, making the dance uniquely her own. It consisted of a woman under attack by spiders. They climbed everywhere, the boldest venturing into her short petticoats, which the dancer scandalously explored for the hidden arachnids she had constructed from cork, India rubber, and whalebone. Novelty, more than artistry, formed much of the performance's appeal.

Whether for repute or her risque dance, Californians were anxious to see Lola perform. In consequence, the gold that miners so laboriously unearthed could be expected to find its abundant way into her purse.

The first entertainer to discover this transmigration quality in California gold was Englishman Stephen C. Massett. On June 22, 1849, "entirely unassisted," he performed in San Francisco's Portsmouth Square a full program of song, recitation, and imitations. Tickets were three dollars and the future "Jeems Pipes of Pipesville,"

A parade of talented women performed in gold rush theatres, including Lola Montez, famed for her titillating "spider dance."

as he chose to call himself, cleared five hundred dollars for his evening's work. Obviously, Massett didn't require a pick and shovel to find a gold mine. Other entertainers quickly followed his example.

Women fared especially well, since audiences consisted largely of men. Talented and beautiful female entertainers frequently received immense sums from the popular practice of fire engine companies buying seats at auction. In 1852, when the lovely songstress Catherine Hayes appeared in San Francisco, the Empire Engine Company bought at auction the best box seat for the flattering sum of $1,150. Miss Hayes, at her departure from California, was estimated to have taken with her a quarter of a million dollars.

Not every entertainer merited theatres and playbills, yet even these lesser lights earned handsome rewards. In the gambling "hells," which frequently provided musical entertainment to attract customers, a woman who played a harp, piano, or violin collected respectable wages for her talent. At a gambling place called the Alhambra, one Frenchwoman violinist daily earned two ounces of gold dust, about thirty-two dollars. Bayard Taylor noted that one young woman, a "Swiss organ-girl, by playing in the various hells, accumulated $4000 in the course of five or six months."

Naturally, the greater rewards were before the crowds eagerly attending San Francisco's several theatres. Lola Montez was booked at the American.

She received mixed reviews. Her charming curtain speeches endeared her to many, but a newspaper critic found her famous dance humorous:

> She unwittingly gets into one of those huge nests of spiders, found during the spring time in meadows, with a long radius of leading spires and fibres, stretching away into an infinity of space. She commences to dance, and the cobwebs entangle her ankles. The myriad spiders, young and old and half grown begin to colonize. . . .
>
> The music, a slow-measured but fascinating amalgamation of polka, waltz, march, mazurka and jig, conforms admirably to the step. The spiders accumulate and the danseuse stamps. They appear in myriads—eleven-legged nondescripts with two heads and no eyes; hairy monsters with fire-clawed feelers and nimble shanks.
>
> They crawl and sprattle about the stage, invading the fringes of Miladi's petticoats and taking such unwarrantable liberties that the spectator imagines an inextricable mass of cobwebs and enraged spiders, and would sympathize with the demoiselle, but she seems to take it so easily herself that one quickly jumps to the conclusion that she is enough for them. It is Lola versus the spiders.
>
> After a series of examinations and shaking dresses, she succeeds in getting the imaginary intruders away—apparently stamps daylight out of the last ten thousand, and does it with so much naivete that we feel [a] sort of satisfaction at the triumph.

The picture winds up with Lola's victory, and she glides from the stage overwhelmed with applause, and smashed spiders, and radiant with parti-colored skirts, smiles, graces, cobwebs and glory.

Whatever anyone thought of the performance, the American Theatre, where Lola trounced the spiders, was grand. Constructed at Sansome and Halleck streets, the American had been built on part of the industrious level-and-fill project the city engaged in so earnestly.

Steam shovels voraciously reduced the city's numerous sand hills by transferring them to the shallow waters of the bay, thereby enlarging the city's perimeter, not to mention salable real estate at exorbitant prices. By 1853 a "water lot" measuring twenty-five by fifty-nine feet could bring as much as sixteen thousand dollars.

The state's first real estate developers, by throwing sand on top of mud, may have laid a fine foundation for their own fortunes, but a poor one for buildings. An observer remarked that the "first brick building erected on this artificial foundation was the American theatre" and on its opening night it "settled bodily two or three inches."

Director of the American was Dr. D. G. Robinson, called "doctor" because of the drugstore he'd been associated with in 1849. In July 1850, in partnership with one James Evrard, he started a "dramatic museum," employing his satirical talents to fine reception.

Robinson and his wife boarded with Jennie Megquier, who was impressed that Mrs. Robinson "at one time had a salary of $150 per week for playing at the theatre. . . . " She held Dr. Robinson in considerably less regard, bluntly writing:

> I was up at Mrs Robinson last night, the Dr said he was coming down to get some medicine for his wife, she was sick at her stomach in the morning. I told him it was enough to make any woman sick to sleep with him . . .

Regardless of Jennie Megquier's distaste for him, Dr. Robinson enjoyed abundant respect in theatrical circles. When his American Theatre opened on October 20, 1851, with seating for two thousand patrons, the *Alta* praised its handsome decoration:

> The draperies of each box are sustained from an eagle's beak above. The front of the first tier of boxes, instead of being panelled, presents a thickly set row of small white pillars whose capitals and bases are

decorated with gilt bands. The front of the second tier is white with moldings at the top and bottom. It has a good ventilation system designed by G. T. Daly, which is unusual.

The American had two balconies, a gallery, a dress-circle, orchestra seats, and several boxes, these upholstered in red plush and draped with red velvet curtains held by the aforesaid eagles' beaks.

Frenchman Albert Benard de Russailh attended the American often, describing it as "extremely agreeable," having thick, soft carpeting and nicely decorated with "paintings and gilt-work."

Benard found California theatre audiences different from those in Europe:

> I must mention here the Americans' strange manner of applauding a
> favorite actor or a good scene. In France, and everywhere else in
> Europe that I know anything about, we clap and sometimes shout
> bravo, and whistle only when we are disgusted. Actors at home are
> terrified and paralyzed if an audience whistles; Nourrit, once so well-
> known in Paris, is even supposed to have died from it. But with
> Americans, whistling is an expression of enthusiasm, and when a San
> Francisco audience bursts into shrill whistles and savage yells, you
> may be sure they are in raptures of joy.

As a Frenchman, Benard felt obligated to support the Adelphi Theatre, "where every Sunday the French Troupe tries hard to put on something worthwhile." The *Alta California* announced in December 1850 that "talented ladies" gave theatrical exhibitions in French at the Adelphi, adding: "It is gratifying to know that there is a disposition in San Francisco to patronise talent, both foreign and native, and we trust that the very deserving artistes . . . will meet with a continuance of patronage. . . ."

Three women directed the company—Mesdames Eleonore, Adalbert, and Racine. Mademoiselle Racine in Benard's opinion had talent. The other two women he considered to "have been on the stage for a long time (I was about to write too long a time), and who have never definitely arrived." Despite the barbs, Benard wrote that Madame Eleonore "is still able to use her old eyes to good effect, which gets over with the public, and Madame Adalbert dresses well enough to make up for the rest." Benard thought they had little to work with but he went to the Adelphi "every Sunday evening eager to find everything wonderful":

I should certainly be the last one to abuse these good ladies, as some
of them treated me with great kindness, and, I might say, generosity.
Need I add that it was not because of my personal charm? To them I
was only a dramatic critic who had to be won over and muzzled, and I
suppose they succeeded well enough. I can't help smiling when I
think of the glowing write-ups I used to give them in Monday's paper,
far better ones than Parisian stars usually receive. The hypocrisy of the
press? Oh well, perhaps. But they are nice people.

The Adelphi was well patronized, Benard observing that the "women
directing the company . . . have not done badly from a financial point
of view, as they now own the building, the lot, and the scenery."

Such theatres as the American and Adelphi contrasted markedly
to the city's first home for dramatic entertainment. It was on January
16, 1850, that San Francisco theatregoers witnessed their first evening
of legitimate theatre. A Sacramento company headed by Mr. and
Mrs. Henry Ray performed *The Wife* and *Charles II* at Washington
Hall, next to the newspaper office on the second floor of a building
destined to become a brothel.

J. M. McCabe, an actor with the Rays' pioneer company, recorded
in his diary that the performances closed at Washington Hall one
week after debuting: "the treasurer, Mr. Mattinson reporting 'No
Salary,' he having lost the entire week's receipts at monte."

Before this unscheduled final curtain, however, the company was
apparently well received for it inspired pioneer entertainer Joseph
Rowe to add dramatic performances to his circus.

Rowe's Olympic Circus had opened in late October of 1849, performing in a crude amphitheatre on Kearny street seating between
twelve and fifteen hundred. The company included Mrs. Rowe, one
of three equestrians riding the two trick horses, Adonis and Mercury.
Two other women known to be in the company were Mrs. Batturs, a
singer, and Signora Levero, a slack-rope dancer.

Gate receipts must have been handsome because Rowe paid good
wages, although William Foley, the clown, quit because he claimed
twelve hundred dollars a month was insufficient to live on in San
Francisco. Or perhaps Foley guessed that an iceberg supporting the
twelve-hundred-dollar pinnacle he received must be rich indeed. In
any event he soon formed a rival company.

After the Rays' successful week at Washington Hall, Joseph Rowe
hastily added a stage to his amphitheatre and dramatic offerings to

ESTABLISHED IN 1849.

ROWE AND CO'S

PIONEER

CIRCUS

OF CALIFORNIA

Display Advertisement for "California's Pioneer Circus"

Joseph Rowe's Pioneer Circus featured his equestrian wife, who rode a trick pony named Adonis.

his bill. He reopened his new and improved Olympic Circus on February 4, 1850, with tickets for private boxes priced at five dollars and not-so-cheap seats at two. Rowe's company performed twelve different dramas in the month of February alone.

This exhausting schedule may have hastened the death of Rowe's singer, Mrs. Batturs. On March 5, 1850, the *Alta* announced that Mrs.

Batturs, "known for some months to the citizens of San Francisco as a pleasing and talented vocalist," had died after a protracted illness. Her death followed that of her twelve-year-old daughter by but a few weeks, the *Alta*'s editor sentimentally observing, "now mother and daughter sleep the sleep of death, side by side, in the silent tomb."

Rowe's dramatic company featured Sarah Kirby, a gifted American actress. Mrs. Kirby, although married to a Mr. Wingard, took her stage name from her deceased first husband, J. P. Hudson Kirby, a popular New York actor.

The theatrical troupe also included Mr. and Mrs. John Hambleton, an Australian couple who achieved immediate popularity. In a dramatic tragedy not intended for public entertainment, on January 14, 1851, Mrs. Hambleton, according to the San Francisco coroner, took her own life by consuming a "large quantity of cyanuret of potassium."

She and John Hambleton, as Sarah Kirby testified after her friend's death, had "lived together very unhappily." Mrs. Kirby reported that a month previous to the suicide Mrs. Hambleton confessed that her husband beat her, showing Sarah Kirby bruises on her neck where he'd tried to choke her.

In her unhappiness, Mrs. Hambleton had formed an alliance with Henry Coad, a member of the company in which the Hambletons and Mrs. Kirby were now employed at the newly opened Jenny Lind Theatre. John Hambleton, discovering the relationship, threatened Coad's life, after which Mrs. Hambleton took poison. Coad, upon learning of her death, also took poison, but recovered when administered an emetic.

Mrs. Hambleton's funeral, according to the *Alta*, was "numerously attended," and "as the procession passed the Jenny Lind Theatre, the orchestra of that establishment played a solemn dirge from the balcony of the Parker House."

Despite the tragedy, the Jenny Lind, under the co-management of Sarah Kirby and James Stark, a well-known tragedian, soon resumed performances, with two women forced to take men's parts because of Henry Coad's departure from the company.

Sometime previous to June 14, 1852, in more private drama, Sarah Kirby's husband, Mr. Wingard, fell from a horse and died, for on that date Mrs. Kirby became Mrs. James Stark in a Sacramento ceremony.

A popular actress joining the Jenny Lind company early in 1852

The Jenny Lind Theatre, where Alexina Baker portrayed Shakespeare's Juliet on February 20, 1852, and found a diamond ring in a bouquet tossed in appreciation.

was Mariette Judah, who also endured personal tragedy. In 1839, her husband, Emanuel Judah, and their two children, drowned in a shipwreck, Mrs. Judah surviving by clinging four days to the wreckage. Although remarried, she retained Judah as her stage name.

Theatrical tragedy was the specialty of two well-known New York actors debuting at the Jenny Lind in February 1852. They were John Lewis Baker and his wife Alexina Fisher Baker. For her performance of Juliet in Shakespeare's tragedy on February 20, patrons showered Alexina with bouquets. One flowery tribute enclosed a diamond ring valued at more than three hundred dollars.

The Jenny Lind first opened on October 30, 1850, bearing the famed Swedish nightingale's name but never her footfall, for the renowned singer never visited the West. The excellent profits to be made from entertaining miners prompted the opening of several theatres. Many perished in the city's recurrent fires, never to reopen, but the Jenny Lind, persistently rebuilt, flourished. Its third incarnation, which opened on October 4, 1851, was a building boasting a facade of finely dressed yellow-tinted sandstone brought from Australia. The *Alta* admired its handsome interior: "The prevailing color was a light pink, which was rendered brilliant and graceful by gilding tastefully applied. The chief feature of the act drop was a picturesque ruin. Richly decorated proscenium boxes added much to the splendid appearance of the whole auditorium."

The Jenny Lind Theatre presented numerous well-known performers, among them Caroline Chapman. Known for her verve and versatility, Caroline was a favorite with audiences. In 1853, when the tempestuous Lola arrived, Caroline Chapman and the clever Dr. Robinson, both now associated at the San Francisco Theatre, determined not to be neglected.

Dr. Robinson, at Lola's debut at the American, wrote a satirical drama titled *Who's Got the Countess? or; The Rival Houses*, designed to burlesque both Lola and the American Theatre's present manager, John Lewis Baker.

The performance featured a wonderfully funny send-up of Lola's famous spider dance, which Robinson called "Spy-dear." At least one citizen objected to the production for lampooning Lola, in light of her generosity in performing firemen's benefits:

> Such performances as the "Spy-dear Dance," though sufficiently nonsensical, are . . . occasionally exceedingly amusing. But a lady!—gentlemen—a lady! If no gratitude is felt for her benevolence, good taste should have decreed at least that her name and character should not be publicly ridiculed and outraged in this community. . . .
>
> Miss Caroline Chapman . . . can play anything and everything . . . and her name is an unfailing source of attraction wherever she appears . . . If she were to "play the Devil," I haven't the least doubt she would do it perfectly . . . *but we don't want to see her in any such character.*
>
> Miss Chapman is a lady, and a most admirable artist, and I cannot believe that lowering her in this manner . . . can be any more agreeable to herself than it is to her admirers. . . .
>
> Give us "Beauty" again, charming Carry. . . .

Some historians suggest that Chapman's parody drove the beautiful Lola from San Francisco. Newspaper accounts indicate, however, that Montez left San Francisco for Sacramento simply because her bay city performances concluded.

Lola had followed her two-week engagement at the American with several benefit performances. Then, in July, she recaptured from Caroline Chapman the attention of the press. *The Golden Era*, on July 3, 1853, announced:

> Mademoiselle Lola Montez, of the whole world, and Patrick Purdy
> Hull, Esq. of the San Francisco *Whig*, were united in the holy bonds of
> wedlock at the Holy Church of the Mission Dolores by the Reverend
> Father Flavel Fontaine. . . ."

Lola had met the California newspaperman aboard the *Northerner*. Her third marriage would prove short-lived and tempestuous, a temporary encumbrance to her California stay.

The day after their marriage the newlyweds left for Sacramento aboard the steamer *New World*. They checked into the Orleans Hotel, not far from the Sacramento Theatre on Third street, where Lola would appear on July 6 in the first of the performances scheduled for her tour of the interior.

It was in Sacramento that California theatre had its beginnings. The Eagle was California's first gold rush theatre, opening in Sacramento in the fall of 1849 and featuring Mrs. Henry Ray, "a celebrated female Tragedian from New Zealand." The Eagle Theatre, hard by the gambling saloon known as the Round Tent, consisted of canvas capped with a metal roof, and looked like an ordinary drinking-house itself but for the sign "Eagle Theatre" nailed to it. Despite its modest appearance, the cost of its erection was estimated at some thirty thousand dollars due to the exorbitant price of the lumber required to construct the tiers of seats.

A rough gallery comprised the "box tier"—tickets, three dollars—seating about a hundred persons; the pit accommodated perhaps three hundred, at two dollars each. Pit-seated patrons on stormy nights, according to one observer, "had the pleasure of enjoying a 'fresh water bath' for the same money," as rainwater collected on a level with the benches.

The theatre's colorful drop curtain, undoubtedly also a costly amenity, exhibited a painting of dark brown trees against lilac-colored mountains and a yellow sky.

The night Bayard Taylor, a New York newspaper correspondent, attended the Eagle, the company presented *The Spectre of the Forest*, in concert with a five-member orchestra, which performed, according to Taylor, with "tolerable correctness."

Taylor's companion for the evening was pioneer entertainer Stephen Massett. Massett's recollection of the orchestra differed from Taylor's in its particulars:

> The orchestra consisting of the fiddle—a very cheezy flageolet, played by a gentleman with one eye—a big drum, and a triangle, that served the double purpose of ringing in the boarders to their meals at the restaurant next door.

Of the drama itself, Taylor wrote:

> The interest of the play is carried to an awful height by the appearance of two spectres, clad in mutilated tent-covers, and holding spermaceti candles in their hands. At this juncture Mrs. Ray rushes in and throws herself into an attitude in the middle of the stage: why she does it, no one can tell. This movement, which she repeats several times in the course of the three acts, has no connection to the tragedy; it is evidently introduced for the purpose of showing the audience that there is, actually, a female performer. The miners, to whom the sight of a woman is not a frequent occurrence, are delighted with these passages and applaud vehemently.

Massett found the lady's accent as curious as Taylor did her frequent entrances:

> To give some idea of the classical style of the lady's pronunciation she replied, upon the question being asked her if she would accept the hand of the bandit chief:
> "Is art is as ard as a stone—and I'd rayther take a basilisk, and rap is cold fangs areound me—than surrender meself to the cold him-braces of a artless willain!"

Despite Taylor's estimate that a full house would net the Eagle nine hundred dollars a performance, management failed to meet the payroll. Lawsuits brought against the Eagle's proprietors forced a sheriff's sale in November 1849. In the settlement of unpaid accounts, the Rays received $1,375 for performing three nights a week for five weeks.

When Lola reached Sacramento with her new husband in tow, she at once provided that city's audiences and newspaper readers with her famed temperamental displays. During one of her performances in Sacramento someone laughed. She left the stage. The next night she was well received but the Sacramento *Daily Californian* intimated the applause was delivered by friends to whom she'd given free tickets:

> The house might be called full, but in looking it over we could distinguish only a few, a very few, of our citizens present. To strangers, impelled by mere curiosity, and the free use of free tickets is she indebted for an audience.

Montez replied in the fiery fashion for which she was famous. (The mention of "women's rights" in her letter probably referred to the women's rights movement inaugurated at New York in 1848, and followed in 1850 with the first national women's rights convention.)

> To the Responsible Editor of the Californian—
> The extraordinary article concerning myself which appeared in your paper this morning requires an extraordinary answer. I use this word 'Extraordinary' for I am astonished that a respectable (?) editor would lie in such a barefaced manner, and be so void of gallantry and courtesy as yourself. I am a woman. I do not advocate women's rights, but at the same time I can right myself by inflicting summary justice upon all jacks and apes!!! After such a gross insult you must don the petti-coats. I have brought some with me, which I can lend for the occasion. You must fight with me. I leave the choice of weapons to yourself, for I am very magnanimous. You may choose between my duelling pistols or take your choice of a pill-box. One shall be poison and the other not, and the chances are even. I request that this affair may be arranged by your seconds as soon as possible, as my time is quite as valuable as your own.
>
> Marie de Landsfeld Hull
LOLA MONTEZ

When her challenge went unaccepted, Lola, on July 15th, left Sacramento to continue her inland tour to Marysville.

Most performers included a tour of the interior on their agendas. In 1852 Caroline Chapman and her brother William had enjoyed a wild, whirlwind tour of the southern mines. Even the smallest camp provided a little theatre of boards and canvas. At Columbia, one of the largest mining camps, the Chapmans were bombarded with buckskin bags of gold thrown upon the stage. And at Sonora, on December 31, 1852, escorted by a thousand miners, they opened the Phoenix Theatre with *She Stoops to Conquer*.

Entertainments came to Sonora long before the Chapmans' resounding success. Nearly a year earlier William Perkins noted the arrival of a Spanish dramatic company "now performing nightly in M. Planel's new theatre; and Madame Abalos, ex-Prima Donna at the opera house in Mexico, sings, aided by her little daughter Sophy. . . . "

Perkins appreciated the contrast that mining camps made with more civilized venues for these touring performers:

> What a change for her; from singing to the gorgeous audiences of the opera house in Mexico, where the blaze of gold and jewels is even more dazzling than in the Theaters of Europe, to the boards of a wooden and canvas theatre filled with red and blue flannel shirts, bowie knives and Colt's revolvers!

Yet, entertainers ventured to far more remote camps than Sonora. To almost everyone Downieville was as far from civilization as the moon, yet it too boasted a little theatre for its touring performers. Wrote J. D. Borthwick:

> There was no lack of public amusements in the town. The same company which I had heard in Nevada [City] were performing in a very comfortable little theatre—not a very highly decorated house, but laid out in the orthodox fashion, with boxes, pit, and gallery—and a company of American glee-singers, who had been concertising with great success in the various mining towns, were giving concerts in a large room devoted to such purposes. Their selection of songs was of a decidedly national character, and a lady, one of their party, had won the hearts of all the miners by singing very sweetly a number of old familiar ballads, which touched the feelings of the expatriated gold-hunters.
>
> I was present at their concert one night, when, at the close of the performance, a rough old miner stood up on his seat in the middle of

the room, and after a few preliminary coughs, delivered himself of a very elaborate speech, in which, on behalf of the miners of Downie-ville, he begged to express to the lady their great admiration of her vocal talents, and in token thereof begged her acceptance of a purse containing 500 dollars' worth of gold specimens. Compliments of this sort . . . which the fair cantatrice no doubt valued as highly as showers of the most exquisite bouquets, had been paid to her in most of the towns she had visited in the mines. Some enthusiastic miners had even thrown specimens to her on the stage.

A "fair cantatrice" played Marysville just before Lola's arrival there. The town extended the cigarette-smoking Montez only a halfhearted reception, perhaps because of her unlucky contrast with the young lady vocalist who had recently captured miners' hearts with senti-mental ballads like *When the Swallows Homeward Fly* and *Young Ladies, Won't You Marry?* Lola's spider dance dropped like a dead weight on men left tearful and homesick by the young singer.

In Marysville, Lola abandoned her tour of the mining towns, and took the first steps to leave her new husband, too. She was rumored by newspaper accounts to have thrown his luggage out an upper window of a Marysville hotel.

Newspapers for the next few days had no news of the Countess. Then, on July 22, the Sacramento *Union*'s Grass Valley correspondent, Alonzo Block, reported: "Lola Montez is here. . . . She is taking the hearts of our people by her affability and good nature."

Grass Valley was on the road from Marysville and when Lola's stagecoach stopped there, she said she liked the place and proposed to remain.

By August the papers were reporting her purchase of a cottage and her divorce from Hull. In December the Grass Valley *Telegraph* announced: "Madam Lola Montez, who, after having traveled the world over, has wisely come to the conclusion that, as a private and romantic residence, a mountain home [in] Grass Valley has no super-iors, and acting upon these convictions she has planned and erected one of the neatest little cottages in this country, in which she now resides in quiet and peaceful retirement."

Lola opened the front door of her cottage to a parade of visitors, holding court for wealthy investors in Grass Valley's Empire Mine, in which she had an interest, as well as theatrical personalities and visiting intelligentsia. She entertained elaborately and frequently.

She adopted a menagerie of pets—a goat, a lamb, parrots, cats, dogs, even a pet grizzly bear, which she fastened by chain to a tree in her yard. Newspapers reported she was "negotiating for a pair of rattlesnakes."

She was seen often in her garden, tending her roses and nurturing cactus specimens collected from rides into the countryside. She appeared to have abandoned the theatre.

In San Francisco, meanwhile, theatre audiences welcomed Catherine Sinclair, the former wife of a famous actor, Edwin Forrest. A jealous and vindictive man, his divorce cost him a yearly alimony of three thousand dollars. As with Lola Montez, Catherine Sinclair's notoriety preceded her appearance in California. Many attended her performances just to see her, according to Jennie Megquier:

> Mrs Sinclair is creating some excitement in the theatrical world, but it is merely curiosity to see one of whom there has been so much said, I saw her in the play of the Stranger . . . but I do not think much of her as an actress, although she is very fine looking but I think her race is not long here as a popular actress.

Jennie Megquier's appraisal proved astute. Catherine Sinclair's achievement in San Francisco theatre was less as an actress than as manager of the Metropolitan Theatre, which opened under her direction in December 1853. She played Lady Teazle in *The School for Scandal*, with Edwin Booth a member of the cast.

Eliza Farnham considered the Metropolitan "the principal theatre of the state." As a consequence of Catherine Sinclair's work, Mrs. Farnham revised her earlier opinion that California entertainment kept "up to decent mediocrity," writing:

> The drama has been nobly served in California, and I am proud to say it, most nobly by one of my own sex. . . . Mrs. Sinclair . . . has served the public in her managerial capacity with a generosity and industry rarely equaled. With a just faith in the value of the drama, she has spared no pains or expense to give it, in her theatre, its noblest power. The best boards of our Atlantic cities do not surpass in excellence and variety the entertainments she has provided for the patrons of the Metropolitan.

The Metropolitan, on Montgomery street, was opulently decorated in red velvet and gold; box tiers formed a horseshoe, and lighting was extravagant coal gas.

San Francisco's opulent Metropolitan Theatre, managed by Catherine Sinclair.

Catherine Sinclair managed the Metropolitan for eighteen months. A series of notable productions and distinguished players made the Metropolitan the premier California theatre, even forcing a temporary closure of the rival American Theatre.

The American was rescued by an unknown but talented young actress named Matilda Heron. A friendless young girl of twenty-three, she arrived alone in San Francisco; her agent George Lewis, with whom she sailed for California, had become ill and died six days before the inbound steamer docked on December 25, 1853.

Having no engagement, unknown and alone, Miss Heron nearly returned on the next steamer. But James Murdock, a noted tragedian with whom she had performed in Boston, was at the Metropolitan. Learning of her plight and attesting to her talents, Murdoch got her an engagement at the American.

She at once became immensely popular. Chroniclers explained her success lay in "her perfect naturalness of manner; the total absence of those screamings, rantings, and gesticulations which have grown up rank and deep-rooted weeds on the dramatic field. . . . "

In response to the American Theatre's unexpected success, Mrs. Sinclair, with much advance publicity, on April 6, 1854, presented at the Metropolitan the brilliant young English actress Laura Keene. Three days later the *Alta* commented that although "Miss Keene has by no means made a failure, it would be useless to deny that she has not made a 'hit.' "

The mixed response to Laura Keene's appearances did little to assist the beleaguered fortunes of the Metropolitan. Neither did Mrs. Sinclair's personal preference for grand opera.

She had every reason to believe San Franciscans would accept operatic performances, based on their enthusiastic reception in 1852 of coloratura soprano Elisa Biscaccianti, the "American thrush" whose voice many critics deemed superior to Jenny Lind's.

Born in Boston and trained in the great musical centers of Europe, Biscaccianti had instantaneous success both as an operatic performer and as a balladist. San Franciscans, according to one critic, nearly swooned at her first performance of a Donizetti aria:

> As her first notes rang out clear and distinct as a bell, the enthusiastic
> house was hushed into profound silence. Thunders of applause,
> showers of bravas and bouquets greeted the conclusion. Again she
> bowed her thanks, and again the audience was electrified by her sweet
> and expressive smile.

Elisa Biscaccianti concluded her program with an encore rendering of "Home, Sweet Home" and her homesick audience fell in love with her. During her year in California her every appearance was show-ered with flowers, fire companies turned out in full regalia in her honor, and she was lauded as the first recognized artist "to brave opinion and try her fortunes on the far shores of California."

She ushered in a parade of renowned female vocalists. Catherine Hayes, the "Swan of Erin," the "Irish Linnet," followed in November 1852. She was a tall woman, with blonde hair and blue eyes. Her imposing appearance and her high soprano voice lent her stage presence unusual drama, and she was the first to introduce to the San Francisco stage costumed operatic presentations. She was first also to perform firemen's benefits, generously establishing a charity fund for volunteer firemen and their families.

Jennie Megquier, who seemed not to miss much of what was happening in San Francisco, heard her sing in December 1852:

> Tuesday eve Mr Snell took me to the concert to hear Miss Hayes, we had a nice time although she cannot compare with Jenny, nor has she the compass to her voice that Madame Biscacianti has, but it is very sweet and she is much better looking.

Of the singer's departure, Mrs. Megquier wrote in May 1853:

> Kate Hayes has sung her last song in Cal in singing the Irish Emi-grants lament, her heart was too full and she was obliged to retire, some say it was for effect, others that she was sincere but she had a fine house, and was escorted to the Hotel by the firemen where they gave her three cheers and parted well satisfied on all sides.

On January 16, 1854, Mrs. Sinclair opened an operatic season at the Metropolitan with but lukewarm reception. Her star performer was Madame Anna Thillon, who, with her five-member Thillon English Opera Company, had enjoyed a career of "unclouded splendor" in Europe. She performed with unabated success in the eastern states for two years before coming to California.

Madame Thillon's company presented six operas in twenty-seven performances but the music critics remained unmoved. One complained that Anna Thillon "sang several arias and scenes, and that was all. She was the opera, and there was nothing of the work of the composer allowed to appear except just as much as was necessary to exhibit Madame Thillon."

In 1855 Catherine Sinclair reintroduced grand opera with Meyerbeer's *Robert the Devil*, with singers of substantial reputation, including Anna Bishop, well known throughout Europe and the eastern states. A series of regular plays followed, and then again Sinclair presented grand opera, with an Italian troupe, this time to her financial undoing.

Her losses created a deficit of nearly fourteen thousand dollars, forcing her to relinquish management of the Metropolitan. The following year she was honored with a farewell benefit before departing for Australia.

Australia's gold rush had followed fast on the heels of California's. Adventurers, miners, and entertainers quickly revised itineraries to include the huge "down under" continent. Catherine Sinclair added it to hers.

So did Lola Montez.

In March 1854 Lola's pet bear bit her. Alonzo Delano composed a brief verse in commemoration:

> *When Lola came to feed her bear,*
> *With comfits sweet and sugar rare,*
> *Bruin ran out in haste to meet her,*
> *Seized her hand because 'twas sweeter.*

Lola sold the bear. It was the beginning of leaving. The townspeople generally would miss the celebrity in their midst, especially the children. At a Christmas party Lola gave them there had been games and gifts and good things to eat. One of the little girls always remembered her kindness.

Another little girl is said to have learned to dance at Lola's knee. Her name was Lotta Crabtree.

The child was six when she and her mother crossed the Isthmus in 1853 to join Lotta's father. Luck eluded John Crabtree, a New York bookseller-turned-goldminer. Mary Ann Crabtree, who had never worked in New York, was forced to keep a boardinghouse in Grass Valley to support the family.

The wealth of her famous neighbor may have inspired Mrs. Crabtree's vision of better prospects than the hard work of her boardinghouse. Dancing was a profitable talent, and little Lotta could dance.

While Lotta may have practiced dancing at Lola's house, she probably learned at Mr. and Mrs. J. B. Robinson's dancing school the jigs and reels that launched her toward fame and fortune. The dancing school opened in Grass Valley in December 1853, and Mary Ann Crabtree certainly knew of the great success enjoyed by the Robinsons' daughter, Sue. Child performers were the rage in California.

In 1853, when Mary Ann and her daughter arrived in California, eight-year-old Susan Robinson (apparently no relation to San Francisco's theatrical Dr. Robinson) was singing and dancing her way through the mining camps to golden acclaim. The following year Kate and Ellen Bateman, ages ten and twelve, played the Metropolitan for several weeks. Experienced comedic and Shakespearean performers, they charmed audiences as well as the *Alta*'s critic: "We had long entertained a latent prejudice against theatrical precocities . . . but we plead guilty to having enjoyed the performance . . . of . . . these lilliputian prodigies."

The Bateman children also toured the interior with great success, only foreshadowing Lotta Crabtree's.

John Crabtree was at Rabbit Creek, which was yielding some miners twenty to thirty dollars a day. Crabtree expected daily to strike it rich, so in the summer of 1854, Mary Ann and Lotta joined him there.

At Rabbit Creek was a saloonkeeper named Mart Taylor, who also ran a small log theatre for touring entertainers.

It was at Rabbit Creek that Lotta Crabtree debuted. Although nearly eight, the tiny girl looked no more than six, and as cute as a leprechaun in the tiny long-tailed green coat, knee breeches, and a tall green hat fashioned by her mother.

In her first appearance, the little red-haired girl, clutching a tiny shillelagh, danced an Irish jig and reel. She thought it such fun that she laughed gaily throughout the performance. Her infectious merriment and obvious delight in performing for her friends captivated the miners. When she came out for a final number wearing a white dress with puffed sleeves and sang a simple ballad, she looked like a little doll.

The delighted miners showered the child with gold.

And Mary Ann Crabtree finally had what she'd come to California for.

Taylor, who played the guitar, found a violinist to complete the small company and taught Lotta more pretty ballads. Then, on muleback, with John Crabtree only a name she once knew, Mary Ann was off with Taylor, the violinist, and her daughter to the remotest mines, where a child performer was guaranteed a triumphant reception.

Lotta performed in saloons and stores, with stages contrived from billiard tables, backdrops from red calico, and footlights from candles stuck in bottles. Taylor played the guitar, the violinist accompanied the ballads, and Mary Ann Crabtree cleaned the stage, promptly gathering into a basket the gold showered upon her daughter.

The mining camps had one of their own to adore, and they did.

Lola Montez often received credit for teaching the child to dance—

although jigs and reels were a Robinson specialty and nothing like Lola's style. It's even been said that Lola wished to take Lotta with her to Australia. There seems little likelihood of Mary Ann Crabtree's entertaining that idea.

But leave for Australia Lola did. Newspapers bid her adieu with as much attention as they'd welcomed her. "Pleasant breezes waft thee, fair Lola," said the San Francisco *Courier* in May of 1855. The *Golden Era* reported that Grass Valley "loses one of its chiefest distinctions in the public eye. A kind nature and many courtesies and charities have made her a favourite with those who knew her well enough to reconcile not a few eccentricities and erratic indications. . . . "

If Lola had at last captured California's good graces, she in turn succumbed to the state's rough charms. She was back in a year.

EIGHT

I MPROPER SOCIETY

A judge here sold his house to some women who came here from San Francisco. It is in a part of town where many men live in their offices. The women have a man servant to clean their house, and they eat in a restaurant. The first few nights they were here they sent their servant out with a drum to excite notice. But they have not been here long and we hear they are going away.
— ELIZABETH GUNN, *Sonora, California, January 1852*

Her name may have been Clara Belle Ryan or it may have been Arabella Ryan. She may have been the daughter of a Baltimore minister. At seventeen, she may have been seduced and abandoned. Her unforgiving father may have cast her out. From Baltimore she may have headed for New Orleans where she bore a child that subsequently died.

That is one account.

A variation favored by a San Francisco police detective is more prosaic. The beautiful girl's parents were respectable, but her father not a clergyman. The impulse that took her to the netherworld of New Orleans originated at a dressmaker's shop on Baltimore's North Street. As a seamstress, her customers included several girls from a place called the Lutz, much favored, it was said, by English sea captains. In this version of the demimonde's shadowy past, the girl discerned that profits lay not in fashioning fancy dresses, but in wearing them. And she went to work at the Lutz.

This version has no child. Further, in it she strayed first to Charleston, where she became the mistress of a man later killed, and then drifted on to New Orleans.

Whatever the truth, the lovely Miss Ryan was in New Orleans in 1849. In that year, or perhaps the year before, she met tall, handsome, black-haired Charles Cora. As his consort, she called herself Belle Cora.

Charles Cora was a gambling man. For men like him, and women like Belle Cora, news of California's gold discovery conjured a feverish vision of raw wealth waiting to be spent on pleasure and amusement. Flocks of gamblers and courtesans abandoned New Orleans on the first ships pointed toward the Isthmus.

In the fall of 1849, Charles Cora, thirty-three, in company with twenty-two-year-old Belle, took passage on the steamer *Falcon*. They crossed the Isthmus by canoe and mule, and at Panama City boarded the sidewheeler *California*. They reached San Francisco on December 28, 1849.

No record survives of Belle Cora's disembarkment. However, the arrival in San Francisco of women of disputed virtue often occasioned comment. In one instance a passenger ship from Panama docked with, according to an observer, "two daughters of Eve of the sort called 'liberated' ":

> No sooner had the anchor been dropped than there broke out a noisy quarrel between the two damsels and the purser. They wanted to come ashore at once; the purser said the arrangement had been that they would pay their passage as soon as they reached this city. The more spirited of the two Yankee girls, acting on the principle that "time is money," said the purser would be held responsible for damages and losses, plus interest, caused by the delay. Whereupon two of the waiting crowd, tired of marking time, clambered on board the ship, and, throwing a bag of gold at the feet of the greedy purser, came back to land with the girls to a general "Hooray!" from the crowd.

No less welcome were the women greeted in May of 1850, as the *Alta California* noted:

> ENLARGEMENT OF SOCIETY—We are pleased to notice by the arrival from sea Saturday, the appearance of some fifty or sixty of the fairer sex in full bloom. They are from all quarters—some from Yankee-land, others from John Bull country, and quite a constellation from merry France. One Frenchman brings twenty—all, they say, beautiful! The bay was dotted by flotillas of young men, on the announcement of this extraordinary importation.

Yet, barely four months after its amiable welcome of the "fairer sex in full bloom," the *Alta* decried their presence, lamenting on September 11: "We must confess our regret at the perfect freedom and unseemly manner in which the abandoned females . . . are permitted to display themselves in our public saloons and streets."

Neither the *Alta* nor society attained a consistent attitude toward prostitutes, or as euphemism perferred, the "fair but frail." The vagaries of public opinion depended much on the time. Early in the rush, a largely male population permitted such women an accord not found in Eastern society. Any woman who could disport herself respectably was treated with utmost esteem simply because she was female. Many European and American prostitutes enjoyed the open admiration of men, even the facade of respect.

Women who spoke Spanish, however, received little courtesy. Evidence that the hierarchy of acceptability went to fair women over their darker-skinned sisters is in this contemporary chronicler's emphatic declaration:

> The Mexicans and Chilians, like the people of negro descent, were
> only of the commonest description. The women of all these various
> races were nearly all of the vilest character, and openly practised the
> most shameful commerce. The lewdness of fallen white females is
> shocking enough to witness, but it is far exceeded by the disgusting
> practices of these tawny visaged creatures.

Many "tawny visaged" pioneer prostitutes sailed from Valparaiso, Chile, a frequent port of call for vessels journeying to and from San Francisco. In August of 1848 Valparaiso had news of California's gold discovery from the Chilean brig *J.R.S.* Another Chilean vessel sailing from San Francisco arrived less than a month later, carrying twenty-five hundred dollars in gold dust. When, on November 4, 1848, the Valparaiso *Mercury* published an article on California's gold mines, the rush was on. During the first six months of 1849, an estimated five thousand Chileans arrived in San Francisco. The boldest men and women took passage at the first opportunity.

Most of their names are lost to history. That of Rosa Montalva survives because Vincent Perez Rosales of Santiago embarked for California December 28, 1848, on the same ship as did she. The port officer tried to stop Rosa from sailing. Rosales, in a journal intended for his mother—which may account for his tone—wrote:

Poor Rosa complains bitterly, swears she is an honest woman of good character and that many on board will testify to this; everyone will say so who has had the good fortune to meet her, and that means most of them. She pleads with one after another, she promises, she weeps, she becomes desperate. Finally, much against our wishes [presumably Rosales and his three half-brothers] she is permitted to continue her auriferous voyage, to the applause of most of the sportive passengers.

Upon arrival at San Francisco Rosales noted:

Rosita has outfitted herself for business with a magnificent silk dress, a cape, and a cap or hat as they call it nowadays. She had won the good will of everyone on board. I do not know what kind of card or letter of recommendation she carried, but everyone on board had had dealings with her, and she with them. All except us, that is. We alone were virtuous, chaste; or finicky and choosy. The truth is, one would have to come to this country and spend days and nights seeing men and only men before he could find the sight of this charming siren tolerable. That is why she has the eyes and attention, now of everyone who happens to see her.

Rosales's scornful attitude—perhaps intended simply to assuage a mother's concerns—obviously was not shared by most men. In fact, because of the shortage of women, some South American prostitutes quickly improved their positions in society. Roberto Cornejo wrote from San Francisco on May 1, 1849, that several Chilean women "from the red light district of Valparaiso have married here and even enjoyed the luxury of choosing among their suitors."

Other South American women fared poorly. Unlike Rosa Montalva, many Spanish-speaking women could not afford the fare to San Francisco. In consequence, hundreds of Latin women, recruited in San Blas and Mazatlan, secured passage through indenture arrangements. Most were destined for the fandango houses, the poor man's brothel.

Jose Fernandez, the first alcalde of San Jose under American rule, wrote:

They did not pay passage on the ships, but when they reached San Francisco the captains sold them to the highest bidder. There were men who, as soon as any ship arrived from Mexican ports with a load of women, took two or three small boats, or a launch, went on board

the ship, paid to the captain the passage of ten or twelve unfortunates
and took them immediately to their cantinas, where the newcomers
were forced to prostitute themselves for half a year, during which the
proprietors took the bulk of their earnings.

Like Chile, China had news of California's gold discovery delivered
under sail in 1848. Not until 1850, however, and the Tai-ping rebellion
in southeastern China, did large numbers of Chinese men—mostly
young, thrifty, industrious agricultural peasants from Kwangtung
Province—emigrate to California in response to reports of high
wages.

According to San Francisco customhouse records, 20,026 Chinese
arrived in that city by sea in 1852. San Francisco's burgeoning Chinatown soon included hundreds of Chinese girls imported for prostitution.

The excesses to which procurement of women for prostitution led
are graphically represented in a painting made in 1852. According to
a description, it shows a group of newly arrived Chinese slave girls
huddled in a horse cart surrounded by a crowd of Chinese men. Two
policemen are beating back men from the cart, while a Yankee ship
captain stands nearby, described as "smugly self-satisfied."

Typically, arriving Chinese girls were taken to a *barracoon*, a base-
ment in Chinatown, and stripped for examination and purchase by
brothel owners or agents for wealthy Chinese seeking a mistress. In
China these girls would have brought prices between thirty and
ninety dollars. Depending on age, beauty, and the prevailing market,
they sold in California for three hundred to three thousand dollars.

A Chinese organization, founded in San Francisco as early as 1852,
trafficked in these "daughters of joy." It recruited primarily from the
poor of Canton, where it was a common practice to sell daughters
into slavery. Other girls came from Hong Kong's prostitution district,
some of them former mistresses of Europeans. Some girls, like Lee
Lan, were simply stolen from the streets.

Lee Lan had, it was believed, gone to visit relatives in Canton and
there been kidnapped, then shipped to San Francisco and sold into
prostitution. She died in San Francisco in 1859 and, because of her
high caste, was accorded an elaborate funeral, rare for most Chinese
women. She was twenty.

Most Chinese prostitutes died young. Their value was in their earning ability. If they became ill, as a great many did, and unable to work, they received no care.

Their only other value was loan security. In 1854 Madame Ah Laon, proprietor of a San Francisco brothel, borrowed $250 from one Ah Chuen. For security, Ah Laon signed a contract pledging "the person of one of my girls; it being hereby mutually agreed between us, that if the said amount is not paid at the expiration of the time aforesaid, the said Ah Chuen can and is empowered to sell the said girl and pocket the proceeds."

The limited worth of Chinese prostitutes reflected the low value of females in China. Like the indentured South American prostitutes, Chinese women were accustomed to marginal regard and held little expectation for improving their position in society. Used to small consideration, and generally sold into hopeless circumstances, Chinese prostitutes rarely anticipated or attained the rewards sought by ambitious and independent professionals like Belle Cora.

Belle delayed her destiny as San Francisco's premier parlorhouse madam by almost immediately abandoning the city for the interior. Within weeks of their arrival, she and Cora went to Sacramento for some big-stakes gambling. Little is known of that sojourn beyond suspicions that Belle may have been bankrolling Charles Cora's losses. But Belle may have told that story in later days.

From Sacramento they moved on to the smaller mining towns. In Marysville Charles Cora shared proprietorship of a gambling house called the New World.

Of Cora's New World venture, one Edward McIlhany recalled: "I remember seeing a bet of $10,000 made at poker by Charles Cora, proprietor of . . . the New World. He won his bet. . . . His wife or mistress, I do not know which, was a pretty woman and seemed very much devoted to him, as I had often seen her with him in the city."

From Marysville, Belle and Charles may have taken temporarily divergent paths. McIlhany says Cora returned to San Francisco. Possibly he went to Shasta, for after his unfortunate fame, the newspaper there noted that "He will be remembered by the old time residents of this place."

Belle apparently went to Sonora. There, using the name Arabelle Ryan, she presided as a madam in a house for prostitutes.

No record survives of Belle's success in the mining town, but many men speculated on how much wealth such women amassed. Wrote traveler Edward Ely from Placerville in October 1851:

> There is a house here owned by a young woman from New Orleans, who has succeeded in bringing to this retired spot about a dozen Sandwich Island girls and although she has not yet been in the place one year, she must be worth a hundred thousand dollars.
>
> It could scarcely be otherwise considering the high price of everything in California, and more especially where there is a monopoly. To speak plainly one night's enjoyment of the society of the charming mistress of the house, costs the man the moderate sum of one hundred dollars, and the same indulgence with the girls, fifty dollars.

Despite the community's apparent acceptance of the Placerville madam, and presumably Arabelle Ryan in Sonora, prostitutes occasionally found themselves unwelcome.

From Rich Bar, for instance, Louisa Clapp wrote to her sister on September 15, 1851:

> Yes! these thousand men—many of whom had been for years absent from the softening amenities of female society . . . looked only with contempt or pity upon these, oh, so earnestly to be compassionated creatures! These unhappy members of a class, to one of which, the tenderest words that Jesus ever spake, were uttered—left in a few weeks, absolutely driven away by public opinon.

Mrs. Clapp makes no mention of it, but a man named Drinkhouse recalled that at Rich Bar also was a man "who had his sister with him, and prostituted her, and the miners were so indignant with him that they ran him out of the place."

Similar to Mrs. Clapp's account at Rich Bar, the people at Cold Springs, in November of 1852, according to William H. Hampton, "tore down a house of ill fame and destroyed all its effects."

But the knife of scorn cut both ways, as Mary Mahaffey proved.

Mary Mahaffey lived in Nevada City in 1850 with her lover, a musician. While visiting Sacramento she captured the heart of a young rancher, who followed her back to Nevada City. Agreeing to marry him, she cooperated in an elaborate hoax upon the unsuspecting and generous suitor who gave her three hundred dollars for a trousseau.

She introduced to the besotted rancher a prominent gambler, who pretended to be a minister and agreed to wed them for fifty dollars. A saloon proprietor, posing as the town clerk, issued a "marriage license" and for it collected a golden ounce from the soon-to-be "bridegroom."

Two bartenders sent to the town's characters, all apparently deserving the title of colonel, this invitation:

> Dear Colonel—A rancher from Bear River will be spliced to Mary Mahaffey this evening. The business will be transacted over at Dawson's Castle, Parson Jack White bossing the affair. You are wanted for to be there, for Mary would feel bad if you wasn't.
> Committee of Inviters.
> P.S.—No guest will have to kiss the bride if he don't want to. Parties will please leave their firearms and cutting implements at home.

The mock ceremony was witnessed on December 31, 1850, by about two hundred men, who then enjoyed drinks and supper courtesy of the deluded "husband." The tab was several hundred dollars. Peter Decker, one of the well wishers, wrote the denouement in his diary:

> After the sucker was thus fleeced, his Deary told him he was a fool, swore he should leave the house or she would shoot him with a pistol she flourished. And not until then the truth flashing on the astonished victim's dull apprehension, after paying about a thousand dollars.

The Mary Mahaffey story is unusual for its portrayal of male gullibility. Much more common were the tales of "fallen" women. William Perkins, at Sonora, heard perhaps the most bizarre story of a woman going astray in California.

According to Perkins, a man named Ransome, like thousands, had left a wife and family behind when he came to California in 1849. Because he moved about frequently, he wrote his wife that she should address her letters to him in care of his friend in Stockton, a man named Moore. Deciding to stay in California, Ransome sent for his family. Moore opened the exchanged letters, learned the arrival date, then met Mrs. Ransome in San Francisco and told her that her husband had sent him. He hired two wagons, put the children in one and took Mrs. Ransome in the other. Wrote Perkins:

From the statement of one of the little boys that the father had got hold of, it appears that Moore by persuasion or force induced the woman to accede to his desires, and afterwards by threats compelled her to accompany him to the mines of the Stanislao, instead of taking her to the Tuolumne. They came up to the mountains, where Moore very shortly tired of his companion, took what money she had, and left her with a party of men, one of whom it seems took possession of her, and carried her off to parts unknown.

The children were recovered at Jamestown but, despite her husband's continuing search, Mrs. Ransome, as far as Perkins learned, was not found. He concluded:

I hardly know whether we ought to wish him success, unless under the supposition that the proceedings of his wife are the result of force. The husband, however, most strenuously believes in his wife's affection, and is convinced that she has been coerced, and is anxious to return to his arms; and he, poor fellow, is ready to pardon every thing and take her again to her household affections and duties.

What strange romances are attached to the history of almost every female who has come to these shores. Mrs. Ransome's is the history of hundreds, modulated or aggravated according to circumstances. Perfect and flawless must be the virtue of the woman that may resist the licentiousness of California!

Perkins's suspicions reflected a common assumption that most of California's single women were unchaste. Eliza Farnham met a young Irish girl, working in a respectable hotel, who became frightened at the conversations of men overheard through the muslin partitions. The girl was distressed to hear men say there were no honest women in California and that "those who professed to be so, were only greater hypocrites or more successful pretenders" and "none were entitled to respect."

The girl, described by Farnham as "religiously educated" and "really good," was terrified of her surroundings. She gratefully accepted another position as a servant in a private family with a mistress "of whose justice and purity she felt no doubt."

Farnham observed:

It is not difficult to see how scores of weaker and worse trained young females might have traveled from such a position in quite an opposite direction, and so justified, in their own lives, the assertions which had at first caused them so much pain.

Such, I doubt not, has been the first cause which has led astray, in California, many innocent feet.

Echoing Eliza Farnham was Mrs. D. B. Bates:

> One can realize the danger likely to be incurred by placing a young, lovely, and attractive female in a country where virtue was regarded by the mass only as a name, and while she was yet too young to discriminate between the respectful homage of sensible gentlemen and the soul-sickening, hypocritical, despicable flatteries which often flow so smoothly from under the moustache of the soulless, "vanity-puffed, shallow-brained apology" for a man.

Fallen to flattery was one Lillie Lee, the fifteen-year-old daughter of a friend of Mrs. Bates. The girl, despite her mother's vigilance, took up with a gambler. "The affection bestowed upon that dissolute gamester was deserving a better object," observed Mrs. Bates.

The girl fled with her lover to one of the interior towns, where her mother tracked them down. The distraught mother, wrote Mrs. Bates, "travelling nearly thirty-six hours without once tasting food, or taking any rest," upon finding her daughter, threatened to shoot the seducer. The girl pleaded for his life, the "deeply dyed villain" repeatedly assured the mother of his intentions to marry Lillie Lee, and the mother spared him.

Many months later, still unwed, Lillie Lee discovered that her lover was already married. His wife had come to California to join him. Heartbroken, Lillie Lee returned to her mother.

Mrs. Bates's story concludes with the girl's "downward track." If Mrs. Bates intended the description as a moral to other young women, however, it seems singularly unpersuasive:

> Her extreme beauty, and her adventurous, fearless course of conduct, won for her a widely extended reputation. One day she would appear in splendid Turkish costume, which admirably displayed her tiny little foot encased in richly embroidered satin slippers. . . . I have seen her mounted on a glossy, lithe-limbed race-horse,—one that had won for her many thousands on the course,—habited in a closely-fitting riding-dress of black velvet, ornamented with a hundred and fifty gold buttons, a hat from which depended magnificent sable plumes. . . . Gold and diamonds were showered upon her.

Showers of gold and diamonds apparently were as frequent San Francisco occurrences as rain. Sarah Royce particularly lamented the practice of rich men giving women "a pretty present" as a way of showing off their own new wealth:

> I blushed to discover, by conversations held in my presence, that there were instances of women watching each other, jealously, each afraid the other would get more or richer presents than herself. This evil became painfully prominent . . . in connection with musical and literary entertainments, school exhibitions, etc. Little girls and young ladies who sung, played, or recited on such occasions often received, thrown at their feet before they left the stage, expensive jewelry, or even pieces of coin. They commonly accepted them; often with looks of exultation; and, still worse, there were mothers, who not merely countenanced the thing, but even boasted of the amount their daughters had thus received. It must indeed be an obtuse moral sense that could not perceive the corrupting tendency of such customs; and I have since seen some sad falls into positive vice of those whose downward course appeared to begin in these and similar practices.

One of the similar practices alluded to by Mrs. Royce may have been the masked ball. At these *soirees* respectable ladies often mixed with their sinning sisters, sometimes each parading as the other behind silk masks. No one remarked that the sinners, by the association, saw the error of their ways and adopted new morals. The opposite transition was thought more probable, given the tenor of the evening. Wrote Frenchman Albert Benard:

> All the women in town appear . . . and one often sees beautiful costumes richly adorned with lace. . . . A masked ball naturally permits a certain freedom, but here the feverish atmosphere of the city produces an abandon I have never seen elsewhere.

The "abandon" of San Francisco was a magnet for prostitutes. The rewards were huge for clever and beautiful women willing to provide the pleasures of female companionship to San Francisco's largely male population.

One of the most beautiful was Belle Cora.

Exactly when she returned to San Francisco is unclear. But it is known from the November 17, 1852, *Alta* that Belle then had a house on Dupont street:

A BOLD THIEF. On Monday evening last, the house of Miss Bella Cora on Dupont street was entered by some daring thief who succeeded in getting richly rewarded for his trouble. He entered the room of Miss Florence Wetmore, and helped himself to a diamond cluster pin, a plain gold chain, a gold waist belt and money to the amount of $120, making the value of all at $185. A gentleman *sleeping* in the same house also lost a gold watch and chain, overcoat, dress coat, vest, pistol, pants and cash to the amount of $45. His loss in all is $350. The amount of property and money stolen amounts to over $800. The thief escaped with his booty and has not been arrested.

The extent of Belle Cora's wealth and prominence is suggested in a description of a house believed to have been hers:

See yonder house. Its curtains are of the purest white lace embroidered, and crimson damask. Go in. All the fixtures are of a keeping, most expensive, most voluptuous, most gorgeous. . . . It is a *soiree* night. The "lady" of the establishment has sent most polite invitations, got up on the finest and most beautifully embossed note paper, to all the principal gentlemen of the city, including collector of the port, mayor, aldermen, judges of the county, and members of the legislature. A splendid band of music is in attendance. Away over the Turkey or Brussels carpet whirls the politician with some sparkling beauty, as fair as frail; and the judge joins in and enjoys the dance in company with the beautiful but lost beings whom, to-morrow, he may send to the house of correction. Every thing is conducted with the utmost propriety. Not an unbecoming word is heard, not an objectionable action seen. The girls are on their good behavior, and are proud once more to move and act and appear as ladies . . . . But the dance is over; now for the supper table. Every thing within the bounds of the market and skill of the cook and confectioner, is before you. . . .
The champagne alone is paid for. The *soiree* has cost the mistress one thousand dollars, and at the supper and during the night she sells twelve dozen of champagne at ten dollars a bottle!

Forty-niner Elisha Crosby recalled one woman in this class, known as the "Countess." She, too, was from New Orleans, and, according to Crosby, employed six or eight "young ladies" from different parts of the world. "Some of these girls," he wrote, "were exquisitely beautiful and very highly accomplished, their conversational powers good and their musical taste and performances were very fine." Crosby noted in particular the fine formality and quality of the "Countess's" invitations:

> The peculiar feature of her early career in San Francisco was her receptions. She would issue her cards of invitation for one of her reception nights, beautifully engraved and embossed envelopes, tied with white Satin ribbon like the most dainty wedding card.

Such invitations were expensive. But ten-dollar champagne paid the bills and multiple sales netted a very nice profit. Wine sales provided parlorhouse madams a polite method of exchange, but not without risk, as the *Alta* reported on September 11, 1851:

> Women and Wine.—A whole bevy of women who live in what they call "respectable boarding houses" in this city were brought up before his honor, Judge Waller yesterday morning, on a citation issued from the Court, charging them with selling champagne without a license. A number of witnesses were summoned, who stated that they had heard of such things being done, had even heard that eucre and other short games had been played for wine, but that none of them had ever been so unfortunate as to "get stuck" at the game, and had therefore never been called upon to fork over the necessary ten dollars which they had heard was the price of the champagne. None of them had ever seen anyone pay for a bottle, and the impression seemed to be conveyed that an unlimited amount of credit must have been granted in these establishments.

The reporter's amusement undoubtedly stemmed from the not-secret success of Belle Cora and other parlorhouse madams. Someone was paying the tariff on the champagne, lots of it; "unlimited credit" didn't furnish those luxurious houses or buy the latest Paris fashions for the residents.

James Garniss wrote that one San Francisco prostitute acquired fifty thousand dollars. She may have been French. As much or more than American women from New Orleans, clientele of the demi-monde favored French women.

Frenchman Albert Benard pridefully noted the preference for his countrywomen:

> Americans were irresistibly attracted by their graceful walk, their supple and easy bearing, and charming freedom of manner, qualities,

after all, only to be found in France; and they trooped after a French woman whenever she put her nose out of doors, as if they could never see enough of her.

France, like China, pounced on the fortuitous discovery of gold in California. France, too, was suffering civil upheaval and consequent economic depression. Its bloody revolution of 1848 left huge numbers unemployed and politically dissident. As one historian observed, the discovery of gold in California must have seemed to the French "a direct act of Providence."

Between November 1849 and April 1851, more than four thousand French migrated to California. Estimates put California's French population by the end of 1853 as high as thirty thousand.

The French government aided this emigration with a lottery called the "L'ingot d'or," the lottery of the golden ingots. Tickets cost one franc and the prizes were solid-gold bars of varying weights. The proceeds paid the passage of three thousand French emigrants to California.

More than a little suspicion attached to the French government's motives. An alarmed U.S. consul at Marseilles wrote to Thomas Butler King, San Francisco's collector of customs, that the lottery was a scheme to relocate French convicts and other undesirables, including "the worst desperadoes of Europe."

Besides the French government, recruiting agents assisted the emigration of French women, as a French journalist reported:

> A speculator of Paris has just arranged the departure of two hundred women for California, and these *houris* of our harems of Paris, Rouen, Lyons, and Havre, will sail for the gold country in a fortnight.

Adding a personal opinion to the announcement, the correspondent wrote:

> Be it understood that these beauties are not diamonds of the first water; but no matter, they leave France with the strong resolution to be good girls. I hope they will stick to it.

To the disappointment of some California miners, at least one of whom penciled an anticipated arrival date for the girls, only about fifty came.

This may have been the arrival witnessed in 1853 by Chilean Benjamin Vicuna Mackenna, who wrote:

> They have done the wildest kinds of business you can imagine in San Francisco, such as auctioning off women in the public square. I got there when matters had settled down somewhat: a ship arrived with sixty French women; none of them had paid her passage, so they offered a girl to anyone who would pay what she owed. Next day they did not have a single one left.

French women were almost universally popular in California. The same chronicler who despised "tawny visaged creatures" credited French women for the general improvement of manners and dress in San Francisco: "The great number of flaunting women of pleasure, particularly the French . . . gave ease, taste, and sprightly elegance to the manners of the town. . . ."

Less admiring was Frenchman Albert Benard who wrote bluntly of his countrywomen that "most of them are quite shameless, often scrawling their names and reception-hours in big letters on their doors."

Many of the French prostitutes, as Benard observed, profitably hired themselves out to stand at gaming tables:

> All in all, the women of easy virtue here earn a tremendous amount of money. This is approximately the tariff.
>
> To sit with you near the bar or at a card table, a girl charges one ounce ($16) an evening. She has to do nothing save honor the table with her presence. This holds true for the girls selling cigars, when they sit with you. Remember they only work in the gambling-halls in the evening. They have their days to themselves and can then receive all the clients who had no chance during the night. . . .
>
> Nearly all these women at home were streetwalkers of the cheapest sort. But out here, for only a few minutes, they ask a hundred times as much as they were used to getting in Paris. A whole night costs from $200 to $400.
>
> You may find this incredible. Yet some women are quoted at even higher prices. I may add that the saloons and gambling-houses that keep women are always crowded and sure to succeed.

The French women's enticing presence provided a formidable competitive advantage to the gambling establishments employing them.

Eliza Farnham, on a sightseeing tour of San Francisco's nightlife, observed the success of the ploy and verbally applauded:

> In one corner, a coarse-looking female might preside over a roulette-table, and, perhaps, in the central and crowded part of the room a Spanish or Mexican woman would be sitting at monte, with a cigarita in her lips, which she replaced every few moments by a fresh one.
> In a very few fortunate houses, neat, delicate, and sometimes beautiful French women were every evening to be seen in the orchestra. These houses, to the honor of the coarse crowd be it said, were always filled!

Less approving but more picturesque is this letter published anonymously in the Missouri *Statesman* of December 14, 1849:

> What would you think to see every house around the Park an open gambling house, monte tables in each corner—faro, A.B.C., and roulette and numberless French games in the center, a splendidly stocked bar—a band of musicians to entertain the crowds, who throng these places so densely, that you find it difficult to press your way through to get near a table. Abandoned women visit these places openly. I saw one the other evening sitting quietly at the monte-table, dressed in white pants, blue coat, and cloth cap, curls dangling over her cheeks, cigar in her mouth and a glass of punch at her side. She handled a pile of doubloons with her blue kid gloved hands, and bet most boldly.

One of the few unadmiring observers was William Perkins, who watched French women at the gaming tables in both Sonora and San Francisco:

> It is fearful to look upon these women at their Lansquenet Tables; to see the forms of angels in the employ of Hell; to witness the anxious and angry glare of disappointment when they lose; the feverish and eager glance of triumph when they win; the efforts to keep a calm exterior and clothe the tongue with honeyed words while the heart is beating with rage! Oh! it is terrible! and enough to make a gambler forswear his unholy trade.

Perkins was a young Canadian who formed strong and lasting attachments to the Spanish-speaking peoples of Sonora. After three years in California he emigrated via Chile to a permanent home in Argentina. He may have formed his opinions of the French based on his sympathies to Latin Americans: "These spanish women are much more elegant, graceful and outwardly correct in their deportment than the Frenchwomen. The latter are more brilliant, lively and talkative, but they are far more profligate."

Perkins held opinions about most of California's women:

> Of the English women from Sidney, and the loose American women from the States, I say nothing; vulgar, degraded and brutish as they are in their own countries, a trip to California has not of course improved them.

The subject of French women, especially, was rarely far from his pen:

> French women . . . are one of the peculiar features of California society. They are to be met with every where, and every where they are the same: money making, unscrupulous, and outwardly well-behaved. . . . Thousands have immigrated to this country as adventuresses. Some few are married and have come out with their husbands, but these generally have few personal attractions. Most are young girls who have found "protectors" in this country with whom they live in all respects as man and wife, and are for the most part excellent helpmates and valuable companions. They are always lady-like in their dress and comportment, and as virtuous as the generality of their class in France think it becoming or necessary in the sex.

Perkins didn't name names, but Albert Benard did. He closed his journal with a list of the French women in California he remembered for their beauty. The name of Simone Jules was not among them, although it probably should have been. Her name lives because she was one of the first French women to work as a gambler rather than just decorate the hall. In 1850, the Bella Union hired the beautiful black-haired Mlle. Jules as a roulette croupier, setting an example that most of the larger gaming establishments soon copied.

Benard does name an Eleonore. Whether she was Eleanore Dumont is pure conjecture, but Eleanore Dumont preserved her own name. She made her mark on Nevada City, arriving there in 1854. A spectator described the young French girl, who was about twenty, as "pretty, dark-eyed, fresh-faced." She checked into a hotel, signing the register as Mme. Eleanore Dumont, then rented an empty store on Broad Street. She furnished it for gambling; her game was *vingt-*

et-un—twenty-one—blackjack. Keeping her gambling house open day and night, she amassed a fortune.

Mme. Dumont was notable in Nevada City for unreproachable character. She was a gambler but her chastity went unquestioned.

Likewise, in Sonora was a young Frenchwoman who worked in a gambling hall without raising questions of impropriety. Elizabeth Gunn wrote that this French girl, only seventeen, had built a house for her mother and younger sister and brother. With no apparent prejudice, Mrs. Gunn observed: "She earns her money by going to the gaming houses and dealing out the cards to the players, and she makes a good deal."

Most women remembered for defying respectability were American or French. However, one Chinese prostitute—her name variously recorded as Ah Toy, Atoy, Attoy, Achoi, and Achoy—shares the distinction.

Unknown is the ship by which she came to the city, or its arrival date. The earliest record of her is a court appearance in 1849 in which she resisted leaders of San Francisco's Chinese community. They claimed to have received a letter from a man in Hong Kong asserting he was Ah Toy's husband and requesting her return. Denying she was married, Ah Toy testified that she was born in Canton, was twenty-one years old, had come to California to "better her condition," and wished to stay. The judge so allowed.

Despite her early arrival, Ah Toy was not the first Chinese woman in San Francisco. That distinction belonged to the servant of Mr. and Mrs. Charles V. Gillespie. The Gillespies arrived in San Francisco on February 2, 1848, aboard the American brig *Eagle*, bringing with them from Hong Kong a Chinese woman servant. Her name has failed to survive.

She and Ah Toy were, according to Bancroft, the only Chinese women in San Francisco in January 1850, despite the October 29, 1849, arrival of "three Chinese ladies of rank" aboard the English bark *Helen Stewart*, noted by the *Alta*. Since it is unlikely these three women left the city, they probably avoided the census takers.

Ah Toy, conversely, was highly visible. A newspaper reporter wrote in 1851: "Everybody has seen the charming Miss Atoy, who each day parades our streets dressed in the most flashing European and American style." A less-admiring chronicler dismissed her briefly and disparagingly: "Every body knew that famous or infamous character, who was alternately the laughing-stock and the plague of the place."

Whatever else people thought of Ah Toy, all agreed she was beautiful. Elisha Crosby recalled her as "a very handsome Chinese girl," adding that she was "quite select in her associates was liberally patronized by the white men and made a great amount of money." Albert Benard wrote of Chinese women that "there are a few girls who are attractive if not actually pretty, for example, the strangely alluring Achoy, with her slender body and laughing eyes." Charles P. Duane remembered her as a "tall, well-built woman. In fact, she was the finest-looking woman I have ever seen."

Beauty aside, Ah Toy was remarkable if only for her frequent court appearances. Her English-language skills and her understanding and employment of the American judicial system set her apart as a most unusual Chinese woman. Chinese people did not "go to law" in their own country. China had no lawyers, as English-speaking people understand the term, and although official courts existed, using them was counted a disgrace. Family councils and village elders tradition-ally settled difficulties. This system prevailed in San Francisco, where most disputes between Chinese were settled by Chinatown leaders.

Ah Toy vigorously resisted such control. She relied on American courts to solve her problems.

In 1849, for example, Ah Toy appeared in Judge George Baker's recorder's court to complain that several of her customers had substi-tuted brass filings for gold dust. In court she displayed the bowl she used for collecting the one-ounce gold dust fee she charged men for looking at her. Since she was not the only Chinese woman in the city—the Gillespies lived nearby and their servant must have been seen frequently—the curious obviously did not come to gaze upon her *countenance*, as a tactful newspaper reporter euphemistically wrote. Some women must have admired her resourcefulness.

In 1850 Ah Toy appeared before Judge R. H. Waller, who dismissed charges filed by some of her neighbors that she was a public nuisance.

It was in 1850, too, on May 22, that the *Alta California* published the following: "Married, in Sonoma, on the 16th inst., Henry Conrad, to the well-known China woman Achoi, from Hong Kong."

No more is heard of Mr. Conrad. Sometime during 1851 Ah Toy formed an alliance with John A. Clark, a brothel inspector for the vigilance committee.

Also in 1851, Ah Toy appeared in court, "blooming with youth, beauty and rouge," to successfully prosecute Chinatown leader Norman Assing for attempting to control her and other Chinese prostitutes through taxation.

In 1852 several hundred Chinese prostitutes arrived, an immigration San Francisco's chronicler blamed on Ah Toy: "Her advices home seem to have encouraged the sex to visit so delightful a spot as San Francisco . . . It is perhaps only unnecessary to say that they are the most indecent and shameless part of the population. . . ."

During 1852 Ah Toy was again in court. To Judge Edward McGowan she complained that John Clark had beaten her for saying she was his mistress. On another occasion she represented a Chinese woman accused of attacking a Chinese man for failing to pay "debts of honor." In August she once more defeated a powerful Chinese man attempting to tax Chinese women. The *Alta* reported:

> Miss Atoy knows a thing or two, having lived under the folds of the
> Star-spangled Banner for three years, and breathed their air of Repub-
> licanism, and she cannot be easily humbugged into any such mea-
> sures. Besides, she lives near the Police Office and knows where to
> seek protection, having been before the Recorder as a defendant
> at least fifty times herself.

For a few years Ah Toy prospered. She moved from the poor Clay Street abode of her first residence in San Francisco. In 1852 a San Francisco city directory listed her address as "Attoy A. board'g h 34&36 Pike," a near neighbor of Belle Cora. Here she was several times cited for keeping a "disorderly house."

In 1854 the city passed its first anti-prostitution law, which was enforced primarily against Chinese, Mexicans, and Chileans. After repeated arrests Ah Toy left San Francisco.

Even before the anti-prostitution law of 1854, court records reveal the frequent appearance of prostitutes on charges of keeping "houses of ill repute." In October 1850, for example, a Sacramento grand jury on separate charges indicted Fanny Seymour and Sarah Hopkins of the "crime of keeping and maintaining a certain common, ill governed and disorderly house. . . ." The indictment specified that men and women "of evil name and fame" were in the house "drinking, tippling, whoring and misbehaving themselves. . . ."

Sarah Hopkins, in a countersuit, contended successfully that the indictment was "defective for not showing upon its face the precise situation and location where said disorderly house is alleged to have been kept." Her best defense, however, ably prepared and cited by attorney C. A. Johnson, was that the "keeping of a disorderly house is not an indictable offence at Common Law."

Fanny Seymour also appeared as a complainant before the district court. In January 1851 the twenty-four-year-old prostitute from Louisiana sued Augusta Ridgeway and Julia Lawrence for four thousand dollars, the amount owed her for four months' rent. She further contended that Ridgeway and Lawrence intended to conceal and dispose of their property to defraud creditors.

Fanny succeeded in her suit against the two young girls. The court attached the property of twenty-one-year-old Augusta, from Missouri, and Ohioan Julia Lawrence, just nineteen. Among the items transferred were eight rocking chairs, six bedsteads, two gilt-framed mirrors, three looking glasses, one settee, and two divans.

A month later Fanny was again in court, once more a defendant. Believing herself insulted by an associate, Mary Chambers, Fanny threw "a large pitcher" at the girl and severely wounded her. Fanny was arrested and conveyed to the station house where she was held on bail of five hundred dollars.

But Fanny Seymour's infractions against proper behavior were as nothing to Irene McCready's.

Irene, like Belle Cora, arrived in San Francisco in 1849 in company with a gambling man. James McCabe, co-owner of the El Dorado, apparently financed the building of Irene's parlorhouse. Like Belle Cora, Irene entertained at her house many of the city's most respectable men. Most of these men, as they did to Belle Cora, extended Irene the deference paid most "fair but frail" women in the earliest days.

But they would not extend it in their wives' presence.

The occasion of Irene's public rebuff was a Benevolent Society entertainment organized by the ladies of the city's four churches as a fund raiser for various worthy causes. Sarah Royce was present and recorded the event:

Introductions, and cordial greetings were turning strangers into friends, and making many, hitherto lonely, hearts feel, that even in California there was a society worth having, when there entered the room a man, prominent for wealth and business-power, bearing upon his arm a splendidly dressed woman, well known in the city as the disreputable companion of her wealthy escort. With cool assurance he proceeded to make her and himself quite at home; but in a few minutes he was waited upon by a committee of gentlemen, who called him aside, and told him they were sent, by the lady-managers to say that they declined to receive as an associate, or to have introduced to their daughters, one who stood in the relation occupied by his companion, and they respectfully requested him to invite her to withdraw with him. . . . It was reported that he had previously boasted that he could introduce "Irene" any where in San Francisco, but the events of that evening proved to him, as well as to others, that while Christian women would forego ease and endure much labor, in order to benefit any who suffered, they would not welcome into friendly association any who trampled upon institutions which lie at the foundation of morality and civilization.

Sarah places this affair on the calendar of 1850 with no specific date. Since she states that Irene's escort respectfully withdrew and the evening went on as before, the date appears not to have been December 20, 1850.

The *Alta* reported that date as the occasion of a similar breach of good taste, one that brought the social event to a close. Again it was a "ladies' fair" fund raiser, which the *Alta* had urged gentlemen to attend, adding, "We feel assured that the taste and refinement of the lady managers and others present, will secure the utmost propriety and taste in all the arrangements and proceedings." The editor's intimated fears of the possibility of breached proprieties proved well founded. The day following the fair, the *Alta* reported:

A suitable deference to public morals and the feelings and characters of the ladies present, did not govern the conduct of some of the visitors. They came there—men who have virtuous mothers and sisters, and who ought, if only for their sakes, to at least *show* respect for virtue and decorum, if they have it—came there, boldly bringing with them the most disreputable companions, such as no virtuous female can look upon except with abhorrence. It is pleasing to know, and honorable to the members of the Guards and other gentlemen present, that they expressed unequivocally their sense of flagrant outrage by causing the sales to be forthwith closed. This insult must not be repeated.

A similar breach of public etiquette spiraled into murder. Evidence of Belle Cora's success is the readiness with which she advanced fifteen thousand dollars in gold to a well-known criminal lawyer to defend Charles Cora for killing U.S. Marshall William H. Richardson.

Richardson's death resulted from an incident at the American Theatre. Mrs. Richardson was insulted at finding the infamous Belle Cora and her paramour seated nearby. Richardson asked the management to insist the Coras leave. The manager refused, the Coras remained and, humiliated, the Richardsons left the theatre.

After two days of trading unpleasantries, Cora shot and killed Richardson and claimed self defense. Richardson's gun was found near his body, cocked and loaded.

Near pandemonium followed. Sam Brannan, urging Cora's instant hanging, was arrested for inciting a riot. Newspapers labeled the killing an "atrocious murder," fixing guilt before a jury could.

Belle's devotion never faltered. She persuaded the defense attorney to stay on the case despite extreme pressure from the newspapers and influential citizens to quit. Daily she sent fresh laundry and meals from her house to the jail. She even tried to bribe eyewitness Maria Knight.

Maria testified during the trial that she was invited to Belle's house, offered wine and tea, and that Belle told her "a pathetic story of her childhood" and how Mr. Cora "had paid for her education." She further testified that when Belle asked for a description of the shooting of Richardson, she interrupted to ask what Richardson had in his hand. When Maria replied that she had seen nothing in his hand, Belle, she testified, jumped up and shrieked, "Woman, if you expect to get out of this house alive you must say that you saw Richardson with a pistol in his hand. That is the only ground we have to save my husband's life!"

More influential in the attempt to save Cora's life was defense attorney E. D. Baker. Belle had been as much on trial as Cora after Maria Knight's testimony, and Baker didn't shy from defending her:

> I will now proceed to grapple with the great bugbear of the case. The complaint . . . is that Belle Cora has tampered with the witnesses. . . . In plain English, Belle Cora is helping her friend as much as she can . . . and in the Lord's name, who else should help him? Who else is there whose duty it is to help him? If it were not for her, he would not have a friend on earth. This howling, raging public opinion would

banish every friend. . . . It is a woman of base profession, of more than easy virtue, of malign fame, of a degraded caste—it is one poor, weak, feeble, and, if you like it, wicked woman—to her alone he owes his ability to employ counsel to present his defense.

What we want to know is, what have they against that? What we want to know is, why don't they admire it?

The history of this case is, I suppose, that this man and this woman have formed a mutual attraction, not sanctioned, if you like, by the usages of society—if you like, not sanctioned by the rights of the Church. It is but a trust in each other, a devotion to the last, amid all the dangers of the dungeon and all the terrors of the scaffold.

The impassioned plea on Belle's behalf cost Baker. Polite society shunned him afterwards and, due to threats on his life, he eventually fled from the city. But Baker's defense won Cora a half-victory. The jury was out forty-one hours before admitting deadlock. Authorities jailed Cora to await a second trial.

Shortly after that, in a twist of fate that sealed Cora's, James P. Casey shot newspaper editor James King of William and set in motion the resurrection of the city's vigilance committee.

And it was the vigilantes who tried Cora next. Belle's money held no sway; Baker's passionate defense would not be repeated. Two vigilantes provided Cora's counsel, and the jury was the vigilance executive committee itself. More important, in vigilance proceedings majority meant conviction. There would be no deadlock this time.

The committee found Cora guilty. The automatic sentence was hanging.

On the day Cora would hang, Belle hurried to Fort Vigilance where she begged, and received, permission to remain with Cora until his execution.

That morning, sometime between 11 a.m. and noon, Father Accolti, a Catholic priest, united Charles and Belle Cora in marriage.

At 1:21 in the afternoon, the bride became a widow.

NINE

LOVE AND MARRIAGE

*i tell you the woman are in great demand in this country no
matter whether they are married or not you need not think
strange if you see me coming home with some good looking man
some of these times with a pocket full of rocks. . . . it is all the go
here for Ladys to leave there Husbands two out of three do it*
—ABBY MANSUR, *Horseshoe Bar, California, May 28, 1853*

In April 1849 the packet ship *Angelique* departed New York with just
twenty-two passengers. Among them was a disappointed Eliza Farnham. Horace Greeley had backed her plan to take a hundred respectable, marriageable women to California. So had William Cullen
Bryant and the Rev. Henry Ward Beecher. Writer Catharine M.
Sedgwick endorsed Mrs. Farnham's proposal and said admiringly,
"She has nerves to explore alone the seven circles of Dante's Hell."

But only two of the two hundred women who responded to Eliza
Farnham's February circular boarded the *Angelique* with her.

The plan seemed sound. Mrs. Farnham wanted only "intelligent,
virtuous and efficient women" over age twenty-five. She required of
them testimonials from clergymen or town officials attesting to their
education and character. Each woman would contribute $250 to
defray the expense of the voyage and accommodations in San Francisco until employed.

Nor could anyone fault Mrs. Farnham's purpose, declared in her
circular's introduction:

The death of my husband, Thomas J. Farnham, Esq., at San Francisco,
in September last, renders it expedient that I should visit California
during the coming season. Having a desire to accomplish some greater
good by my journey thither than to give the necessary attention to my
private affairs, and believing that the presence of women would be

one of the surest checks upon many of the evils that are apprehended
there, I desire to ask attention to the following sketch of a plan for
organizing a party of such persons to emigrate to that country.

Many Californians shared Mrs. Farnham's belief in the civilizing
influence of women. Introduce sufficient women into a frontier mining camp and a community emerged. Women required schools for
their children, they attended churches, formed benevolent societies
for the needy.

Women's presence encouraged stability, observed Peter Burnett,
an Oregon pioneer who emigrated to California and became the
state's first governor:

> I had seen society in Oregon, without means, without spiritous
> liquors, and without a medium of exchange; but there was a due
> proportion of families, and the people rapidly improved in every
> respect. In California, however, there were few women and children,
> but plenty of gold, liquors, and merchandise, and almost every man
> grew comparatively rich for the time; and yet, in the absence of female
> influence and religion, the men were rapidly going back to barbarism.

The *Alta California*, on October 4, 1849, affirmed Burnett's belief:

> Woman to society, is like a cement to the building of stone. The
> society here has no such a cement; its elements float to and fro upon
> the excited, turbulent, hurried life of California immigrants, or rather,
> we should say, gold hunters, of all colors and shape, without any
> affinity. . . . But bring woman here and at once the process of
> chrystalization . . . will set in the society. . . .

Eliza Farnham's noble intentions to contribute "cement" to California's turbulence failed, undermined by gossip and suspicion. Conser-
vative Eastern society hinted at the potential for immorality, and
insinuated that Mrs. Farnham's California Association of American
Women was but a ploy for prostitutes.

Meanwhile, Californians had got wind of her plan to bring women
to them, not knowing its failure. The *Alta*'s editor waxed ecstatic:

> This is the most gladdening intelligence of the day . . . the girls are
> coming, and the dawning of brighter days for our golden land is even

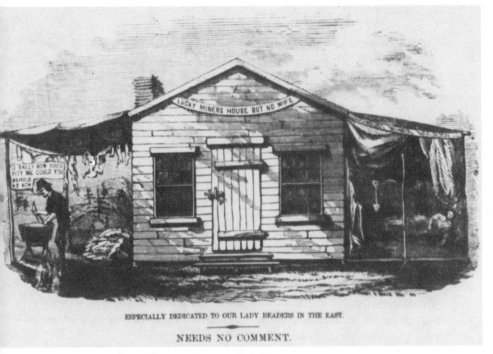

ESPECIALLY DEDICATED TO OUR LADY READERS IN THE EAST.

NEEDS NO COMMENT.

Miners published this cartoon to accompany a poem entitled "We Miss Thee, Ladies"—a proposal of marriage to willing women.
ELEANOR McCLATCHY COLLECTION, CITY OF SACRAMENTO, MUSEUM AND HISTORY DIVISION

now perceptible! The day of regeneration is nigh at hand. . . . We shall . . . prepare ourselves to witness the great change which is shortly to follow, with feelings akin to hilarious joy. . . .

Echoing these sentiments for a similar, though later, anticipation, was San Francisco lawyer John McCrackan, who wrote in a letter to his sister Mary on April 14, 1850:

We find we are to enjoy at last, what we have so much needed, the sweet, the gentle, the saving influence of woman. . . . We look upon woman as the only agent that can rescue us amid the . . . quicksands that surround us. We have already arrivals of more than two thousand women by sea, many more have come across the country. I heard not long since of the arrival of an old Lady & her five daughters. They came in a wagon & seemed quite happy to think there were such chances to get well married.

Many women found husbands in California. In 1851, after an acquaintance of just two weeks, schoolteacher Abigail Tuck married pioneer John Marsh. She thus accomplished an intent revealed in a letter written in the early 1840s while teaching in the South:

> You say you hope I shall have a Yankee for a husband, but I do not know about that, I know one thing, that a Yankee, a good one, is worth more than ten Southern gentlemen in general. You just spread the word for me . . . but I never shall stay North unless I get a Yankee for a husband.

Abigail made a good marriage, for not only did the educated John Marsh share her interest in books, his Contra Costa cattle ranch was worth a half million dollars. Marsh adored his wife and built a mansion for her as evidence of his esteem.

Women new to California soon learned their value, and one put a high price on it. She placed the following advertisement in an 1849 issue of a Marysville newspaper:

A HUSBAND WANTED

BY A LADY WHO can wash, cook, scour, sew, milk, spin, weave, hoe, (can't plow), cut wood, make fires, feed the pigs, raise chickens, rock the cradle, (gold-rocker, I thank you, Sir!), saw a plank, drive nails, etc. These are a few of the solid branches; now for the ornamental. "Long time ago" she went as far as syntax, read Murray's Geography and through two rules in Pike's Grammar. Could find 6 states on the Atlas. Could read, and you can see she can write. Can —no, *could*—paint roses, butterflies, ships, etc. Could once dance; can ride a horse, donkey or oxen, besides a great many things too numerous to be named here. Oh, I hear you ask, could she scold? No, she can't you, you———— ————good-for-nothing————!

Now for her terms. Her age is none of your business. She is neither handsome nor a fright, yet an *old* man need *not* apply, nor any who have not a little more education than she has, and a great deal more gold, for there must be $20,000 settled on her before she will bind herself to perform all the above. Address to DOROTHY SCRAGGS, with real name. P.O. Marysville.

Women's value, whatever the price they might individually assign themselves, escalated with their scarcity. California's 1850 census reported female residents at about 8 percent, although the actual

Women were not entirely absent from mining communities. Butte County numbered 72 women over the age of 18 in its census of 1850; Calaveras counted 194.

figure was probably higher, since some tabulators ignored prostitutes.

Contributing to women's apparent absence were the numbers of San Francisco women living unseen aboard ships. Anne Booth was one, but even in 1849 she found more women in the city than she expected:

> We were led to believe there were but a very few ladies, if any, in this place; I have met with several ladies myself, that do credit to, and highly adorn any society, however fastidious its demands; surely this fact need excite no particular surprise; generally speaking, they are not actuated by any love of adventure; and only obey the dictates of duty and inclination to accompany their husbands, wherever their interests may call them. . . . the ladies, with a very few exceptions, are all married. . . .

Further contributing to women's assumed scarcity was their reluctance to venture into the public thoroughfares and endure unpleasant gawking. Wrote one sympathetic man:

> The side-walks are narrow and generally crowded to such an excess as to render it really difficult and tiresome to travel them. To the ladies, shopping . . . is especially annoying and tedious, for they are designedly balked or hindered in their course by a set of well-dressed vagabonds who promenade the *trestoir* from morning to night for the sole purpose of staring in their faces.

Women made uneasy by unwelcome attention shared Eliza Farnham's feelings, expressed upon arrival in 1849:

> At that period in the history of San Francisco, it was so rare to see a female, that those whose misfortune it was to be obliged to be abroad felt themselves uncomfortably stared at. Doorways filled instantly, and little islands in the streets were thronged with men who seemed to gather in a moment, and who remained immovable till the spectacle passed from their incredulous gaze.

Mrs. Farnham's California arrival fell far short of the one she must have imagined when first devising her plan to bring good and proper women to its shore. Certainly her reception paled sadly against that of Mrs. Sheppard.

She was the wife of John McCrackan's law partner. McCrackan's witty correspondence home announced the great occasion:

> The Steamer Oregon arrived this morning and Mrs. Sheppard came passenger. Yes! she has at last arrived, the identical Mrs. Sheppard, that is, as they say, so Mr S says, and I presume he is a good judge. I have not yet seen her Ladyship. She went directly from the landing to the House which I believe was in readiness to receive her, at any rate Mr S has been up there often enough of late to get everything to rights. Sheppard of course is delerious with joy. being a small man, and like all small men a little pompous, it is a subject of speculation with his bachelor friends, what portion of the street he will require if he should conclude to come to the office tomorrow, all fear he will bend his back now in walking, so that he will jeopardize his head.

Sheppard's promenade would have required one of the city's planked streets, for no others in January 1851 could accommodate such an inflated stroll. Mud frequently left most thoroughfares impassable, as an editorialist complained:

> From the Point to the sandy eastern suburbs of the city there is one vast fathomless sea of mud, and from the water's edge to Portsmouth Square men and animals struggle and flounder and splash and spatter. . . . Its composition is heterogeneous, its character antipellucid, its adhesive qualities immense and antagonistic to a composed state of nerves. Its ingredients are dust and water, egg shells, cabbage leaves, potato parings, onion tops, fish bones, and other articles too numerous to mention. Mud is the element in which we are now compelled to exist. It is utterly impossible to do anything without thinking of mud, to go anywhere without stirring the subject, for, sober or muddled, a man is sure to put his foot in it. It is in every street, and a man is crossed by it at every crossing.

A Frenchman complained indignantly of the city's mud:

> This is not a town, it is a quagmire; it is chaos! . . . San Francisco literally floats on an ocean of mud. One finally chances it, one either walks somewhat in advance or else copies those who have preceded you or follows the pedestrians who know the way, putting one's foot where they put theirs. . . . It is your misfortune then if your foot slips or if, deceived by the mire, you just miss the proper place to step!

Women with no need to go out in such conditions simply did not. Margaret De Witt, whose husband Alfred had opened a store in the city, wrote her mother of the muddy conditions of January 1850: "It has done nothing but rain . . . —Alfred came home the other day with mud above the knees—and said he had been where there was no bottom."

Jennie Megquier similarly wrote her daughter that winter: "O the mud, it is dreadful, man and beast get stuck in the slush and cannot move it is like glue takes their boots off their feet it is a foot deep. . . ."

Although the business district boasted extensive boardwalks and a plank road by the end of 1850, unimproved outlying areas continued to impose muddy hazards. Bridging with large timbers provided a temporary solution, but crossing them required more temerity than

San Francisco, 1851.

some women possessed. Mrs. D. B. Bates, obliged to traverse above a muddy drop, wrote:

> I grow dizzy even now, thinking about it. . . . It was proposed to cross . . . on a hewn timber, which, at least, must have been nearly one hundred feet, and at a height of twelve feet, I should think, from the green slimy mud. . . . I succeeded pretty well, until about halfway over, when, finding myself suddenly becoming very dizzy, I was obliged to stop, get down on my knees, and hold on to the timber. I was afraid to proceed, lest I should fall into the mud and water below, and, for the same reason, unable to retrace my steps. After much crying on my part, and coaxing and scolding on the part of the gentleman, I succeeded in reaching the terminus of the timber. That was my introduction into the town of San Francisco in 1851.

Women's fashions of long, full skirts and dainty shoes ill-suited San Francisco's muddy streets. Women determined to be out, however, frequently temporized the dictates of fashion with the necessity of conditions. The *Alta California* commented approvingly on March 14, 1850:

> Desirous of saving their soles [women] have in many instances adopted the style of boots worn by men—a very admirable substitute for their delicate, paper soled, consumptive breeding shoes—and in one or two cases we have detected *bona fide* pantaloons peeping out from beneath the 'flowing skirts'. . . . If ladies do go out in such dreadful weather as we have been having recently—and it is very hard to expect them to be housed all the time—no objection ought certainly to be urged to their appearance in boots and whatdycallems to protect them from the mud.

The *Alta* even editorialized in favor of "whatdycallems," Amelia Bloomer's controversial design:

> Several very respectable ladies have "put on the apparel" . . . and when the rains commence, we may of course expect very large acces- sions to the Bloomer ranks. Ladies will then be obliged to go in boots, unless something is done by the street commissioner, (of which there is not the slightest probability, we may cheerfully add) to prevent the mud from accumulating knee-deep in all our thoroughfares.
>
> About this costume—we are still quite undecided as to the practica- bility of putting it in general use. We have before suggested the propriety of a compromise . . . something between the kirtle or actual Bloomer, and the long "train" dresses so much in vogue. . . . To the ladies of San Francisco it is becoming an important question—What shall be worn in the street when the rains begin? Certain it is that if the winter is at all severe, our ladies will be debarred to a great extent, from out-door exercise and privileges through four or five long months, unless they conform to some of the *habits* of the long-booted sex. We predict that many of them will come to the short skirts, and be compelled, besides, to wear long boots. . . .

Emigrants frequently found their wardrobes wanting for appropriate dress, whether the occasion was a promenade or the much-favored dances and balls. Luzena Stanley Wilson reported that the dress of "amusement-loving people" in the early days of her town was "quite unique":

The *Alta California* approved "whatdycallems," Amelia
Bloomer's controversial fashion, for San Francisco ladies. This Currier & Ives lithograph appeared in 1851.

> The ladies came in calico dresses and calf boots; a ribbon was unusual,
> and their principal ornaments were good health and good nature; the
> gentlemen came ungloved, and sometimes coatless.

Coatless or ungloved gentlemen must have seemed almost formal in
comparison to even earlier times. In California's youngest days and
remotest camps, gold-rushing men adopted far more unusual dress
for a dance. With few or no women present, some men obligingly
took the female part. Various artifices distinguished who among the
men were ladies. One method for temporarily canceling manhood
was a strategically tacked patch of calico upon the "ladies'" trousers.

Even the grand ball organized for California's constitutional convention in 1849 required creativity of attendees. Bayard Taylor attended the Monterey ball, which boasted some sixty or seventy ladies and an equal number of gentlemen. He thought the ladies' gowns showed "considerable variety," as did most men's dress:

> A complete ball-dress was a happiness attained only by the fortunate few. White kids could not be had in Monterey for love or money, and as much as $50 was paid by one gentleman for a pair of patent-leather boots. Scarcely a single dress that was seen belonged entirely to its wearer, and I thought, if the clothes had power to leap severally back to their respective owners, some persons would have been in a state of utter destitution. For my part, I was indebted for pantaloons and vest to obliging friends.

Jessie Benton Frémont also attended the party:

> The dressing for this ball was a serious matter to these native California ladies. They had already all these expensive gowns, but they wished something absolutely new and in our fashion. . . . An American who had lived there many years asked me to show her "in strictest confidence" my ball dresses; she did not believe me when I told her I had none with me; she said that she would show them to no one else, that only her dressmaker and herself should see them. . . . I could not convince her that it was not unwillingness on my part to share "the fashions" with her; she looked upon it as an excuse. When I said "really I had no evening dresses with me," she broke out with "What have you got in all those trunks, then . . . ?" I . . . insisted that she should look. When she saw only morning and walking dresses and underwear, she exclaimed as though it had dawned upon her that I was a sort of social imposter: "Why, you was *pore* when you left the States! Why, I have thirty-seven satin dresses, and no two off the same piece."

Music for Monterey's grand affair consisted, observed Taylor, of "but three pieces alternately, for waltz, contra-dance and quadrille." Two violins and two guitars made up the orchestra.

Townspeople in the interior readily organized entertainments, too, for the social mingling of the sexes. In April 1850 more than a hundred men and an impressive forty ladies attended a Sacramento ball. The *Alta*'s editor, so anxious for women to provide "cement" to California, approvingly reported the event: "Sacramento is only a year old, but boasts a good society, and it is refreshing to observe its rapid progression and wide-extended refining influences."

San Francisco's "good society" almost exhausted John McCrackan. In a letter to his sister Lottie he confided that he'd been "forced into quite a round of dissipation, private balls, house warmings, champagne frolics," and was anticipating a ball at which twenty-five ladies would be present, including "the fascinating widow." McCrackan's pleasure at women's company apparently did not extend to their children. He noted that Mrs. Brooks would attend the ball "if she can think of any way to dispose of little Willey for the Eve.—these children what a plague they are. It has been proposed to put him in a bag & carry him on her arm, the principal objections however seem insurmountable."

At Santa Cruz, however, no entertainments lightened Eliza Farnham's life. The impetus for her California journey was not the bringing of marriageable women west, but the settlement of her late husband's estate. That property included a large tract of land at Santa Cruz, including a *casa* which impressed Mrs. Farnham with its failings:

> . . . not a cheerful specimen even of California habitations—being made of slabs, which were originally placed upright, but which have departed sadly from the perpendicular in every direction. There is not a foot of floor, nor a pane of glass, nor a brick, nor anything in the shape of a stove. The fire is made upon the ground, and the smoke departs by any avenue that seemeth to itself good, or lingers in the airy space between our heads and the roof, which is beautifully done in bas relief of webs. . . .
>
> The dimensions of the entire structure are about twenty-five feet in length by fifteen feet in width at one end, and diminishing by beautiful convergence, to about ten feet at the other. A partition of slabs, thrown across the narrow end, rather divides the house than makes a room, of which the other three walls are so imperfect that you may walk through them almost where you will.

The first necessity at Santa Cruz—which Eliza, her two sons, and Miss Sampson, her companion, reached on February 22, 1850—was installing the stove brought for heat and cooking. Eliza hired a man named Tom to haul it the two miles from Santa Cruz bay where her goods were unloaded. He then attempted to "put it up."

Tom discovered that some of the stove's parts had been damaged, but he persevered in trying to install it. Night fell and he gave up. The next day Miss Sampson unsuccessfully tried assembling it. Then Eliza engaged it:

> On the third day, it was agreed that stoves could not have been used in the time of Job, or all his other afflictions would have been unnecessary. But our spirits were now so thoroughly tamed by it, and our demands upon it so humbled, that we agreed to come to its terms without further parley, and abandon the use of the refractory rods, plates, etc., which before had been thought indispensable to its perfect action. No sooner was this done than the question was amicably settled; and it shows how, often, difficulties that seem insuperable, are in truth more imaginary than real—that in an hour from this concession we had our stove well heated and its oven doing duty upon a generous pan of biscuit, very comforting to our eyes. This was a great triumph.

A great triumph and not her last. Her family needed a new house.

Lumber sawn for her was delivered July 1. By the fourth, she had marked out the foundations of a house thirty-seven feet wide, twenty-seven deep, with a wing thirteen by twenty-one, plus a six-foot piazza across the front:

> It seemed to me a great step taken, actually to see my future house defined on the very ground it was to cover. It was more real than any plan on paper could have been. Here I stood in the parlor, there was the dining-room, yonder the bath-room, here a sleeping-chamber, and, in the pleasantest yet most secluded corner . . . my library. Already, in imagination, I saw its walls lined with the contents of my well-stored boxes . . . forgetful, in that first dream, of the days and weeks of toil that must be performed before I could invite my guests or sit down with them; for—let not ladies lift their hands in horror—I designed supplying the place of journeyman carpenter with my own hands.

Mrs. Farnham hired three Sonorans to level the site, cut sills, and assist her. Then she set to work:

> My first participation in the labor of its erection was the tenanting of the joists and studding for the lower story, a work in which I suc-

ceeded so well, that during its progress I laughed, whenever I paused for a few moments to rest, at the idea of promising to pay a man $14 or $16 per day for doing what I found my own hands so dexterous in.

Regardless of self-sufficiency, a widow was not likely to remain unmarried in California's matrimonial climate. Eliza Farnham married William Fitzpatrick on March 23, 1852. On June 25, 1853, she gave birth to a daughter, Mary.

Unfortunately, the marriage was not a happy one. Fitzpatrick, it was rumored, mistreated her. Then, in 1855, Eliza's ailing son, Eddie, died and, shortly after, so did two-year-old Mary. The double tragedy swept from Eliza the energies necessary to continue teaching the Santa Cruz school. Financial entanglements overwhelmed her, as did the continued failure of her farming venture. Neither could she longer tolerate her husband's abuse.

In 1856 Eliza Farnham filed for divorce.

Hers was by no means an unusual solution to marriage difficulties in California. Indeed, the readiness with which couples severed the bonds of holy matrimony astonished even California citizens.

The frequency of divorce was in part due California's permissive divorce law, passed by the state legislature in 1851. The divorce bill, heatedly debated, prompted a vehement protest from the *Alta California* and the prediction of "evil, much evil, and only evil" as its consequence:

> Divorce has become of so easy attainment nowadays that men take wives with as much *sang froid* as they purchase a horse, knowing that if they become dissatisfied their *bargain* can as easily be unmade again. And women with similar impressions fish for partners with as much unconcern as ever Isaak Walton flung a fly upon the surface of a brook. We are sick of all such legalized immorality.

In concert with the affronted editor, San Francisco street preacher William Taylor railed against the "desolating evils in domestic life in California." Taylor blamed Satan for the decline in the sacred sanction of matrimony. The devil, he claimed, used four tools to destroy connubial fidelity. The first was the "insidious Mormon devil of Polygamy." The second was the doctrine of Andrew Jackson Davis, author of *Great Harmonia*, which held that the only valid matrimonial tie was a spiritual bond ordained by the Creator, and the best evidence that two people were not naturally and eternally married was that by living together "they generate discord, discontent, disrespect, and unhappiness." The third tool of the devil, according to Taylor, was California's legislation exempting men from legal penalties for seduction. The fourth was none other than California's "very accommodating divorce laws."

Even judges grew impatient with the incessant request for divorces, as the Sacramento *Daily Union* revealed in publishing Judge Monson's decision in the case of Margaret E. Avery vs A. G. Avery:

> Our Legislature has prescribed a number of causes for which the
> marriage contract may be dissolved; whether or not they have adopted
> the true policy—whether or not they have consulted the good of
> society in allowing divorces for other causes than that of adultery, is
> not for me to decide. My duty is only to construe and give effect to the
> law as enacted. . . . [However], take away from the marriage contract
> the stamp and impress of permanency—encourage the idea that it
> is not a relation as permanent as the lives of the parties—that it is not
> an engagement for better or worse . . . and we shall find, if we have
> not discovered it already, that we have adopted the very method "to
> encourage family dissensions and a contemptuous disregard of those
> duties imposed by the marriage relation". . . . The suffering party
> must endure in some degree the consequences of an injudicious
> connection. . . . As yet, but few divorces have been granted by this
> Court. The number of applications, however, are so rapidly increasing, that I have written out a decision in this case in order that all
> applying may know my views in regard to it. The application for a
> divorce in this case is denied.

A spirited defense of California's divorce law appeared in the *Pioneer* of April 1854. The writer attacked those opposed to the divorce bill as "representatives from the shores of fogydom," advocates of "some old worn-out system of theology." Praising California's population as "selected from the choice young men of all the most active nations of the world" and thereby embodying "the great principle of progress," the writer asserted:

> We live faster than other people. We think more promptly. . . . Our
> passions are stronger; our intellects keener; our prejudices weaker.
> . . . We think for ourselves on religious subjects; dreading not the
> verdict of village scandal-mongers, we enjoy to the full our present
> opinions; glorying in the isolation of our social position and our

comparative freedom from social formalities. . . . It is for us in California—the freest of the free—to choose between authority and reason; between other men's dicta and our own convictions.

California law gave district courts exclusive jurisdiction in granting divorce. Grounds were natural impotence, minority, adultery, extreme cruelty, habitual intemperance, desertion, willful neglect, consent obtained by force or fraud, and conviction for a felony.

A divorce petition specifying cruelty was heard in Coloma, where the wife claimed that while crossing the plains her husband made her fetch wood and water. Both testified that en route they agreed to separate, but after arriving in California the husband changed his mind. The judge viewed marriage as a civil contract, advising the jury that, as such, it could be entered into and broken at the will of the parties. Thus, "if an engagement had been entered into on the plains to separate, and the defendant afterwards refused to do so, the jury must find for the plaintiff." The jury, thus admonished, found for the plaintiff without having to decide whether fetching wood and water constituted cruelty.

In Weaverville, Franklin Buck sat on the jury of a "famous divorce case," with grounds more interesting than cruelty. On one day of trial, jurors sat through eight hours of "hearing the lawyers squabble," Buck wrote his sister, but as they received "three dollars cash each day and as the testimony is very *piquant* we don't care." Since the judge also allowed jurors to "smoke and whittle," Buck rather enjoyed himself. Although charged not to say anything about the case, Buck thought no harm done by sharing it with his sister:

Susan Teresa R. vs. Phillip R., are from Tiffin, Ohio. Married two years ago and started for California. They commenced quarreling on the steamer because she was too thick with a young fellow and had quarrelled ever since last January when, as his partner testified, he came down to the claim one morning and said the d_____d bitch has gone. She went to live with a single gent who has a ranch. One of her bosom friends, a Mrs. Broom, quite a pretty young woman, was so embarrassed that the court room had to be cleared of spectators before she could answer some of the questions and then she made a clean breast of it and told of some of the richest conversations she had had with Susan, touching the *qualifications* of her husband, the unfortunate Philip, who it seems couldn't satisfy her at all.

The alacrity with which women exchanged husbands fostered jealousy in insecure men, like Martha Hitchcock's husband. Mrs. Hitchcock wrote from San Francisco on June 30, 1851, that her husband had "quite recovered from his jealous fit—I hope he is ashamed of it—I am ashamed of it, for him."

Thoroughly out of patience with the opposite sex, she added: "The more I see of men, the more I am disgusted with them—they are rather worse too, in California, than anywhere else—This is the Paradise of men—I wonder if a Paradise for poor *women*, will ever be discovered—I wish they would get up an exploring expedition, to seek for one."

In the same letter, however, she noted: "I must not forget to tell you that I have been invited to a wedding here—Col Stevenson (of the N.Y. Regt) married a very pretty woman, who got a divorce from one husband, to marry him—And the Mrs *Bonner* who ran away from her husband with a Mr *Plume*, in Columbus, is living here with him—married, of course."

California's frequent divorces kept lawyers occupied—and well paid. John McCrackan wrote his sister in January 1851 that he was busy examining a divorce case "on behalf of the lady of course." He was only waiting for a retainer of five hundred dollars, and expected it to be "forthcoming in a day or two." He added:

> You are not perhaps aware of the peculiar character of our laws here in
> regard to "Women." I presume there is no "State in the Union"
> where the Laws are so liberal, so just. For instance, when the husband
> and wife are doing business of any kind together, the law considers
> her an equal partner, and as such gives her one half of all the profits
> and she can sue for them, and collect them from her husband, should
> he refuse to account to her for them. Beside which, she can employ
> her own capital in a business apart from her husband, and she is
> protected in her right to the fullest extent. So you see we are particu-
> larly well disposed towards the ladies.

Some critics of California's divorce law laid the blame for the state's numerous divorces at the feet of the delegates to the constitutional convention at Monterey in 1849.

That body had indeed, as John McCrackan informed his sister, guaranteed women's right to own property, thus freeing women from an economic dependency that otherwise forestalled many a divorce.

California's constitutional provision protecting women's property rights was not unique. A few states provided similar protections through constitutions and legislation. The concept of women's rights in 1849 was, however, sufficiently advanced to elicit lively debate.

It was on September 27, 1849, that a committee at the Monterey constitutional convention introduced a section on women's rights among "Miscellaneous Provisions," to wit:

> All property, both real and personal, of the wife, owned or claimed by
> her before marriage, and that acquired afterwards by gift, devise, or
> descent, shall be her separate property, and laws shall be passed more
> clearly defining the rights of the wife, in relation as well to her
> separate property as that held in common with her husband. Laws
> shall also be passed providing for the registration of the wife's sepa-
> rate property.

Delegates speaking to the issue advanced two cogent arguments on behalf of the provision. The delegate from San Luis Obispo, Henry Tefft, cited California's existing laws, in which Mexican civil law guaranteed native California women separate property rights. James M. Jones, the Stockton-area delegate, argued that marriage constituted a civil contract, a partnership in which both parties shared equally. Henry Hallack, Monterey's delegate, was rebuked for his argument, best judged as enlightened self-interest:

> Having some hopes that sometime or other I may be wedded . . . I
> shall advocate this section in the Constitution, and I would call upon
> all the bachelors in this Convention to vote for it. I do not think we can
> offer a greater inducement for women of fortune to come to Califor-
> nia. It is the very best provision to get us wives. . . .

Charles Botts vociferously opposed the provision, asserting that there "must be a head and there must be a master in every household." Botts protested to the assembly that woman "takes her husband for better, for worse; that is the position in which she voluntarily places herself, and it is not for you to withdraw her from it." Continuing, he pleaded, "I beg you, I entreat you, not to lay the rude hand of

Eliza Farnham

legislation upon this beautiful, and poetical position." Such a trespass upon the "laws of nature," Botts argued, could lead only to divorce.

To these "rhapsodies about poesy," delegate Jones directed this rejoinder:

> What is the principle so much glorified, but that the husband shall be a despot, and the wife shall have no right but such as he chooses to award her. It had its origin in a barbarous age, when the wife was considered in the light of a menial, and had no rights. But in this age of civilization, it has been found that the wife has certain rights. . . .

Eliza Farnham apparently married a despot. Fortunately, in California the mistake was easily rectified. Santa Cruz County granted her one of its first divorces and she prepared to return East with Charles, her only surviving child.

But before she left she wrote a book about her experiences in California. Despite her multiple disappointments, a failed farm, a failed marriage, the deaths of two children, the woman who had once conceived a plan to bring marriageable women to California's shores retained her visionary optimism. She concluded her book about California (1856) with these words:

> But let the "talking-wires" span free soil from the Atlantic to the Pacific, and let free labor, with its enterprise, progress, and intelligence, possess and build up Kansas and Nebraska, through which California will ultimately be connected, by railroad, with the East, and in a few years she will be garden of the Union. There is no prosperity to which she cannot attain, with true manhood to control, and true womanhood to preserve her.

TEN

WEAVING THE SOCIAL FABRIC

maybe I can be able to cast my influence in favor of religion, temperance, and good morals: I feel that no person can live in any community without exerting a little influence, for we are so formed that it is impossible: and what little influence I have I am resolved shall be good, if possible. —CLEMENTINE BRAINARD, *Columbia, California, October 23, 1853*

Georgiana Bruce was an educated, sophisticated Englishwoman who had lived three years at the transcendentalist community of Brook Farm near Boston. There she had known Emerson, and she counted among her acquaintances reformer Margaret Fuller.

Another reformist friend was Eliza Farnham.

The two women had worked together at Sing Sing Prison's women's division, and when Eliza went west in 1849 she soon wrote to her friend "Geordie" to join her.

In March of 1851 Georgiana wrote to friends in the East, too:

> I have never regretted coming—not even when I was living on short meals with a long grace at the deplorable washing establishment where I ironed shirts, cooked & slept on the kitchen floor for $75 per month [but] now . . . I luxuriate in the unparalled [sic] freedom of turkish pants & tunic. . . . By the way it is my belief that this modification of the Turkish & Albanian dress which Mrs F & I find so convenient will eventually become the fashion here for you see we are amenable to no vulgar public opinion &—I say it with all due modesty—we are *the* people of the place—live more like civilized beings than any one else & if any thing worthy *does* come to S.C. it comes to our house

Thirty-five-year-old Georgiana Bruce wed Richard Kirby, owner of a prospering Santa Cruz tannery, on the same day that Eliza Farnham

Georgiana Kirby

---

married William Fitzpatrick, to Georgiana's great disapproval: "She married the greatest blackguard in the country who strikes and otherwise ill treats her."

The friends had a falling out for a time, and Georgiana confessed to her journal the sorrow occasioned by the rift:

> Every good woman needs a companion of her own sex, no matter how
> numerous or valuable her male acquaintances, no matter how close
> the union between herself and husband; if she have a genial, loving
> nature, the want of a female friend is a sad void. . . . If I had a nice
> friend with me it would recall me from my vague dreaming to the
> worth of the actual present.

Women's letters and diaries written from lonely camps and cabins often echoed Mrs. Kirby's wistful desire. However less eloquently they might express it, many women yearned for friends and homes left behind. Wrote Mary Ballou at Negro Bar:

> Clarks Simmon wife . . . came in here last night and said, "Oh dear I am so homesick that I must die," and then again my other associate came in with tears in her eyes and said that she had cried all day. she said if she had as good a home as I had got she would not stay twenty five minutes in California. I told her that she could not pick up her duds in that time. she said she would not stop for duds nor anything else but my own heart was two sad to cheer them much.

Even in a large town like Sacramento, Mary Crocker shared Mrs. Kirby's longing:

> There is but one drawback to my *perfect* happiness, that is my great distance from all other *dear* friends, here I am with one of the dearest but an ardent, strong desire is often felt to see the others.

In the absence of friends left behind, women eagerly sought new attachments. Clarissa Burrell wrote from her remote mountain home that her neighbors were all "of the bachelor order" until a Mr. Wayland brought his mother and sister to live there. "It is very pleasant to me," she wrote to her sister, "to have some female neighbors. . . ."

In thinly populated Napa Valley, Rebecca Woodson found "great comfort" when the Larkin Cockrill family moved nearby. She soon got acquainted with them and enjoyed "many happy hours" spent with Mrs. Cockrill: "There was scarcely ever a day we were not together. We did not think we could start a new dress or start piecing a quilt without consulting each other."

When the McDaniel family arrived at Grass Valley, Mrs. Shelton, who kept a boardinghouse there, rushed to greet them. Young Kate McDaniel observed the meeting:

> She helped mother out of the wagon and as mother got down from her high seat, she was embraced affectionately as though she had been a long lost sister. This poor, pioneer woman was overjoyed to see another woman come into the camp and she said, "O my dear, you seem just like an angel come to me in my loneliness."

In her own loneliness Georgiana Kirby freely admitted that she longed for the "pleasant and healthy excitement caused by the friction of mind on mind." In a fledgling attempt to gain it, even on an elementary level, she started a girls' school in her home. One ten-year-old child irked her exceedingly:

> She staid away on the least excuse and no one at home paid any attention to her coming over at the right hour. [Her family] represent pretty well the "poor white trash" of the slave states where the parents were born and married. Get up late, dawdle about and do forever a long string of nothings. Let the children drink tea and coffee and up as late as the parents. Live principally on buckwheat cakes, send the children to school a week and keep them out two months, borrow incessantly everything from indigo to a pair of stockings to go to party in. I believe I've given up trying to do anything for them.

She didn't give up, however. Georgiana Kirby, like many pioneers, was committed to the establishment of schools.

Schools, from the beginning of American interest in California, had captured the energies and convictions of people determined to have them. Walter Colton, Monterey's alcalde in 1847, for example, designed Monterey's first schoolhouse, "sixty feet by thirty—two stories, suitably proportioned, with a handsome portico. The labor of convicts, the taxes on rum, and the banks of gamblers, must put it up. Some think my project impracticable; we shall see."

With the financial support of citizens, the school eventually opened.

San Franciscans of 1847 opened California's first public school-house, building it on the southwest corner of Portsmouth Square. To teach in it they hired Thomas Douglas, a Yale graduate, who began instruction on April 3, 1848. Classes ceased soon after. A teacher's salary offered little attraction after Marshall's discovery at Coloma.

Despite this temporary recess, the fact that a public school opened in San Francisco in 1848 drew praise from Englishman Frank Marryat:

> What better illustration can we find in proof that the Americans stand out in strong colors on this point? what better proof that they are good colonists, when under such adverse circumstances, in the midst of riot, dissipation, and ungodliness, the first and only approach to a sense of responsibility was shown in a fostering care of the young and helpless children *not their own*.

Such fostering care in California was first provided by Olive Mann Isbell, niece of the famous educator Horace Mann. She is credited with establishing California's first English-speaking school.

Mrs. Isbell and her husband were among the nearly two hundred emigrants who spent the winter of 1846 in the dark, damp confines of the Santa Clara mission, waiting out the conflict that would secure California for the Americans. Margaret Hecox with her husband Adna and four children had crossed the plains from Illinois that year. Mrs. Hecox's memory of the terrible winter the emigrants spent imprisoned in the mission included a special appreciation of Olive Isbell:

> Mrs. Isbell was a woman who won the everlasting gratitude of us all that winter for her excellent help in caring for our children. Mrs. Isbell organized a little school in one of the old buildings and succeeded in keeping the children occupied and out of mischief and imparted much useful information to the little ones.

Sarah Royce was another pioneer teacher. In 1849, on her dreadful trek across the forty-mile desert she had stopped amid the immense litter of abandoned property to admire a few "very beautifully finished trunks." She thought a company of merchants must have intended the contents for sale in California, but like so many others had left their goods behind to save their own lives. Of these things, she wrote:

> There was only one thing, (besides the few pounds of bacon) that, in all these varied heaps of things, many of which, in civilized scenes, would have been valuable, I thought worth picking up. That was a little book, bound in cloth and illustrated with a number of small engravings. Its title was "Little Ella." I thought it would please Mary, so I put it in my pocket. It was an easily carried souvenir of the desert; and more than one pair of young eyes learned to read its pages in after years.

Mrs. Royce taught school in Grass Valley. Her son Josiah, who became a noted philosopher, writer, and historian, first attended school in his own home. An older sister taught him to read, and his mother was his earliest teacher in philosophy.

Among the first women emigrating to California with the intent to

teach school was one the *Alta California*'s editor awaited with anticipation. Her gender was considered newsworthy for the issue of
January 28, 1850:

> Education—We perceive by some of the eastern papers that Mrs. M. E.
> Tullos, late principal in Tuscaloosa, Alabama, is en route for this place,
> with the intention of devoting herself to the education of her sex in
> this distant and infant state. *Werry* kind in Mrs. Tullos, certainly. We
> are also happy to learn that "Mrs. T is an accomplished lady in the full
> acceptation of the term, and is zealous in the philanthropic but ardu-
> ous mission which she has undertaken." The sex, which is doubtless
> honored in the possession of a philanthropic Mrs. Tullos, will be
> deeply gratified for the "arduous mission" she has undertaken.
> Wonder if Mrs. T. is a "vidder," and wouldn't like to give lessons to
> some nice young man in the school of matrimony!

The need for teachers on the frontier prompted the National Board of
Popular Education in the decade following 1846 to send nearly six
hundred women west to teach school. Of these, the names of 250
women survive, but of them, disappointingly, only one, Susan A.
Lord, is known to have come to California. She helped establish at
least two California schools, serving as principal of the Young Ladies'
Seminary in Benicia when it opened in 1852. The Benicia Seminary
apparently solicited donations, for Thomas Larkin was reminded in a
letter dated August 16, 1852, that he had offered the Seminary one
hundred dollars toward the purchase of a "piano forte." After establishing this seminary, which survived to become Mills College, Susan
Lord moved to a frontier mining community in Butte County and
started her own female academy.

Many teachers started their own schools. In June 1851, the *Alta*
announced that Mrs. C. M. Parker intended to open a private school
for girls. The help of Mrs. Parker must have been appreciated by Mr.
and Mrs. John Cotter Pelton, whose San Francisco school in February
1851 numbered 160 children aged three to fifteen.

Eliza Farnham observed that the Peltons' school "became so large
that Mr. P and his wife were unable to give anything like the requisite
attention to the pupils, who represented every continent and the
islands of the sea, and spoke nearly all the languages of Christen-
dom."

John Pelton had assumed responsibility for the schoolhouse on the
plaza, where in April 1849, the Rev. Albert Williams had opened

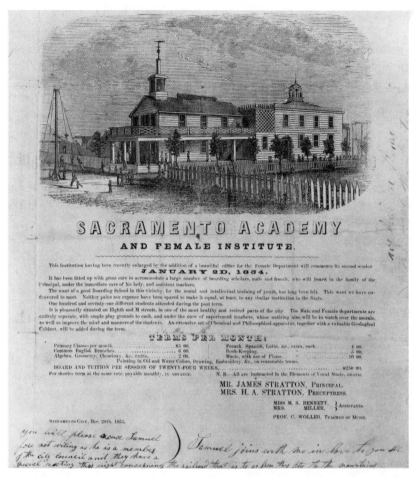

By 1854 Sacramento schools had enrolled more than five hundred students.
CALIFORNIA STATE LIBRARY

private classes. After church duties required all Williams' time, the position went to Pelton, a young Massachusetts schoolteacher and Baptist Church layman. With the help of his wife, Pelton continued the school as private, depending upon voluntary subscriptions and donations.

In April 1850, however, Pelton appealed to the city for financial assistance. San Francisco eventually recompensed him from the public treasury a salary of five hundred dollars a month, payable in city scrip, which had a cash value of about thirty cents on the dollar. The city's apparently generous five hundred dollars translated to not much more than $150 for the united services of Mr. and Mrs. Pelton and their assistants.

San Francisco's population of children increased so rapidly that by May 1854 its citizens supported seven public schools and twenty-seven private schools. Enrollment in that month totaled 1,574 children in public schools and 947 in private.

In Sacramento, by July 1854, more than five hundred students were attending public and private schools.

Public education benefited greatly by female energies. The ladies of Nevada City in 1853 sponsored a dinner and music festival to raise funds for a public school. A man named Bill Stewart attended the event and, addressing those assembled, confessed that he and many others had not expected the women to "succeed in this enterprise":

> We now think that we were very unreasonable in doubting. We ought to have taken into consideration the fact that the ladies of Nevada [City] are California ladies, and have had the enterprise and daring to come to a country supposed in the Atlantic States to be out of the world, or at least to be in the most wild and uncivilized part of it, and that whatever they had attempted must and would succeed. Your present efforts establish the fact that no one has a right to doubt your success in any enterprise that may engage your attention.

Women's attentions focused on many good works on behalf of society, for which Mallie Stafford praised her pioneer sisters: "It was due largely to their influence and exertions that churches flourished, Sunday schools were inaugurated, and many societies for the relief of the sick, friendless and distressed were organized."

Women organized fund-raising events for numerous good causes. In San Francisco they tirelessly promoted benevolent organizations, among them four Hebrew societies, one Chinese, two Irish, one Swiss, one German, and one French, as well as three devoted exclusively to women. The German and French associations both had good hospitals. The Sisters of Mercy supervised the city and county hospital. In 1851 San Francisco women established by their support two orphan asylums.

Women helped organize churches even before the gold rush. Mary Jones, an overlander of 1846, recalled that in 1848 a "body of Christians" held "regular service every Sabbath":

Margaret De Witt helped organize a fund-raising fair to help pay the $16,000 cost of San Francisco's First Presbyterian Church, erected in 1850.

Some of us were Cumberland Presbyterians, some Methodists some Baptists, and we had a Methodist preacher at first. But he went away soon and then there was a Rev. Douglas came from New York, who was a Congregationalist, who . . . was paid a large salary and he organized the first Sabbath school in California. . . .

In 1848 the Rev. T. Dwight Hunt arrived in San Francisco from the Sandwich Islands. The California city's "unenviable notoriety for wickedness," according to its chroniclers, attracted Hunt as the first clergyman bent on reform. He was followed by numerous missionaries eager to do battle with California's evils.

By 1849 San Franciscans supported several churches. The Rev. Albert Williams organized the First Presbyterian Church on May 20 with six members, three of them women. During that summer, congregation member Alfred De Witt assumed the responsibility of procuring a church building from New York. It arrived in the fall of 1850; freight, building, and lot cost an estimated sixteen thousand dollars. Margaret De Witt wrote home that the ladies of the church "formed a sewing society to make articles, to sell for the debt on the church—They had a fair—and succeeded very well."

The Rev. O. C. Wheeler established the First Baptist Church on June 24, 1849. Anne Booth attended services there on September 23, noting a "large congregation, very respectable, about one dozen ladies, all of whom were perfectly genteel in appearance."

The Rev. T. Dwight Hunt's efforts resulted in the organization of the First Congregational Church in July 1849. Grace Chapel opened on Sunday, December 30, 1849, the labor of the Rev. Dr. Ver Mehr, a missionary sent by the Protestant Episcopal Church.

In 1849, too, the Rev. S. F. Mines, an Episcopalian, formed Trinity Church. Within a few months the congregation erected a building at a cost of approximately eleven thousand dollars. It measured about sixty by thirty feet, its exterior painted "stone color" and embellished with Gothic windows. Inside was a small altar, "prettily furnished." The unfinished interior had no gallery, the choir taking the front row of rough benches. Four or five of these seats were sold, reported member John McCrackan, and "were cushioned and improved by the owners."

Townspeople in smaller communities proved equally industrious on behalf of religion, although their early church edifices rarely rivaled those of San Francisco. At the gold-mining camp of Agua Fria, west of Mariposa, Enos Christman on Sunday, May 12, 1850, attended a "meeting in the forest and listened to a good sermon," with "six ladies and about fifty gentlemen."

In San Jose, a Presbyterian Church was "built" by Mrs. Bascom:

> I built it all alone, with my own hands, and the only tool I had was a good stout needle! It was the famous 'Blue Tent'. . . . Mr. Blakeslee asked me if I could make it, and I told him of course I could. He bought the cloth and cut it out. It was of blue jean, and cost seventy-five cents a yard.

Mrs. Charles Crocker attested that Sacramento churches in 1853 were well attended. Proudly, and somewhat defensively, she wrote:

[Our churches] would put some of the Eastern Congregations to the blush, there where they think of California as only inhabited by the offscourings of the earth, persons who pay no attention to the usages nor proprieties of civilized life. We are not so very far behind other people after all.

In 1852, members of Stockton's First Presbyterian Church, built in 1849, organized a choir and brought a melodeon from San Francisco for accompaniment. In the choir were Mrs. Woods, wife of the Rev. Mr. Woods, and Henry Kroh's musically gifted wife and five daughters, Mary, Emma, Margaret, Sarah, and Lauretta.

Mary Kroh's one regret in accompanying her family to California was the piano left behind. When a knock was heard on the Kroh door during Christmas dinner in 1852, Henry Kroh sent Mary to answer it. A teamster with an immense case tied on his wagon gave her a note: "A merry Christmas and a happy birthday for Miss Mary Matilda Kroh, from her father and many friends who have appreciated her noble sacrifice of the musical environment of her Eastern home. This instrument is given as a partial compensation for her cheerful and noble performance of her duty to her parents and as full appreciation." It was signed by her father and seventeen townsmen.

Mary, overcome, retreated upstairs where her sister Sarah found her in prayer. Finally, she sat at the uncased piano and tried to play, but her head sank. "Then the tears gushed forth," observed her sister Margaret, "the spell was broken and after a short time she was able to proceed."

Henry Kroh had occasion that evening to answer the door and "to his surprise," wrote Margaret, "the sidewalks and porch were filled with old and young men. Along the side of the house stood scores of men in the street as far as the eye could see and some were sobbing" from the sweet sounds of the Kroh family singing around Stockton's first piano.

The piano cost twelve hundred dollars, but fortunes were being made in California and subscribing its purchase was probably not difficult. The constant focus on commerce, however, distressed some women because merchants conducted business on Sundays. In 1853 Deborah Mulford lamented: "I never would be willing to make a home of Nevada [City] if for no other reason than its non observance of the Sabbath."

The rising influence of women like Deborah Mulford eventually accomplished such goals as Sabbath observance. In September 1854 the Nevada City office of Wells, Fargo & Company first observed Sunday closings. An announcement declaring that "the office will be opened after the arrival of the Sacramento stage for the delivery of Letters and Packages, but no Banking Business will be done on Sunday's" was signed by the Wells, Fargo & Company agent. He was Charles Mulford.

The earliest project Nevada City women undertook on behalf of Sabbath observance was a fund-raising bazaar for the building of their community's first church.

Charles Ferguson was among the men paying the two-dollar entrance fee. Inside, at the bazaar's post office, Miss Bowers, the "pleasant postmistress," said she held a letter for him:

> I was young and felt quite flattered when notified by that young lady, in her most winsome manner, that she had in her official keeping a letter for me. I stepped up and received a letter at her hands, and was in the act of returning her gracious smile . . . when she said, in the sweetest of womanly accents, "Two dollars and fifty cents." I paid it with alacrity. When I opened it I found it to be written in Dutch or Indian, not a word of which could I make out. I was not wise enough to keep the joke to myself, but must go and tell her. "Dear me, how stupid I was," said she; "but here is your letter," handing me another. I was innocent enough to receive it, when the same sweet seductive voice repeated: "Two dollars and a half," and I again discharged my obligation to the post-office without shedding a tear.

From Miss Bowers's post office, Ferguson visited Mrs. Phelps's pie and coffee stand. But he "was not long in falling in with Mrs. Scott, who kept the scales":

> "Dear me," said that lady, "is that you? Why I hardly knew you. Have you been sick?" I innocently said, "No." "How I had fallen away!" I thought not, but she was sure I had. "Just step on the scales and she would see." I did not drop to her little game, but like a simpleton mounted the scales as she requested, and weighed five pounds more than usual. "Well, well, I was mistaken," but smiling, she said: "People are liable to be deceived. Two dollars, please."

An hour's attendance at the ladies' church bazaar cost Ferguson about thirty dollars. In recalling the event he couldn't remember how much the fair netted, "but it was something enormous":

> The miners were captivated with the smiles of the ladies and were willing to pay liberal for one; nor were the ladies sparing of their blandishments, so long as the miners' money held out. The gamblers, too, came in for their share, and got as handsomely fleeced as they ever fleeced a poor miner.

Women intent on organizing and supporting churches effectively supplanted the Sunday activities of the earliest miners, which Luzena Wilson recalled:

> The old-time Sabbath amusements of riding bucking mustangs into the saloons, drinking all day at the various bars, running foot-races, playing poker, and finishing the day with a free fight are things of the past. The sobering influence of civilization has removed all such exciting but dangerous pastimes as playing scientific games of billiards by firing at the balls with a pistol, [and] taking off the heads of the decanters behind the counter with a quick shot. . . . Now when the individual members of the enlightened population play cards, as perhaps they sometimes do, it is in the seclusion of the back-room, out of range of prying eyes.

The "prying eyes" undoubtedly were female. California wives, upon arrival, attacked unacceptable male habits as if they were so much household dirt. Women literally and figuratively rolled their sleeves and went to work to tidy up society.

Fertile fields awaited them. California's numerous saloons and gambling hells attracted hordes of customers. Lights, music, excitement, warmth, and companionship understandably enticed thousands of men from miserable tents or crowded, foul-smelling boardinghouses. And the men drawn to drinking, gambling, and bad company drew the ire of respectable women, clerics, and temperate brothers.

The first target of reformers was Sunday gambling. They suppressed the practice in San Francisco in September 1850.

Such prompt excision of evil struck Frank Marryat, a cultivated Englishman on tour, as understandable, given its extent:

It is said that one surfeit of raspberry-tarts will produce, in the pastry-cook's boy, a permanent nausea for these luscious things; thus with Californians, they have seen vice and debauchery in so awful a shape, that in the reaction of feeling[,] more good is being done to the country as regards sweeping reform, than would have happened in twenty times the time had the early colonists been at the first but ordinarily virtuous.

A sermon delivered in Sacramento by the Rev. J. A. Benton graphically delineated Marryat's charge of "vice and debauchery":

Ah, if such as dwell far away, if parents and guardians, if wives and children, if brothers, sisters, and those other loving ones, should hear concerning your habits of drinking, your revels, and your debauches, would they believe? If they heard that your evenings were passed in the saloon, and that all the proceeds of your labor and the profits of your business were swept into the coffers of gamesters, deceptive, deft and adroit, could they receive it as true? If they should be made to know, as we too well know, your indifferences, your delinquencies, your sensualities, your gross infidelities, what havoc would there be of human happiness, human hopes, human hearts: How would love slighted and trust betrayed turn to indignation and abhorrence, which years could scarce abate? Beware, yet whose feet are in these paths of death, lest, while ye destroy yourselves, ye dash many another's cup with bitterness, and bring down grey hairs with sorrow to the grave!

The Rev. Benton's tongue, observed a contemporary, was "not too bitterly charged with denunciation," and the pouring spirits barely slowed. Although temperance meetings were held in San Francisco as early as January 1849, and Sacramento formed a temperance society in 1850, California remained notorious for prodigious imbibing.

In 1854 this excess of indulgence attracted a brave crusader, Sarah Pellet, M.D., a graduate of Oberlin. Franklin Buck, after hearing her speak in Weaverville, wrote to his sister:

Miss Pellet has been here. She came in town Sunday and lectured in front of the hotel . . . on a dry goods box. . . . No dog fight ever drew together such a crowd. Perhaps you have seen Miss Pellet, as she hails from Maine. She is not bad looking, dresses in the Quaker style, has a fine voice and a great flow of language. Did I say flow? It is a perfect torrent. She talked for an hour and never stopped to draw breath. . . . We drew a long breath when she got through and thanked our stars we were not tied to her for life.

San Franciscans apparently shared Buck's view. Although Sarah Pellet's first lecture at the Music Hall there was well attended, only twenty-two listened at her second.

In March 1855, at the Capitol's assembly chamber, she addressed Sacramentans. The *Daily Union* ignored her message and praised her syntax: "Her grammar as well as pronunciation are scrupulously correct."

In Downieville, however, Calvin McDonald, editor of the *Sierra Citizen*, championed her cause. Sarah forthwith made her way to remote Downieville, a town Major William Downie called "a vast field for labor in the cause of temperance." Downieville men, under Miss Pellet's influence, adopted an opposite extreme and for a time deemed total abstinence the only correct behavior. They formed a Sons of Temperance group and, despite some objections to female speakers, honored Miss Pellet with an invitation to deliver the Fourth of July oration.

Her eventual departure from the town, wrote Major Downie, was "much regretted, and the cold-water brigade dwindled down for want of a leader, and the Sons of Temperance became an order of the past."

Nonetheless, California's roster of civilities was fast enlarging. San Francisco numbered among its polite and genteel behaviors the practice of New Year's calls.

The custom caught one lady by surprise.

She was Mary Smith, who had come around the Horn, reaching San Francisco in October 1852. Her first social endeavor was a Thanksgiving dinner, featuring a turkey sent by a friend from the interior. Told she could sell it for twenty dollars, she declined: "What is twenty dollars, compared with a Thanksgiving dinner?" Roasting the bird required "skillful management," she wrote, since the stove was too small to contain it: "I succeeded by leaving the oven door open from which different parts of the fowl would at different times protrude. . . ."

This social success behind her, Mrs. Smith employed the time between Thanksgiving and New Year's Day in the fashioning of a "golden brown brocade" into a new dress: "The hours I spent plying my needle were full of the vain glorious dreams of how proudly I should walk forth with my husband on New Year's morning arrayed like one of Solomon's lilies."

Mrs. Smith's beautiful brocade gown lay on her bed, "rustling with stiffness," on the morning of January 1, 1853. Before she had time to change into it from her morning dress, she heard a knock at the door:

> I opened it. There was a small company of men dressed rather better style than usual. Some of them had had their whiskers trimmed and a few wore "biled" shirts. I made myself as agreeable as possible in my husband's absence. Another knock and another company, the first disappearing to make room for the others. I did not understand until the day was too far advanced to parade my new wardrobe and my walk was indefinitely postponed, that I had been the honored recipient of New Year's calls.

Even in distant Columbia "good society" emerged. A surprised Clementine Brainard noted in her diary of December 1853:

> Attended a party last Thursday evening at Mr. Brown's: a large company present about twenty-five ladies, all married, everything passed off pleasantly, a very good supper no liquors sayed to be the first party in Columbia where they had no liquors think this is a proof that C is improving would not have believed that a party could have been got up in a mining town in Cal. in so good style.

In Santa Cruz, however, Georgiana Kirby returned home from a social outing in despair. After an evening at the home of a man she called a "shallow, conceited, dogmatic, insolent, pro-slavery braggart" she wrote:

> I came home quite sad and hopeless about the progress of truth and justice in this country, where it is the universal custom to call sin virtue—to boast of oppression and brag of the freedom of this great country, all in a breath—to hate with a wolfish hatred whose who

dare to advocate the most obvious right, what reason have we for hope? I despair. . . . I should live where I have the sympathy of abolitionists.

On September 9, 1850, President Fillmore had signed the bill admitting California to the Union as a free state. The delegates at Monterey's constitutional convention had voted unanimously for the clause which read "neither slavery nor involuntary servitude, unless for the punishment of crimes, shall ever be tolerated in this state."

Despite the state's constitution, buying black people in California was not unusual, even though purchasers understood slavery to be illegal in the state. The Bascom family in San Jose paid eight hundred dollars for a cook. Mrs. Bascom recalled that people told them he wouldn't stay—"for, of course, he was free in California." He did stay, however, living with them four years.

In Sacramento in 1850 interested purchasers were invited to inquire at the Vanderbilt Hotel for J. R. Harper who was selling there an eighteen-year-old girl "of amiable disposition, a good washer, ironer and cook."

In 1852 the Sacramento *Democratic State Journal* carried the following advertisement:

Negro for Sale.—On Saturday the 16th inst., I will sell at public auction a Negro Man, he having agreed to said sale in preference to being sent home. I value him at $300, but if any or all of his abolition brethren wish to show that they have the first honorable principle about them, they can have an opportunity of releasing said Negro from bondage by calling on the subscriber, at the Southern House, previous to that time and paying $100. I make this great sacrifice in the value of the property, to satisfy myself whether they prefer paying a small sum to release him, or play their old game and try to steal him. If not redeemed, the sale will take place in front of the Southern House, 87 J St., at 10 o'clock of said day.

Although committed abolitionists did frequently purchase and free slaves, ideals of justice did not underlie most Californians' opposition to the southern institution. Walter Colton, Monterey's alcalde, identified Californians' opposition to slavery as nothing more than implied inferiority for white men who labored beside slaves. Wrote Colton bluntly:

The causes which exclude slavery from California lie within a nut-shell. All here are diggers, and free white diggers won't dig with slaves. They know they must dig themselves: they have come out here for that purpose, and they won't degrade their calling by associating it with slave-labor: self-preservation is the first law of nature. They have nothing to do with slavery in the abstract . . . not one in ten cares a button for abolition . . . all they look at is their own position; they must themselves swing the pick, and they won't swing it by the side of negro slaves. That is their feeling, their determination, and the upshot of the whole business.

A measure of the rightness of Colton's conclusion is the "free Negro" amendment debated during California's constitutional convention. Adopted in committee was a provision to exclude from California residence *free* Negroes as well as enslaved:

The Legislature shall, at its first session, pass such laws as will effectu-ally prohibit free persons of color from immigrating to and settling in this State, and to effectually prevent the owners of slaves from bring-ing them into this State for the purpose of setting them free.

Only one delegate argued opposition to the provision based on its conflict with the U.S. constitution. More persuasive were those op-posed to instructing the legislature; they argued the inappropriate-ness of constitutional convention delegates dictating to the legislature what laws it should pass and when. Other delegates feared that including such a provision would impede congressional approval of statehood. After considerable debate, delegates defeated the "free Negro" amendment thirty-one to eight, with nine abstentions.

Had the "free Negro" amendment been adopted, California would have denied residence to a remarkable woman: Mary Ellen Pleasant.

Her accepted birthdate is August 19, 1814. One account has her born in Philadelphia to a Negro mother and a well-educated merchant from the Sandwich Islands. Another, more commonly accepted, says she was born a slave in Virginia or Georgia.

Delilah Beasley, who gathered records of California's pioneer blacks, wrote that Mary Ellen picked cotton on a Georgia plantation until a man named Price discovered her quick intelligence. That account says Price purchased her freedom for six hundred dollars and sent her to Boston for an education.

In Boston, where she became acquainted with abolitionists, she married Alexander Smith, a plantation owner thought to have been Cuban. They were apparently living in Boston when he died, bequeathing her a fortune of approximately forty-five thousand dollars. These funds, according to accepted accounts, she was to use to aid abolitionists.

She then married John Pleasant (or Pleasants), reportedly an overseer on Smith's plantation, and sometime around 1849 went west to San Francisco.

There she opened a boardinghouse. Said to be an excellent cook, and with good accommodations scarce in those days, she prospered. Delilah Beasley states that Mrs. Pleasant added to her fortune by lending money at 10 percent interest. Another historian suggests she expanded her boardinghouse business into houses of assignation.

Among her boarders were several men who rose to political and financial prominence in California. From some of these she purportedly gleaned important information and advised others on financial matters.

She also gained a reputation for assistance to the Negro community, rescuing slaves held illegally and seeking legal recourse to equality.

One goal was equal-testimony rights. In 1852 she and other politically minded San Francisco blacks organized the Franchise League in a first attempt to gain the right to testify in court cases involving whites. The law they opposed had been passed by the state legislature in April 1850. It specified procedures for deciding civil and criminal matters and stipulated that "no black or mulatto person, or indian, shall be permitted to give evidence in any action to which a white person is a party, in any Court of this State."

One of the first to be injured by the discriminatory legislation was eighteen-year-old Sarah J. Carroll. In December 1850 she was living in Sacramento where she rented a room from a Mrs. Moss on Second Street. A man named William H. Potter lived with her, and some took the couple for married although Sarah claimed she never said she was Potter's wife.

On December 12, 1850, Sarah Carroll, filing a charge of grand larceny, testified to Justice of the Peace Charles C. Sackett that Potter had stolen from her trunk seven hundred dollars in gold coin. Potter, she swore, had admitted to her he had taken it, and was at the moment in possession of it aboard the steamer *New World*, then lying at wharf in Sacramento. Sackett issued an immediate warrant of arrest, and Potter was brought before the magistrate.

Sackett had presumed Potter was Negro. When Potter appeared in court and Sackett saw that he was white, he dismissed the charge. He instructed the court clerk to write on the complaint: "Defendant discharged, he proving himself a white man & none but Colored testimony against him."

The campaign by California blacks for equal-testimony rights remained a constant struggle throughout the 1850s. Not until 1863 and the Civil War did the California legislature institute reform.

Not only did California exclude blacks from equal justice under the law, it denied them education. Black children were for several years denied education in California's public schools although state law, which required school attendance, specified no exclusion because of race. In Nevada City, when a mulatto girl applied to the district school for admission, school commissioner Edwin Budd proposed a separate schoolroom for her, since so many citizens objected to "mixing the two colors in such close contact and direct equality."

Private education for the black community was easier than forcing the issue in public schools. Elizabeth Thorn, a black woman from New Bedford, Massachusetts, was among the earliest to fill this need. In 1854 she established the first elementary school for blacks in Sacramento. Fourteen students enrolled in the private school she opened in her home. A year later, when she married and gave up teaching, Sacramento had thirty black children eligible for the school. The Rev. Jeremiah B. Sanderson succeeded Miss Thorn, relocating the school to the A.M.E. church.

Legal and educational discriminations reflected the social degradation endured by many black people. Undoubtedly not isolated was an incident involving a woman named Julia, one of five Negroes brought to Nevada City from Missouri in 1850 by the Gregory family. In August of 1851, Alexander "Sandy" Brown, a Southerner and part-owner of Nevada City's Empire Saloon, overheard Julia arguing with Susan Gregory in the Gregorys' boardinghouse. Incensed by Julia's violation of his idea of appropriate behavior, in which blacks did not talk back, Brown burst into the hotel and knocked Julia down. Fiercely upbraiding her manners, he punctuated his lecture with kicks.

Julia, like Sarah Carroll, could not bring suit. The assault went unpunished except for the intercession of Daniel Smith, who paid heavily for his affronted sensibilities. Smith, a miner from New England, hearing of the attack on Julia, confronted Brown at a faro table in the gambler's saloon. Smith wanted to fight and grabbed Brown as he rose from his chair. Breaking away, Brown pulled a pistol and shot the miner point blank.

Brown pleaded self-defense at his trial, and the jury found him not guilty. Smith survived, and Brown paid some of his medical bills. The miner, however, could no longer work and had no money. A benefit raised funds to send him home to his family.

Compounding the legal and social inequities endured by black people was the constant threat of return to the South and servitude. California was not exempt from the national fugitive slave law, but in 1852 its legislators passed a state fugitive slave law.

The California census of 1852 revealed a black population of over two thousand, more than double that of 1850 which counted 962, ninety of them women. While most blacks were men in the mines, the 1852 census listed 338 blacks living in Sacramento and 444 in San Francisco.

As the black population increased, California's pro-slavery forces gained sufficient support to pass the repressive 1852 state fugitive slave law. By its terms, slaves who were in California prior to its admission as a free state were fugitives.

Free blacks as well as enslaved lived in constant dread of arrest. In 1852, at Grass Valley, a free black woman named Jane Jones was kidnapped and held for extortion. She escaped the threat only because she had taken the precaution of recording her freedom papers with the county clerk.

A similar case occurred in San Francisco in 1853, which the *Alta* reported on April 20:

A person by the name of Brown attempted to have a negro girl
arrested in our town a few days since as a fugitive slave, but was taken
all a-back by the girl's lawyer, F. W. Thomas, producing her Freedom
Papers. Brown's father set the girl at liberty in 1851, and it is thought
by many that the son knew the fact, and thought to catch the girl
without her Freedom Papers but fortunately for her he did not.

Blacks without freedom papers were at constant risk of return to slavery and many became runaways. Elizabeth Ware advertised in the

San Francisco *Herald* in 1852 a one-hundred-dollar reward for a runaway black girl named Hagar.

A Nevada City washerwoman named Mary appealed to the townspeople for help when the man who had brought her to California decided to return to the States. Several men contributed toward the woman's purchase price of eight hundred dollars and then gave Mary her freedom.

In 1852 in Sonoma County, Mary Ann Israel-Ash raised eleven hundred dollars to free a family of slaves threatened with return to the South.

Slaves also purchased their own freedom from owners who permitted them to obtain the necessary funds through their labor. Ellen Mason, who accompanied her master to California in 1849, bought her freedom from the fifty cents a week agreed upon with him, and then bought her sister's freedom.

By working at night, a woman belonging to a Doctor Langhorn purchased herself, her husband, her daughter, and three grandchildren.

Slavery continued in California because the constitutional provision prohibiting it was not well served by the state's laws. California law did not condone slavery, but neither did it emancipate the slave. From the first the state tacitly permitted slavery by employing an "in transit" principle which held that slave owners could retain slave property if they were "in transit" through a free state.

One especially cruel instance of the "in transit" claim was the arrest of a mulatto woman as a fugitive slave. She was brought as a slave to California in 1850 from Missouri. In 1852 she married a free black man and ran away with him. The Missourian who brought her to California claimed that he was "in transit," had her arrested, and she was returned to slavery.

A return to slavery was a threat Biddy Mason faced from Robert Smith. In 1838, when Biddy was twenty years old, she bore her first child, Ellen. By thirty, she was the mother of two more daughters, eight-year-old Ann and infant Harriet. The family was then living in Mississippi. A man named Robert Smith owned them.

In that year, 1848, Smith and his wife, converted by Mormon missionaries, left Mississippi and headed to Salt Lake City with their personal property, which included nine people: Biddy and her three daughters, and a woman named Hannah and her four children.

In 1851 the Smiths moved west again, joining a wagon train to the Mormon community established at San Bernardino, California. They took with them the black people they owned as well as several head of stock. Biddy, with her three children to care for, followed the wagons on foot down the long, dusty trail from Salt Lake City to southern California, herding the cattle.

Whether she knew it or not, she was walking toward freedom.

A few years later, when Smith decided to move his entourage to Texas, Biddy sought legal confirmation of her equality. Although she had not thus far enjoyed freedom in California, its laws held the promise—but not the laws of Texas.

It is not clear whether Biddy sought Mrs. Rowen's intervention, but it was Elizabeth Rowen of San Bernardino who advised the Los Angeles County Sheriff that Smith was taking slaves to Texas.

Sheriff Frank DeWitt obtained a writ to prevent Smith from taking Biddy, Hannah, and their children out of the state and served it on him while Smith and his slaves were camped in a mountain canyon near Los Angeles.

The case went to court before Los Angeles district judge Benjamin Hayes. At issue was the freedom of fourteen persons, including the child born to Hannah in Utah and the three born to her in California, as well as the two-year-old girl born in California to Hannah's daughter Ann.

After due deliberation, Judge Hayes decided he had "satisfactory proof to the Judge here that all the said persons of color are entitled to their freedom and are free and cannot be held in slavery or involuntary servitude. . . ."

On January 19, 1856, Judge Benjamin Hayes declared that all of Robert Smith's slaves "are entitled to their freedom and are free forever."

The former slave's future in the state that gave her freedom was rich with promise. She would amass personal wealth, found Los Angeles's first A.M.E. church and its first elementary school for black children, and devote her life to philanthropy.

Biddy Mason's triumph represented a great victory for the "progress of truth and justice in this country," which Georgiana Kirby so despaired of three years earlier. But it was a skirmish, not the battle. Two years after Biddy Mason won freedom, Georgiana lamented:

I heard last week that there was a fuss in the common school at Watsonville about two colored children, nice, intelligent, well-behaved children all say, but disgraced by their skin. I understand that the children are admitted but put off by themselves, poor things, and not allowed to take places no matter how much they out-spelled those above them. The more violently pro-slavery do not permit their children to go to the school at all. The ignorant, white people from the slave states are the curse of California, they are so stupid and so conceited they think one man (to-wit, themselves) just as good as another, providing there be not the least drop of African blood in them.

Still, the state's society did accommodate a steady change—albeit a slow one—including, finally, Georgiana herself. "Am growing by degrees more cheerful and at rest," she confided to her journal in 1859, "not so frantic as I used to be for want of the finest people for friends. Begin to realize that a little progress is a good thing and it's no use looking for strides."

POSTSCRIPT

*Some one struck up the song, "The sun shines bright on my
California home," and I longed for the lonely ranch, even to the
coyotes and the grizzly bears. I begged my husband to make a
visit and go back, but he said again he never put his hand to the
plow and looked back. . . . I have never ceased to remember
with pleasure my loved home in the land of
sunshine and flowers.* —Virginia Ivins, *Keokuk, Iowa*

By the end of 1853, a contemporary historian estimated California's
female population at approximately sixty-five thousand, and "perhaps 30,000 children." In San Francisco women numbered about
eight thousand.

By that time, energy and gold had transformed San Francisco from
the "city of tents" of 1849 into a major metropolis. "To give a general
notion of . . . the city at the close of 1853," wrote a San Francisco
chronicler of the time, "we here present a variety of miscellaneous
facts," and appended these among them: 626 brick or stone buildings
within the limits of Broadway and Bush street, Stockton street and
the waterfront—350 of them two stories in height, 154 of three stories,
34 at four stories, 3 at five stories, and 1 at six; 160 hotels and public
houses; 66 restaurants and coffee saloons; 63 bakeries; 13 foundries
and iron works; 19 banking firms; 9 fire, life, and marine insurance
companies; resident consuls for 27 foreign governments; 12 daily
newspapers; and "regular lines of omnibuses on the plank roads,
which run to the mission every half hour."

San Francisco was no longer a hamlet and California no longer a
frontier. Its people no longer were only transient miners. Men were
bankers and businessmen, lawyers and doctors, farmers and manu-
facturers. They intended to stay. So did the women, as Mallie Stafford
recalled: "Very few, if any, in those [first] days contemplated perma-

217

"I believe you have a sketch of San Francisco in 1851," wrote this correspondent of 1854 on an illustrated lettersheet, adding, "I send this that you may see the improvements. . . ."

nently settling in the country. . . . But as time wore on . . . they came to love the strange, new country . . . and found that they were wedded to the new home, its very customs, the freedom of its lovely hills and valleys."

And beyond the hills and valleys, in the wild country, it was the grizzly bear that was feared—and already being slaughtered into extinction—not the fabled elephant.

That enticing, frightening, ghostly pachyderm had faded into memory. Of the thousands who came to see it, only a handful left a history of their sighting, of their trek, their adventures, their misfortunes—of their lives.

A few sprinkled the thinnest trail to the evidence of their presence, to be tracked through musty libraries and dusty attics. Historical society archives, too, certainly yet secrete the untold stories of men and women who joined the great adventure.

All the names that survive in family Bibles, a few manuscript collections, the rare published diary or reminiscence, only hint at the many thousands who, unknown or long forgotten, came west to create homes, communities, a state.

Following are the histories surviving some of them, women who—by choice, chance, or circumstance—found themselves in California during the great adventure. They few must represent the many—the thousands of women who saw the elephant.

JULIETTE BRIER

Following their miraculous survival from the death-threatening desert of Death Valley, the Brier family settled briefly in southern California. They sold twelve oxen and with the proceeds purchased a half interest in a Los Angeles hotel.

They soon moved north to Marysville, and Juliette bore three more children. She was, however, destined to outlive all but one of the six born to her.

In 1903, she invited surviving Jayhawkers to her home in Lodi for their annual reunion. "Rheumatism and other ills have been effectual in pulling down the house in which I have lived for 88 years and 8 months," she wrote them. "All signs of a sudden fall are perceptible—dullness of sight, hearing and memory abide. Notwithstanding all these, life is not unpleasant and I still like to meet friends of Long Ago."

Despite advancing age she lived to attend the Jayhawker reunion of 1911. She died at Lodi in 1913, at ninety-nine.

LOUISA CLAPP

In 1852 "Dame Shirley," author of the wonderful letters written from the California mines, returned to San Francisco with her husband. There she remained when, their marriage ties rapidly unraveling, Fayette Clapp departed for the Sandwich Islands.

When an acquaintance, Ferdinand C. Ewer, started up a new periodical, she offered him copies of the letters she'd written to her sister. They appeared in each issue, from January 1854 through December 1855, when the *Pioneer* ceased publication. The *Pioneer* also published two articles written by her, but like previous and subsequent writings were marred by an ornate and erudite style. Nothing else she ever wrote compared with the unadorned letters from the mines.

In 1854 Mrs. Clapp started teaching in the San Francisco public schools. In 1856 she filed a petition for divorce, which was granted on April 4, 1857.

In 1878, her health poor, Mrs. Clapp retired from teaching and returned east. In 1881 a periodical published by the Hellmuth Ladies' College, an Anglican institution, printed a series of articles written by her. One of them, "Our Summer in the Valley of the Moon," described a vacation enjoyed twenty years earlier in Sonoma with her brother's children.

In 1897 Mrs. Clapp moved to Overlook Farm, a home for the elderly, near Morristown, New Jersey. She died there on February 9, 1906, at eighty-six.

The first collection of her lively and vivid accounts of California mining life was published privately in 1922. A small edition printed by San Francisco's Grabhorn Press appeared in 1933. The first widely distributed copies of the letters were published in New York in 1949 by Alfred A. Knopf. Each edition identified the author of the Shirley letters as Louise Amelia Knapp Smith Clappe.

In 1964 historian Rodman Paul, in preparing a profile of her for *Notable American Women, 1907–1950* (Harvard University Press, 1971), researched the details of her life, largely unknown. He discovered that her husband's family name was Clapp, spelled without an *e*. On her divorce petition, Mrs. Clapp gave her name as Louisa A. K. S. Clapp, which has been herein respected and adopted.

LUCY RUTLEDGE COOKE

Lucy and William Cooke, with their daughter Sarah, after reaching Placerville in 1853, settled at the nearby mining camp of White Rock. William earned $3.50 a day as a hired miner. They rented a room in the back of a grocery for eight dollars a month. "Through the cracks in the boards," wrote Lucy, "we could see men in the grocery playing cards all night, and frequently when we awoke next morning the candle would be burning and the men still at cards."

William and a hired carpenter built a house and the Cookes moved in "soon as the frame was up." They lived two years at the mining camp, where a second daughter, Mary, was born on July 12, 1855. The family then moved to Placerville where Lucy taught private school and music.

When William bought a mining claim they moved to Weber Creek and there, on January 22, 1857, Lucy gave birth to a son, Willie, third of the eight children born to her. Rains ruined the claim and the family moved to Placer County where William joined a company fluming the American River. This venture failed and William went into public service.

In 1874 the Cooke family was living at Dutch Flat, and there Lucy's sister, Marianne Willis, visited. She brought a gift: the letters Lucy wrote to her while crossing the plains. In the 1880s the Cookes moved to Virginia City, Nevada, where William served as judge and justice of the peace.

After William's death in 1898, Lucy moved to San Francisco where two of her children lived. She was blind in 1914 when interviewed by a reporter for the Healdsburg *Tribune*, who wrote "though the light of her eyes has been extinguished . . . this old lady shows marvelous interest in the world's activities of today, and her mind is alive with plans and hopes for the future." He quoted Lucy Cooke as saying, "Oh, if I just had my sight. I feel I could set the world on fire!"

Despite blindness, she wrote poetry, penning these lines in San Francisco on August 23, 1914:

> *There's a spot on the hillside,*
> *So near the old home,*
> *Where our loved ones*
> *We lay down to rest.*
> *No spot more befitting*
> *The old pioneer or the son*
> *On the slope they knew best.*
>
> . . . .
>
> *Years forty-nine*
> *In rain and sunshine,*
> *Together life's pathway we pressed.*
> *Here I would lie*
> *Side by side with the one*
> *Who in life was the dearest and best.*

Lucy Cooke died October 22, 1915, at eighty-eight.

Her remarkable letters, preserved by her sister Marianne—and now by the California Historical Society—were first published in 1923 by Lucy's son Frank Cooke, a teacher of printing and journalism in Modesto. Students set the type.

In 1980, the Plumas County Historical Society reprinted the letters, courtesy of Robert S. Cooke, of Taylorsville, Lucy's grandson, who provided a copy to the author in 1986. Lucy Cooke's letters are included in *Covered Wagon Women*, Vol. 4 (see bibliography).

BELLE CORA

Seven carriages followed the hearse drawn by four black horses in the funeral Belle arranged for Charles Cora. He was buried in a silver-trimmed mahogany coffin at Mission Dolores.

Two days later the San Francisco *Bulletin* printed a letter to the vigilance committee signed "Many Women of San Francisco." The letter asked the committee to request Belle Cora to leave town: "The women of San Francisco have no bitterness toward her, nor do they ask it on her account, but for the good of those who remain, and as an example to others. Every virtuous woman asks that her influence and example be removed from us."

The request was ignored. Belle continued to live in San Francisco, and to conduct business at her house on Waverly street. Sometime in the late 1850s she learned that the cemetery at Mission Dolores was too crowded to permit her burial next to Cora. She had his body removed to Calvary Cemetery and there was buried beside him in February 1862, following her death from pneumonia. She was thirty-five.

In 1916 Pauline Jacobson, a journalist for the San Francisco *Bulletin*, visited the overgrown and untended graves at Calvary Cemetery, and described the headstone Belle had commissioned before her death: it "stretched the width of both graves, was engraved with two figures—a young man and a young woman—standing with heads bowed, under a weeping willow tree."

Through Miss Jacobson's instigation the bodies of Charles and Belle Cora were removed to Mission Dolores Cemetery. They are buried together there under the headstone Belle purchased for them.

LOTTA CRABTREE

In November 1856 the diminutive red-haired performer appeared with the Chapmans in a mixed program at San Francisco's American Theatre. The one-night engagement was followed by constant appearances at music halls throughout California where Lotta honed her talents.

Belle Cora's tombstone, San Francisco's Mission Dolores

At seventeen she performed a farewell benefit in San Francisco which netted about fifteen hundred dollars. Mary Ann Crabtree then took her daughter to New York, where she appeared in a play manufactured from Dickens' *The Old Curiosity Shop*. Lotta, playing both Little Nell and the Marchioness, was an instant success. In London and throughout America her performances delighted audiences. Lotta returned in triumph to San Francisco and donated a fountain to the city, erected at Kearny and Market streets.

She continued to perform in plays with great success, always managed by her mother who carefully protected her daughter from any admiring men. An army officer Lotta fell in love with found no favor in her mother's eyes. The engagement eventually dissolved.

Lotta retired from the stage in 1891, at the age of forty-four. She supported her mother until Mary Ann's death in 1905. Her brother lived with her until his death, after which Lotta was alone with her wealth.

When she died in Boston in 1924, at the age of seventy-seven, her estate was valued at four million dollars.

SOPHIA EASTMAN

The Bancroft Library purchased Sophia Eastman's letters as part of the Robert B. Honeyman Collection. Neither the collection nor the Bancroft's acquisition records contain further information about Sophia or Harrison Eastman beyond Sophia's letter dated December 15, 1851.

California's census of 1852 counted Harrison Eastman, age twenty-eight, occupation "artiste," and Mrs. Eastman, age twenty-one, both previously of New Hampshire. An 1854 San Francisco directory listed Harrison Eastman as a "designer & engraver" living on Taylor, "3 doors from Clay." In 1856 a directory identified him as a "landscape painter." In 1862 he had an engraving shop in the Golden Era Building at 151 Clay. The last directory listing for Harrison Eastman was 1885–86: "landscape painter, r. 1123 Clay."

The events of Sophia Eastman's life after 1851 await the interested delver's determined prowl through old newspapers, city and county records, and vital statistics compilations.

ELIZA FARNHAM

Following the publication of *California, In-doors and Out*, when she returned to New York in 1856, Mrs. Farnham started work on *Woman and Her Era*, in which she asserted the superiority of the female sex. On May 13, 1858, she addressed the National Woman's Rights Convention in New York City on the topic.

She also wrote a fictionalized account of her painful childhood, originally published in 1859 as *My Early Days* and in 1864 under the title *Eliza Woodson*.

She returned to California in 1859, touring as a public lecturer on spiritualism, female valor, and contemporary civilization. In April 1861 she accepted the position of matron for the Stockton Insane Asylum's female department.

In 1862 she again returned to New York, becoming active in the Women's Loyal National League and joining the abolitionists seeking a constitutional amendment to end slavery.

She had enrolled in medical studies at the start of the Civil War, and in 1863 answered a call for volunteer nurses to the battlefields. She served at Gettysburg until forced by ill health to return to New York City. There, on December 15, 1864, she died of tuberculosis. She was forty-nine.

The two-volume *Woman and Her Era* was published in 1864. Published posthumously was *The Ideal Attained*, a fictional rendering of Mrs. Farnham's ideas about manhood and womanhood. Her literary accomplishments also included the publication in 1846 of *Life in Prairie Land*, written from her experiences in Illinois where she lived after marrying Thomas Jefferson Farnham.

JESSIE BENTON FRÉMONT

In the mid 1850s the gold-rich, seventy-square-mile Mariposas tract—purchased by proxy for John C. Frémont in 1847 before the gold discovery—made the Frémonts wealthy beyond imagining.

In 1856 Frémont was the first Republican candidate for president, losing to James Buchanan. He returned to California to oversee the Mariposas mines while Jessie and their children visited Europe. "Love me in memory of the old times when I was so dear to you," she wrote her husband, revealing her pain at the separation and apparent estrangement. "I love you now much more than I did then."

Upon her return Jessie and the children acceded to Frémont's insistence that they live at Mariposas. Despite an initial reluctance, Jessie, marital wounds apparently healed, wrote cheerfully from her plain white-washed cottage that she was "very contented." At Bear Valley, she planted honeysuckle, tended the vegetable garden, and adapted to country living: "I used to fear caterpillars & spiders but I do not mind a housesnake or a chapparal snake now since I have seen the fresh trail of a rattlesnake crossing the patch to the kitchen."

Sometime in 1859 legal entanglements began draining the mines of their profits. For a time, however, the Frémonts lived lavishly, first in San Francisco at Black Point and then in the East, at Pocaho, a magnificent Hudson River estate.

By the mid 1870s Frémont had lost his fortune through poor management and a failed railroad venture. Jessie, at fifty, started writing her reminiscences and children's stories, which she sold to support herself and her husband.

They moved to Los Angeles in 1888, and in 1890 John Frémont died in a New York City boardinghouse where he was staying on one of his trips to petition the government for a military pension.

Jessie, at seventy-eight, died in Los Angeles on December 27, 1902. She is buried next to her husband at Rockland Cemetery, near Pocaho.

Margaret Frink

MARGARET FRINK

Although Margaret and her husband Ledyard failed to find California's gold so plentiful that citizens there "kept flour-scoops to scoop the gold out of the barrels that they kept it in," the Frinks did prosper in the golden state.

In Sacramento, where they opened "Frink's Hotel" and put free milk on the table to attract customers, they established their first permanent home. In 1851 they purchased two lots at the corner of M and Eighth streets and erected a "ready-built cottage" they had sent via the Horn. In that year, too, they sold the hotel, purchased another twenty-five cows, and went into the dairy business. Mrs. Frink was a charter member of Sacramento's First Baptist Church.

Margaret Frink's journal ends with 1851, but years later she appended this note: "The progress of time only confirmed us more strongly in our choice of a home, and we never had occasion to regret the prolonged hardships of the toilsome journey that had its happy ending for us in this fair land of California."

She died in Oakland on January 16, 1893, at the age of seventy-four, survived by her husband. Ledyard Frink, in response "to the many requests made by relatives and friends for a history of our journey across the plains to California, made in the summer of 1850," published his wife's journal in 1897.

The journal was reprinted in 1983 in *Covered Wagon Women*, Vol. 2 (see bibliography).

ELIZABETH GUNN

In 1851 Elizabeth Gunn had traveled around the Horn with four children to join her husband in Sonora. There, in 1853, at age forty-two, she gave birth to a fifth child, Anna Lee.

The Gunn family left Sonora in August 1861 and settled in San Francisco, where Lewis Gunn was appointed Deputy Surveyor of the port. After the Civil War, Gunn received an appointment as San Francisco's Assessor of Internal Revenue. The increased salary permitted Elizabeth to engage a servant and the family to move to a fine hilltop house at the corner of Jones and Washington streets.

Lewis Gunn soon returned to the newspaper business as supervising editor of the San Francisco *Times*. In 1871 Gunn, exhausted by the hours and responsibility, "broke down completely and was obliged to give up all work." Advised to take a sea voyage, he and Elizabeth went east to visit her sisters in Philadelphia. After their return to California they relocated to San Diego. There, Douglas, their oldest son, had purchased a part interest in the San Diego *Union*, which he edited until 1886.

In 1873 the Gunns' daughters, Sarah and Lizzie, opened a private school, the San Diego Academy, where they were soon joined by their younger sister Anna Lee. Sarah and Lizzie both married in 1876. In 1878 Anna married and the school was then closed.

Lewis Gunn died in San Diego in 1892. Elizabeth survived him by fourteen years, living her last years with her youngest daughter, Anna Lee Marston. "Her old age was very peaceful and beautiful," wrote Mrs. Marston. "The children remember her best with her knitting in her hands, an open book on the rest before her, and flowers on her table. Even with failing memory, these were a delight to her."

Nancy Kelsey

Elizabeth Gunn died in San Diego in October 1906. She was ninety-five.

In 1928 daughter Anna Lee Marston, then seventy-five, published her father's gold rush diary and her mother's letters written from the cargo ship *Bengal* and from Sonora. *Records of a California Family* was reprinted in 1974 courtesy of the Donald I. Segerstrom Memorial Fund.

NANCY KELSEY

In 1841 Nancy Kelsey, carrying her infant daughter Ann, crossed the Sierra on foot, the only woman in the first organized overland emigrant party to California. Her adventures had barely begun. In 1843 the Kelseys and a small party started for Oregon. En route, Indians stole twenty-five of their horses and a fight ensued. "I counted twelve of them as they went down before our guns," reported Mrs. Kelsey.

In 1844 Benjamin Kelsey, unable to settle long anywhere, returned from Oregon with Nancy, Ann, and a newborn daughter to Napa Valley. Again Indians attacked. "While the arrows were flying into our camp," said Nancy, "I took one babe and rolled it in a blanket and hid it in the brush and returned and took my other child and hid it also."

In 1848 Benjamin went to the mines and brought back a thousand dollars in gold. He returned to the mines with a flock of sheep, which he sold for sixteen thousand dollars. In 1850 the family sold the stock from their ranch near Sonoma (from which the present-day town of Kelseyville took its name) and moved to the Humboldt area. That venture was not profitable, "but we helped start the towns of Eureka and Arcata," claimed Nancy. They returned to Sonoma in 1851. By 1859 Mrs. Kelsey "had enough incidents happen to me to make a book."

In 1859 the Kelseys went to Mexico and in 1861 "drifted into Texas, where we were attacked by the Comanche Indians." Nancy's twelve-year-old daughter was scalped in the raid.

The family returned to California, and the injured daughter died in Fresno at age eighteen. The Kelseys lived at Owens Valley for a time, and Benjamin died in Los Angeles in 1888.

After his death, Nancy Kelsey lived alone in a remote cabin high in the mountains of Santa Barbara County, supporting herself by raising chickens and vegetables. An admiring neighbor interviewed her and sent the article to the San Francisco *Examiner*, which published it on February 5, 1893. "I have enjoyed riches and suffered the pangs of poverty," she told him. "I have seen U. S. Grant when he was little known; I have baked bread for General Fremont and talked to Kit Carson; I have run from bear. . . ."

Doctors at Santa Barbara and Santa Maria diagnosed incurable cancer on her face, which she attributed to a bad bruise to her cheek received years earlier after being thrown against the side of a stagecoach during a ride through rough country. "Up to within a few weeks of her death," wrote a friend, "she would mount her pinto pony and ride across the mountains to help bring a baby into the world, bind splints on a broken leg or minister to a fever-ridden child."

She died in 1896, in her seventy-third year. She was buried at the

A crude concrete gravestone marks the burial place of Nancy Kelsey, the first woman to cross the plains to California.

head of Cottonwood Canyon, in the desolate and beautiful Cuyama River valley. For more than forty years the only stone marking her grave was rough concrete crudely etched "Kelsey 1823–1896." Above it, in 1937, a chapter of the Native Daughters of the Golden West mounted a bronze plaque to commemorate the first woman to cross the plains to Californa.

GEORGIANA BRUCE KIRBY

Between the ages of thirty-five and forty-seven, Georgiana Kirby, Eliza Farnham's dear friend, bore five children at Santa Cruz.

In 1869, when Wyoming Territory granted women suffrage and both the National Woman Suffrage Association and the American Woman Suffrage Association were founded, Mrs. Kirby organized in Santa Cruz the first local society of suffragists.

Between 1870 and 1872 Mrs. Kirby wrote articles for the *Santa Cruz Sentinel*, *Overland Monthly*, and *Old and New*. In later years she commenced *Years of Experience*, an autobiography which includes vivid accounts of her formative years in England, her residence at Brook Farm, her work at Sing Sing, her teaching experiences in Missouri, and the anti-slavery movement. Her hands crippled with arthritis, Mrs. Kirby could barely hold a pen. So difficult and painful was the task of writing that she closed her book with her departure from New York in 1850. Her autobiography says of California only that there she passed the remainder of her life. *Years of Experience* was published in 1887.

A record of her early California experiences survived in a journal kept between 1852 and 1860, published by the Santa Cruz County Historical Trust in 1987.

On January 27, 1887, Georgiana Bruce Kirby died at age sixty-eight. She was buried in Santa Cruz at the Odd Fellows Cemetery.

BIDDY MASON

In Los Angeles in 1856, former slave Biddy Mason undertook her first work on her own behalf. Dr. John S. Griffin hired her as a "confinement" nurse and midwife. From her wages she frugally saved $250 with which she purchased, on November 28, 1866, two parcels of land on Spring Street. There she built a two-story brick building with storerooms below and living quarters above. Rents from the storeroom supplemented her investment funds as she continued to purchase the Los Angeles property that eventually made her a wealthy woman.

Her eldest daughter, Ellen, married Charles Owens, son of Robert and Minnie Owens, a pioneer black family from Texas who moved to Los Angeles in 1853.

Both the Owens family and Biddy Mason prospered, and the two names are paired in the founding in 1872 of the first African Methodist Episcopal Church (A.M.E.) in Los Angeles. Biddy Mason is also credited with helping to establish the first elementary school for black children in Los Angeles.

She gave generously of both her time and her substance, frequently visiting hospitals and jails and providing food and shelter for the needy.

She died in 1891 at seventy-three, and was buried at Evergreen Cemetery near Los Angeles.

In 1988, in recognition of her generous contributions to the community, the First A.M.E. Church of Los Angeles erected a monument on her grave at Evergreen Cemetery. Los Angeles Mayor Tom Bradley was among the three thousand persons participating in the dedicatory service to honor Biddy Mason as a philanthropist and humanitarian.

In addition to this belated recognition, two public art projects dedicated to Biddy Mason, supported by the National Endowment for the Humanities, have been planned for the structure being erected on the site of her former Spring Street home.

Mary Jane Megquier

In 1849, when Jennie Megquier and her husband, Dr. Thomas Lewis Megquier, left Maine for California, they intended to "make a pile" and go home. After two years they returned to Maine, but only to visit. They sailed again for California in 1852. In 1854, the doctor's health failing, the two again traveled east. The doctor stayed, but not Jennie; she returned to California without him. Dr. Megquier died in Winthrop in 1855.

Mrs. Megquier's letters from San Francisco are in the manuscript collection of the Henry E. Huntington Library. The final letter is dated June 19, 1856, and the library has no information about her after this date. Her letters were published in 1949 under the title *Apron Full of Gold*. Editor Robert Glass Cleland took the title "from Mrs. Megquier's laughing promise . . . to 'come trudging home with an apron full' of gold."

Lola Montez

After Lola's two-year sojourn in the golden state, she departed for Australia where her initial success at Sydney's Royal Victoria Theatre on August 23, 1855, was not sustained.

She returned to California aboard the *Jane A. Falkinburg*, arriving in San Francisco on July 26, 1856, and enjoyed a successful two-week engagement at the American Theatre followed by performances in Sacramento. In September she is believed to have sold her Grass Valley residence, and San Francisco newspapers announced her re-

Evergreen Cemetery, Los Angeles. Members of the First A.M.E. Church of Los Angeles erected this monument in 1988.

tirement from the stage and an auction of her jewelry. She left California for New York in November.

In the East Lola commenced a career as lecturer, reading from an autobiography written for her by Charles Chauncey Burr, a retired minister, and speaking on such subjects as "Gallantry," "Wits and Women of Paris," and "Heroines of History."

In the fall of 1859 she suffered a stroke, and on January 17, 1861, she died. She was forty-two years old.

A plain marble slab marks her grave in Greenwood Cemetery, Brooklyn, New York, on Summit Avenue, near the 37th Street gate. The inscription reads "Mrs. Eliza Gilbert."

MARY ELLEN PLEASANT
In 1858 Mary Ellen Pleasant went east and was briefly at Chatham, Canada. There she allegedly gave thirty thousand dollars to John Brown to finance the plan that culminated in his capture at Harpers Ferry. The story remains unproven.

Mary Ellen Pleasant

Mrs. Pleasant returned to San Francisco and supported numerous black causes there. She assisted runaway slaves, obtained servant positions for blacks, filed a lawsuit for access to streetcars, reportedly helped fund a cultural center known as the Atheneum Institute. She was a generous contributor to organizations dedicated to improving the status of black people, such as the Convention of Colored Citizens of the State of California.

After 1870 Mrs. Pleasant's reputation centered on her association with San Francisco banker Thomas Bell, for whom she worked as housekeeper for many years. She supposedly dominated the banker and enjoyed access to his money.

In 1881 notoriety attached to Mrs. Pleasant when Bell's rival, William Sharon, who had at one time boarded with her, was sued for divorce by Sarah Althea Hill. A state court granted property divison based on a marriage contract produced by Hill. Upon appeal a federal circuit court ruled the contract a forgery and the judge laid the fraud to Mrs. Pleasant: "This case, and the forgeries and perjuries committed in its support, have their origins largely in the brain of this scheming, trafficking, crafty old woman."

After Bell's death, the woman familiarly known as "Mammy Pleasant" lived, apparently impoverished, with a San Francisco acquaintance. She died at the home of Lyman Sherwood on Filbert street in January 1904. The San Francisco *Call* of January 4 noted that "One last request of 'Mammy Pleasants' was that there be placed above her grave a tombstone bearing her name, age, nativity, and the words: 'She was a friend of John Brown's.' "

Mary Ellen Pleasant was buried in Tulocay Cemetery in Napa, California.

LOUISIANA STRENTZEL

The Strentzels, with their two-year-old daughter Louise and infant son John, left Texas for California on March 22, 1849, arriving in San Diego via the southern wagon road through present-day New Mexico and Arizona.

The family continued north to the Tuolumne River valley near the mining camp of LaGrange. There, for two years, they ran a hotel, store, and ferry. The Strentzels then purchased six hundred acres on the Merced River, but a flood washed out their holdings. Moving north again, they settled in a valley near Martinez, paying ten thousand dollars for twenty acres on which they set out fruit trees. Over the years they purchased additional acreage and developed a substantial orchard.

In 1857 their son John died of diptheria.

Daughter Louise attended the Atkins Seminary for Young Ladies in Benicia. On April 14, 1880, she married John Muir.

The famous naturalist briefly managed the Strentzel property but its success and the Strentzels' encouragement soon permitted his fulltime devotion to exploring and writing about the Sierra Nevada he so loved.

John Theophil Strentzel died on October 31, 1890, aged sixty-nine. In 1897 Louisiana died in her seventy-sixth year.

SUSANNA TOWNSEND

Little Ellen Beulah's death sorrowed Susanna Townsend doubly because she and her husband Emory were "rather *old folks* to have the first one." In 1853, at thirty-six, Susanna again suffered heartache when a stillborn baby boy was born to her.

In 1859 the Townsends moved to Lake County. Despite her late start, Susanna bore three more daughters—Beulah, Fannie, and Jessie—and these survived. Her letters continue from Lake County until 1867. They were presented to the Bancroft Library in 1957 by a granddaughter.

LUZENA WILSON

When Luzena and Mason Wilson came overland in 1849 they had two young sons. Two more children were born to Luzena after the family established an inn on the road between Benicia and Sacramento. Born in Vacaville in 1855 was a third son, Mason. In 1857, also in Vacaville, Luzena bore her only daughter, Correnah.

Twenty-four years later Luzena told her daughter, "the rags and tatters of my first days in California are well nigh forgotten in the ease and plenty of the present. . . . [And] dear old friends are falling asleep one by one; many of them already lying quietly at rest under the friendly flower strewn California sod; day by day the circle narrows, and in a few more years there will be none of us left to talk over the 'early days.' "

It was 1881. The occasion was a long convalescence for Correnah, suffering a serious illness. To help pass the time Luzena recounted for her daughter the trip across the plains in 1849, her first days in Sacramento, the founding of the prosperous "El Dorado" hotel in Nevada City, the purchase of land from Vaca. Correnah laboriously recorded her mother's narration, adding to the last page: "I have written my mother's story as nearly as I could in her words. Correnah Wilson, April, 1881."

Years later Correnah gave a typed and bound copy of the reminiscence to the library at Mills College, her alma mater. No accompanying information had been added, no details of her mother's last years, no death dates for either parent.

Correnah Wilson Wright died in Yokohama, Japan, in 1934. The Eucalyptus Press of Mills College published her mother's memoirs three years later, in 1937.

ACKNOWLEDGMENTS

Within libraries large and small, public and private, resides the history of human endeavor. The dedicated caretakers of that knowledge make possible books such as this. To librarians I met, and those I never shall, I am indebted. My special appreciation goes to the anonymous tenders of interlibrary loan, which bestows the astonishing gift of the nation's libraries delivered locally. Truly, the best of all possible worlds.

Grateful acknowledgment is also made to the following for permission to reprint from manuscripts and previously published material—

The Bancroft Library: for permission to quote from Anne Willson Booth's journal of a voyage from Baltimore to San Francisco, 1849; typescript diary of Clementine N. Brainard; Emeline Hubbard Day, Journal, 1853–1856; letters of Margaret De Witt in De Witt Family Papers; Mary Durant, letter of 24 December 1853, in Durant Family Papers; Sophia A. Eastman letters in Maria M. Eastman Child Correspondence; Mary Ann Elliot letter, January 1850, in Van Ness Family Papers; Martha Taliaferro Hitchcock Papers; typescript, Mary Ann Jones, Recollections, ca. 1915; John McCrackan's letters to his family, 1849–1853; Mary Pratt Staples, Reminiscences and related papers, 1886; Susanna Roberts Townsend correspondence, 1838–1868; Abigail Tuck letters in Marsh Family Correspondence; and Sarah Walsworth letter, 14 July 1853, in Walsworth Family Papers.

California Historical Society: for permission to quote from an unsigned letter written to Catherine D. Oliver, manuscript #1596.

Mills College: for permission to excerpt from its Eucalyptus Press edition of *Luzena Stanley Wilson,'49er.*

California State Library: for quotations from Mary Crocker's letter of March 25, 1853; the reminiscence of Mrs. James Caples; Mary Fetter Hite Sanford's "A Trip Across the Plains, March 28 - October 27, 1853"; and the Kate Furniss reminiscence.

Regents of the University of California and the University of California Press: for permission to quote from *Three Years in California: William Perkins' Journal of Life at Sonora, 1849–1852.*

Arthur H. Clark Co.: for permission to quote from Eliza McAuley's diary in *Covered Wagon Women*.

Robert S. Cooke: for permission to quote from his grandmother's letters in *Covered Wagon Days—Crossing the Plains in 1852*, by Lucy Rutledge Cooke.

Theron Fox: for permission to quote from *California Caravan: Overland Memoirs by Margaret M. Hecox*.

The Huntington Library: for permission to quote from the journal of Mary Stuart Bailey and from Angeline Ashley's "Crossing the Plains in 1852" in Sandra L. Myres, *Ho for California! Overland Diaries from the Huntington Library*; from Catherine Haun's diary in Lillian Schlissel, *Women's Diaries of the Westward Journey*; from *Memoirs of Elisha Oscar Crosby*; and from *Apron Full of Gold: The Letters of Mary Jane Megquier from San Francisco, 1849–1856*.

Santa Cruz County Historical Trust: for permission to quote from the journal of Georgiana Bruce Kirby in *Georgiana, Feminist Reformer of the West*.

Department of Special Collections and University Archives, The Stanford University Libraries: for permission to quote from the Lucena Pfuffer Parsons Journal typescript (M85).

Western Americana Collection, The Beinecke Rare Book and Manuscript Library, Yale University: for quotations from the journal of Sarah Davis and for excerpts from the letters of Mary Ballou in *I Hear the Hogs in My Kitchen*.

Yale University Press: for permission to quote from *A Frontier Lady: Recollections of the Gold Rush and Early California* by Sarah Royce.

BIBLIOGRAPHY

Ackley, Mary E. *Crossing the Plains and Early Days in California: Memories of Girlhood Days in California's Golden Age*. San Francisco: privately printed, 1928.

Altrocchi, Julia C. *The Spectacular San Franciscans*. New York: E. P. Dutton & Co., 1949.

Alverson, Margaret Blake. *Sixty Years of California Song*. San Francisco: Sunset Publishing House, 1913.

Asbury, Herbert. *The Barbary Coast*. New York: Alfred A. Knopf, 1933.

Bailey, Mary Stuart. "Journal, 1852." In *Ho for California! Women's Overland Diaries from the Huntington Library*, edited by Sandra L. Myres. San Marino, Calif.: Huntington Library, 1980.

Bailey, Paul. *Sam Brannan and the California Mormons*. Los Angeles: Westernlore Press, 1943.

Ballou, Mary B. *I Hear the Hogs in My Kitchen: A Woman's View of the Gold Rush*. New Haven, Conn.: Frederick W. Beinecke Library, Yale University, 1962.

Bancroft, Hubert H. *California Inter Pocula*. San Francisco: History Co., 1888.

————. *History of California*. 7 vols. San Francisco: History Co., 1886. Reprint. Santa Barbara: Wallace Hebbard, 1963.

————. *Popular Tribunals*. 2 vols. San Francisco: History Co., 1887.

Barnhart, Jacqueline B. *The Fair but Frail: Prostitution in San Francisco 1849–1900*. Reno: University of Nevada Press, 1986.

Barry, T. A., and B. A. Patten. *Men and Memories of 1850*. San Francisco, 1873. Reprint. Oakland, Calif.: Biobooks, 1947.

Barth, Gunther. *Bitter Strength: A History of the Chinese in the United States, 1850–1870*. Cambridge: Harvard University Press, 1964.

Bates, Mrs. D. B. *Incidents on Land and Water, or Four Years on the Pacific Coast*. Boston: E. O. Libby & Co., 1858. Reprint. New York: Arno Press, 1974.

Beasley, Delilah L. *The Negro Trail-Blazers of California*. Los Angeles, 1919. Reprint. San Francisco: R and E Research Associates, 1968.

Behrins, Harriet Frances. "Reminiscences of California in 1851." In *Let Them Speak for Themselves: Women in the American West, 1849–1900*, edited by Christiane Fischer. Hamden, Conn.: Shoe String Press, 1977.

Beilharz, Edwin A., and Carlos U. Lopez. *We Were 49ers! Chilean Accounts of the California Gold Rush*. Pasadena, Calif.: Ward Ritchie Press, 1976.

Belden, Josiah. *Josiah Belden, 1841 California Overland Pioneer: His Memoir and Early Letters*. Edited by Doyce B. Nunis. Georgetown, Calif.: Talisman Press, 1962.

Belden, L. Burr. *Death Valley Heroine: And Source Accounts of the 1849 Travelers*. San Bernardino, Calif.: Inland Printing & Engraving Co., 1954.

Benard de Russailh, Albert. *Last Adventure: San Francisco in 1851*. Translated by Clarkson Crane. San Francisco: Westgate Press, 1931.

Bennett, William P. *The First Baby in Camp*. Salt Lake City: Rancher Publishing Co., 1893. Reprint. Seattle: Shorey Book Store, 1967.

Berry, Mrs. John. "A Letter from the Mines." *California Historical Society Quarterly* 5 (1927): 293–295.

Berthold, Victor M. *The Pioneer Steamer California, 1848–49*. Boston: Houghton Mifflin Co., 1932.

Bidwell, John. *Echoes of the Past About California*. Chicago: Lakeside Press, 1928.

———.*Life in California Before the Gold Discovery*. Palo Alto, Calif.: Lewis Osborne, 1966.

Black Angelenos: The Afro-American in Los Angeles, 1850–1950. Los Angeles: California Afro-American Museum, 1988.

Bodeen, DeWitt. *Ladies of the Footlights*. Pasadena, Calif.: Pasadena Playhouse Association, n.d.

Booth, Anne Willson. "Journal of a Voyage from Baltimore to San Francisco . . . , 1849." The Bancroft Library, University of California, Berkeley.

Borthwick, J. D. *Three Years in California*. Edinburgh: William Blackford & Sons, 1857. Reprint. Oakland, Calif.: Biobooks, 1948.

Bowman, Alan P., ed. *Index to the 1850 Census of the State of California*. Baltimore: Genealogical Publishing Co., 1972.

Bowman, Mary M. "California's First American School and Its Teacher." *Historical Society of Southern California* 10 (1915–1916): 86–94.

Brainard, Clementine H. Diary, October 1853–October 1855. Typescript, The Bancroft Library, University of California, Berkeley.

Bristow, Gwen. *Golden Dreams*. New York: Lippincott & Crowell, 1980.

Brooks, Elisha. *A Pioneer Mother of California*. San Francisco: Harr Wagner Publishing Co., 1922.

Brooks, Sarah Merriam. *Across the Isthmus to California in '52*. San Francisco, 1894.

Brown, Dee. *The Gentle Tamers*. New York: G. P. Putnam's Sons, 1958. Reprint. Lincoln: University of Nebraska Press, 1981.

Brown, Lucilla Linn. "Pioneer Letters." Edited by Gaylord A. Beaman. *Historical Society of Southern California Quarterly* (March 1939): 18–26.

Bruff, J. Goldsborough. *Gold Rush: The Journals, Drawings, and Other Papers of J. Goldsborough Bruff, April 2, 1849–July 20, 1851*. Edited by Georgia Willis Read and Ruth Gaines. New York: Columbia University Press, 1949.

Bryant, Edwin. *What I Saw in California*. New York: D. Appleton & Co., 1848. Reprint. Lincoln: University of Nebraska Press, 1985.

Buck, Franklin A. *A Yankee Trader in the Gold Rush*. Boston: Houghton Mifflin Co., 1930.

Burchell, R. A. *The San Francisco Irish 1848–1880*. Berkeley and Los Angeles: University of California Press, 1980.

Burnett, Peter H. *Recollections and Opinions of an Old Pioneer*. New York: D. Appleton & Co., 1880. Reprint. New York: Da Capo Press, 1969.

Burrell, Clarissa W. *The Burrell Letters*. Edited by Reginald R. Stuart. Oakland, Calif.: privately printed, 1950.

Calhoon, F. D. *49er Irish*. New York: Exposition Press, 1977.

"California Emigrant Letters." *California Historical Society Quarterly* 24 (December 1945): 347.

Caples, Mrs. James. Reminiscence. California State Library, Sacramento.

Caughey, John W. *Gold Is the Cornerstone*. Berkeley and Los Angeles: University of California Press, 1948.

————. *Their Majesties the Mob*. Chicago: University of Chicago Press, 1967.

Christman, Enos. *One Man's Gold: The Letters & Journal of a Forty-Niner*. Edited by Florence Morrow Christman. New York: McGraw-Hill Book Co., 1930.

Clappe, Louise Amelia Knapp Smith. *The Shirley Letters from the California Mines, 1851–1852*. New York: Alfred A. Knopf, 1949.

Clark, Arthur H. *The Clipper Ship Era*. New York: G. P. Putnam's Sons, 1911.

Cleland, Robert G. *A History of California: The American Period*. New York: Macmillan Co., 1926.

Clyman, James. *James Clyman, Frontiersman: Adventures of a Trapper and Covered-Wagon Emigrant*. Edited by Charles L. Camp. Portland, Ore.: Champoeg Press, 1960.

Cogan, Sara G. *The Jews of San Francisco and the Greater Bay Area, 1849–1919*. Berkeley, Calif.: Western Jewish History Center, 1973.

Collins, Carvel, ed. *Sam Ward in the Gold Rush*. Stanford, Calif.: Stanford University Press, 1949.

Colton, Walter. *Three Years in California*. New York: A. S. Barnes & Co., 1850. Reprint. Oakland, Calif.: Biobooks, 1948.

Comstock, David A. *Brides of the Gold Rush: The Nevada County Chronicles 1851–1859*. Grass Valley, Calif.: Comstock Bonanza Press, 1987.

————. *Gold Diggers & Camp Followers: The Nevada County Chronicles 1845–1851*. Grass Valley, Calif.: Comstock Bonanza Press, 1982.

Conlin, Joseph R. *Bacon, Beans, and Galantines: Food and Foodways on the Western Mining Frontier*. Reno: University of Nevada Press, 1986.

Cooke, Lucy Rutledge. *Covered Wagon Days: Crossing the Plains in 1852*. Edited by Frank W. Cooke. Modesto, Calif., 1923. Reprint. Plumas County Historical Society, 1980. Reprint. Glendale, Calif.: Arthur H. Clark Co., 1985.

Crocker, Mary. Letter, March 25, 1853. California State Library, Sacramento.

Crosby, Elisha. *Memoirs of Elisha Oscar Crosby: Reminiscences of California and Guatemala from 1849 to 1864*. Edited by Charles Albro Barker. San Marino, Calif.: Huntington Library, 1945.

Cummings, Mariett Foster. "Journal." In *The Foster Family, California Pioneers*, edited by Lucy Ann Sexton. Santa Barbara, Calif: Press of the Schouer Printing Studio, 1925. Reprint. In *Covered Wagon Women*, vol. 4. Glendale, Calif.: Arthur H. Clark Co., 1983.

Curtis, Mabel Rowe. *The Coachman Was a Lady: The Story of the Life of Charley Parkhurst*. Watsonville, Calif.: Pajaro Valley Historical Association, n.d.

Dana, Julian. *The Sacramento—River of Gold*. New York: Farrar & Rinehart, 1939.

Davis, Sarah. "Diary, 1850." In *Covered Wagon Women*, vol. 2, edited by Kenneth L. Holmes. Glendale, Calif.: Arthur H. Clark Co., 1983.

Davis, W. N., Jr. "Research Uses of County Court Records, 1850–1879: And Incidental Intimate Glimpses of California Life and Society." *California Historical Quarterly* 52 (Fall 1973): 241–266.

Day, Emeline Hubbard. Journal, 1853–1856. The Bancroft Library, University of California, Berkeley.

de Graaf, Lawrence B. "Race, Sex, and Region: Black Women in the American West, 1850–1920." *Pacific Historical Review* 49 (May 1980): 285–313.

Delano, Alonzo. *Across the Plains and Among the Diggings*. 1853. Reprint. New York: Wilson-Erickson, 1936.

Delavan, James. *Notes on California and the Placers*. New York: H. Long & Bro., 1850. Reprint. Oakland, Calif.: Biobooks, 1956.

Derbec, Etienne. *A French Journalist in the California Gold Rush: The Letters of Etienne Derbec*. Edited by A. P. Nasatir. Georgetown, Calif.: Talisman Press, 1964.

DeVoto, Bernard. *The Year of Decision: 1846*. Boston: Little, Brown & Co., 1943.

De Witt, Margaret. Letters. De Witt Family Papers. The Bancroft Library, University of California, Berkeley.

Dickenson, Luella. *Reminiscences of a Trip Across the Plains in 1846 and Early Days in California*. San Francisco: Whitaker & Ray Co., 1904. Reprint. Fairfield, Wash.: Ye Galleon Press, 1977.

Dobie, Charles C. *San Francisco's Chinatown*. New York: D. Appleton-Century Co., 1936.

Downie, Major William. *Hunting for Gold*. San Francisco: California Publishing Co., 1893. Reprint. Palo Alto: American West Publishing Co., 1971.

Durant, Mary. Letter of 24 December 1853. Durant Family Letters. The Bancroft Library, University of California, Berkeley.

Eastman, Sophia A. Letters. Maria M. Eastman Child Collection. The Bancroft Library, University of California, Berkeley.

Egan, Ferol. *The El Dorado Trail: The Story of the Gold Rush Routes across Mexico*.

New York: McGraw-Hill, 1970. Reprint. Lincoln: University of Nebraska Press, 1984.

Elliot, Mary Ann. Letter, January 1850. Van Ness Family Papers. The Bancroft Library, University of California, Berkeley.

Ely, Edward. *The Wanderings of Edward Ely, a Mid–19th Century Seafarer's Diary*. Edited by Anthony and Allison Sirna. New York: Hastings House Publishers, 1954.

Faragher, John M. *Women and Men on the Overland Trail*. New Haven, Conn.: Yale University Press, 1979.

Farnham, Eliza W. *California, In-Doors and Out; or, How we Farm, Mine, and Live generally in the Golden State*. New York: Dix, Edwards & Co., 1856. Reprint. Nieuwkoop, The Netherlands: B. DeGraaf, 1972.

Ferguson, Charles D. *California Gold Fields*. Cleveland, Ohio: Williams Publishing Co., 1888. Reprint. Oakland, Calif.: Biobooks, 1948.

Ferguson, Tabitha. "Mrs. Tabitha Ferguson Bingham." *Records of the Families of California Pioneers* 2:12–14. California State Library, Sacramento.

Field, M. H. "Grandma Bascom's Story of San Jose in '49." *Overland Monthly* 9 (May 1887): 543–551.

First Steamship Pioneers. San Francisco: H. S. Crocker & Co., 1874.

Foley, Doris. *The Divine Eccentric: Lola Montez and the Newspapers*. Los Angeles: Westernlore Press, 1969.

Frémont, Jessie Benton. *A Year of American Travel: Narrative of Personal Experience*. New York: Harper & Bros., 1878. Reprint. San Francisco: Book Club of San Francisco, 1960.

———. *Mother Lode Narratives*. Edited by Shirley Sargent. Ashland, Ore.: Lewis Osborne, 1970.

Frink, Margaret A. *Journal of the Adventures of a Party of California Gold-Seekers, Indiana to Sacramento, March 30, 1850 to September 7, 1850*. Oakland, 1897. Reprint. In *Covered Wagon Women*, vol. 2. Glendale, Calif.: Arthur H. Clark Co., 1983.

Frizzell, Lodisa. *Across the Plains to California in 1852*. Edited by Victor H. Paltsits. New York: New York Public Library, 1915.

Furniss, Catherine McDaniel. "From Prairie to Pacific." Reminiscence. California State Library, Sacramento.

Gagey, Edmond M. *The San Francisco Stage: A History*. New York: Columbia University Press, 1950.

Gardiner, Howard C. *In Pursuit of the Golden Dream: Reminiscences . . . 1849–1857*. Edited by Dale L. Morgan. Stoughton, Mass.: Western Hemisphere, Inc., 1970.

Gentry, Curt. *The Madams of San Francisco*. New York: Doubleday & Co., 1964.

Giffen, Helen. *Trail-Blazing Pioneer: Colonel Joseph Ballinger Chiles*. San Francisco: John Howell—Books, 1969.

Goode, Kenneth G. *California's Black Pioneers*. Santa Barbara, Calif.: McNally & Loftin, 1974.

Gray, Charles G. *Off at Sunrise: The Overland Journal of Charles Glass Gray*. Edited by Thomas D. Clark. San Marino, Calif.: Huntington Library, 1976.

Gray, Dorothy. *Women of the West*. Millbrae, Calif.: Les Femmes, 1976.

Gregson, Eliza M. "The Gregson Memoirs." *California Historical Society Quarterly* 19 (June 1940): 113–143.

Griswold, Robert L. *Family and Divorce in California, 1850–1890: Victorian Illusions and Everyday Realities*. Albany: State University of New York Press, 1982.

Groh, George W. *Gold Fever*. New York: William Morrow & Co., 1966.

Grunsky, Charles and Clotilde. "From Europe to California: Being Extracts from the Letters of Charles Grunsky and His Wife, Clotilde, 1844–53." Translated by C. E. Grunsky. *Society of California Pioneers Quarterly* 10 (1933): 9–44.

Gudde, Erwin G. *Bigler's Chronicle of the West*. Berkeley and Los Angeles: University of California Press, 1962.

————. *California Gold Camps: A Geographical and Historical Dictionary*. Berkeley and Los Angeles: University of California Press, 1975.

Hammond, George P. *The Weber Era in Stockton History*. Berkeley, Calif.: Friends of the The Bancroft Library, 1982.

Hanson, Woodrow J. *The Search for Authority in California*. Oakland, Calif.: Biobooks, 1960.

Hargis, Donald E. "Women's Rights: California 1849." *Historical Society of Southern California* 37 (December 1955): 320–334.

Haun, Catherine. "A Woman's Trip Across the Plains, 1849." In *Women's Diaries of the Westward Journey*, by Lillian Schlissel. New York: Schocken Books, 1982.

Heath, Minnie B. "Nancy Kelsey—The First Pioneer Woman to Cross Plains." *Grizzly Bear* (January 1937): 3.

Hecox, Margaret M. *California Caravan: Overland Memoirs by Margaret M. Hecox*. Edited by Richard Dillon. San Jose, Calif.: Harlan-Young Press, 1966.

Herr, Pamela. *Jessie Benton Fremont: A Biography*. New York: Franklin Watts, 1987.

Hester, Sallie. "The Diary of a Pioneer Girl." *Argonaut* (September, October 1925). Reprint. In *Covered Wagon Women*, vol. 1. Glendale, Calif.: Arthur H. Clark Co., 1983.

Hitchcock, Martha. Letter of 30 June 1851. Martha Taliaferro Hitchcock Papers. The Bancroft Library, University of California, Berkeley.

Hodgson, Mary A. "The Life of a Pioneer Family. A True Account by Mary A. Hodgson." California State Library, Sacramento.

Holdredge, Helen. *Mammy Pleasant*. New York: G. P. Putnam's Sons, 1953.

Holliday, J. S. *The World Rushed In: The California Gold Rush Experience*. New York: Simon & Schuster, 1981.

Hutchings, James M. *Seeking the Elephant, 1849: James Mason Hutchings' Overland Journal*. Edited by Shirley Sargent. Glendale, Calif.: Arthur H. Clark Co., 1980.

Ide, Simeon. *A Biographical Sketch of the Life of William B. Ide*. 1888. Reprint. Glorieta, N.M.: Rio Grande Press, 1967.

Ivins, Virginia W. *Pen Pictures of Early Western Days*. n.p., 1908.

Jackson, Joseph H. *Anybody's Gold: The Story of California's Mining Towns*. New York: D. Appleton-Century Co., 1941.

————. Introduction to *The Life and Adventures of Joaquin Murieta*, by John Rollin Ridge. Norman: University of Oklahoma Press, 1955.

Jacobson, Pauline. *City of the Golden 'Fifties*. Berkeley and Los Angeles: University of California Press, 1941.

Jeffrey, Julie Roy. *Frontier Women: The Trans-Mississippi West, 1840–1880*. New York: Hill & Wang, 1979.

Jensen, Joan M., and Darlis Miller. "The Gentle Tamers Revisited: New Approaches to the History of Women in the American West." *Pacific Historical Review* 49 (May 1980): 173–212.

Johnston, Wm. G. *Overland to California*. 1892. Reprint. Oakland, Calif.: Biobooks, 1948.

Jones, Mary Ann. Recollections, ca. 1915. The Bancroft Library, University of California, Berkeley.

Kaufman, Polly Welts. *Women Teachers on the Frontier*. New Haven, Conn.: Yale University Press, 1984.

Kelly, William. *A Stroll Through the Diggings of California*. London, 1852. Reprint. Oakland, Calif.: Biobooks, 1950.

Kemble, Edward C. *A Kemble Reader: Stories of California, 1846–1848*. San Francisco: California Historical Society, 1963.

Kemble, John H. *The Panama Route, 1848–1869*. Berkeley and Los Angeles: University of California Press, 1943.

Kirby, Georgiana Bruce. "Journal, 1852–1860." In *Georgiana, Feminist Reformer of the West*, edited by Carolyn Swift and Judith Steen. Santa Cruz, Calif.: Santa Cruz Historical Trust, 1987.

————. *Years of Experience: An Autobiographical Narrative*. New York, 1887. Reprint. New York: AMS Press, 1971.

Lapp, Rudolph M. *Blacks in Gold Rush California*. New Haven, Conn.: Yale University Press, 1977.

Latta, Frank F. *Death Valley '49ers*. Santa Cruz, Calif.: Bear State Books, 1979.

Levy, JoAnn. "Crossing the 40–Mile Desert: Sorrowful Recollections of Women Emigrants." *The Californians* 5 (September/October 1987): 26–31.

Lewis, Oscar. *Lola Montez: The Mid-Victorian Bad Girl in California*. San Francisco: Colt Press, 1938.

————. *Sea Routes to the Gold Fields: The Migration by Water to California in 1849–1852*. New York: Alfred A. Knopf, 1949.

————. *Sutter's Fort: Gateway to the Gold Fields*. Englewood Cliffs, N.J.: Prentice Hall, 1966.

Lewis, W. David. "Eliza Wood Burhans Farnham." In *Notable American Women 1607–1950: A Biographical Dictionary*. Cambridge: Harvard University Press, 1971.

Long, Margaret. *The Shadow of the Arrow*. Caldwell, Idaho: Caxton Printers, 1950.

Lotchin, Roger W. *San Francisco 1846–1856: From Hamlet to City*. New York: Oxford University Press, 1974.

Lothrop, Gloria. "True Grit and Triumph of Juliette Brier." *The Californians* 2 (November/December 1984): 31–35.

Lyman, George D. *John Marsh, Pioneer*. New York: Charles Scribner's Sons, 1931.

Lynch, Alice Kennedy. "Memoirs." In *Notes on California and the Placers*, by James Delavan. Oakland, Calif.: Biobooks, 1956.

McAuley, Eliza Ann. "Diary, 1852." In *Covered Wagon Women*, vol. 4, edited by Kenneth L. Holmes. Glendale, Calif.: Arthur H. Clark Co., 1983.

McCrackan, John. Letters to his Family, 1849–1853. The Bancroft Library, University of California, Berkeley.

McGlashan, C. F. *History of the Donner Party*. 1880. Reprint. Palo Alto, Calif.: Stanford University Press, 1940.

Manly, William Lewis. *Death Valley in '49*. San Jose, Calif.: Pacific Tree and Vine Co., 1894. Reprint. n.p.: Readex Microprint Corporation, 1966.

Mann, Ralph. *After the Gold Rush: Society in Grass Valley and Nevada City, California 1849–1870*. Palo Alto, Calif.: Stanford University Press, 1982.

Mansur, Abby. "Ms Letters Written to Her Sister, 1852–1854." In *Let Them Speak for Themselves: Women in the American West 1849–1900*, edited by Christiane Fischer. Hamden, Conn.: Shoe String Press, 1977.

Margo, Elisabeth. *Taming the Forty-Niner*. New York: Rinehart & Co., 1955.

Marryat, Frank. *Mountains and Molehills*. New York: Harper & Bros., 1855. Reprint. Palo Alto, Calif.: Stanford University Press, 1952.

Marston, Anna Lee, ed. *Records of a California Family: Journals and Letters of Lewis C. Gunn and Elizabeth LeBreton Gunn*. San Francisco: Johnck & Seeger, 1928. Reprint. San Diego: Donald I. Segerstrom Memorial Fund, 1974.

Massett, Stephen C. *The First California Troubador*. Oakland, Calif.: Biobooks, 1954.

Mattes, Merrill J. *The Great Platte River Road*. Nebraska State Historical Society, 1969.

Megquier, Mary Jane. *Apron Full of Gold: The Letters of Mary Jane Megquier from San Francisco, 1849–1856*. Edited by Robert Glass Cleland. San Marino, Calif.: Huntington Library, 1949.

Monaghan, Jay. *Chile, Peru, and the California Gold Rush of 1849*. Berkeley and Los Angeles: University of California Press, 1973.

Morgan, Martha M. *A Trip Across the Plains in the Year 1849, with Notes of a Voyage to California by Way of Panama*. San Francisco: Pioneer Press, 1864. Reprint. Fairfield, Wash.: Ye Galleon Press, 1983.

Munkres, Robert. "Wives, Mothers, Daughters: Women's Life on the Road West." *Annals of Wyoming* 42 (October 1970): 191–224.

Myres, Sandra L. *Westering Women and the Frontier Experience 1800–1915*. Albuquerque: University of New Mexico Press, 1982.

Nevins, Allan. *Fremont, The West's Greatest Adventurer*. London: Harper & Bros., 1928.

Ogden, Annegret. "The Frontier Housewife—Stereotype vs. Reality." *The Californians* 4 (May/June 1986): 8–13.

Oglesby, Richard. Introduction to *The Shirley Letters*. Salt Lake City: Peregrine Smith Books, 1983.

"Our Divorce Law, By C. T. H." *Pioneer* 1 (April 1854): 213–220.

Parsons, Lucena. "The Journal of Lucena Parsons." In *Covered Wagon Women*, vol. 2, edited by Kenneth L. Holmes. Glendale, Calif.: Arthur H. Clark Co., 1983.

Paul, Rodman W. "In Search of 'Dame Shirley.' " *Pacific Historical Quarterly* 33 (May 1964): 127–136.

People vs. Ida Vanard. Case File 228, California Sixth Judicial District Court, 1853. Archives & Collections, Sacramento History Center.

Perkins, William. *Three Years in California: William Perkins' Journal of Life at Sonora, 1849–1852*. Berkeley and Los Angeles: University of California Press, 1964.

Perlot, Jean-Nicolas. *Gold Seeker: Adventures of a Belgian Argonaut during the Gold Rush Years*. Edited by Howard R. Lamar. New Haven, Conn.: Yale University Press, 1985.

Peters, Charles. *The Autobiography of Charles Peters*. Sacramento: LaGrave Co., 1915.

Pfeiffer, Ida. *A Lady's Visit to California 1853*. 1856. Reprint. Oakland, Calif.: Biobooks, 1950.

Phillips, Catherine C. *Coulterville Chronicle: The Annals of a Mother Lode Town*. San Francisco: Grabhorn Press, 1942.

———. *Jessie Benton Fremont: A Woman Who Made Destiny*. San Francisco: John Henry Nash, 1935.

Pomfret, John E., ed. *California Gold Rush Voyages, 1848–1849: Three Original Narratives*. San Marino, Calif.: Huntington Library, 1954.

Pratt, Sarah. "Daily Notes." In *Covered Wagon Women*, vol. 4, edited by Kenneth L. Holmes. Glendale, Calif.: Arthur H. Clark Co., 1983.

Read, Georgia Willis. "Diseases, Drugs and Doctors on the Oregon-California

Trail in the Gold-Rush Years." *Missouri Historical Review* (April 1944): 260–276.

———. "Women and Children on the Oregon-California Trail in the Gold-Rush Years." *Missouri Historical Review* (October 1944): 1–23.

Records of the Families of California Pioneers. 27 vols. Compiled by The Genealogical Records Committee, D.A.R. of California. California State Library, Sacramento.

Reid, Bernard J. *Overland to California with the Pioneer Line: The Gold Rush Diary of Bernard J. Reid.* Edited by Mary M. Gordon. Palo Alto, Calif.: Stanford University Press, 1983.

Riley, Glenda. *Women and Indians on the Frontier 1825–1915.* Albuquerque: University of New Mexico Press, 1984.

———. "Women on the Panama Trail to California, 1849–1869." *Pacific Historical Review* 55 (November 1986): 531–548.

Rix, Alfred. Rix Family Letters. The Bancroft Library, University of California, Berkeley.

Rix, Chastina. Diary. California Historical Society, San Francisco.

Robinson, Fayette. *California and its Gold Regions.* New York: Stringer & Townsend, 1849. Reprint. New York: Promontory Press, 1974.

Rolfe, Emily Lindsey. "Reminiscences of Emily Lindsey Rolfe." *Nevada County Historical Society Bulletin* 20 (December 1966).

Root, Virginia V. *Following the Pot of Gold at the Rainbow's End in the Days of 1850.* Edited by Leonore Rowland. Downey, Calif.: Elena Quinn, 1960.

Rose, Rachel C. Diary, 1852. California State Library, Sacramento.

Rosenberg, Charles E. *The Cholera Years.* Chicago: University of Chicago Press, 1962.

Rourke, Constance. *Troupers of the Gold Coast, or the Rise of Lotta Crabtree.* New York: Harcourt, Brace & Co., 1928.

Rowe, Joseph A. *California's Pioneer Circus: Memoirs and Personal Correspondence Relative to the Circus Business Through the Gold Country in the 50's.* Edited by Albert Dressler. San Francisco: H. S. Crocker Co., 1926.

Royce, Josiah. *California from the Conquest in 1846 to the Second Vigilance Committee in San Francisco.* Boston and New York, 1886. Reprint. New York: Alfred A Knopf, 1948.

Royce, Sarah. *A Frontier Lady: Recollections of the Gold Rush and Early California.* New Haven, Conn.: Yale University Press, 1932. Reprint. Lincoln: University of Nebraska Press, 1977.

Sanford, Mary Fetter Hite. "A Trip Across the Plains, March 28 - October 27, 1853." California State Library, Sacramento.

Sanger, William W., M.D. *The History of Prostitution.* New York: Eugenics Publishing Co., 1937.

Savage, W. Sherman. "Mary Ellen Pleasant." In *Notable American Women 1607–1950: A Biographical Dictionary.* Cambridge: Harvard University Press, 1971.

Sawyer, Francis. "Journal." In *Covered Wagon Women*, vol. 4, edited by Kenneth L. Holmes. Glendale, Calif.: Arthur H. Clark Co., 1985.

Scamehorn, Howard L., ed. *The Buckeye Rovers in the Gold Rush*. Athens: Ohio University Press, 1965.

Secrest, William B. *Juanita*. Fresno, Calif.: Saga-West Publishing Co., 1967.

Severson, Thor. *Sacramento, An Illustrated History: 1839–1874*. San Francisco: California Historical Society, 1973.

Seymour vs. Ridgeway and Lawrence. Case File 789, California Sixth Judicial District Court, 1851. Archives & Collections, Sacramento History Center.

Shinn, Charles Howard. *Mining Camps: A Study in American Frontier Government*. New York: Charles Scribner's Sons, 1885. Reprint. New York: Alfred A. Knopf, 1948.

Shumate, Albert. "'A Lady is More Observed Here': Maria Tuttle of Birds Valley." *The Californians* 5 (March/April 1987): 6–7.

Simmons, Marc. "The Old Santa Fe Trail." *Overland Journal* 4 (Summer 1986): 61–69.

Smith, Mary. Letter. In *Nantucket Inquirer*, February 14, 1903. Typescript, California State Library, Sacramento.

Snyder, David L. "Negro Civil Rights in California: 1850." Sacramento: Sacramento Book Collectors Club, 1969.

Soule, Frank, John H. Gihon, and James Nisbet. *The Annals of San Francisco*. 1855. Reprint. Palo Alto, Calif.: Lewis Osborne, 1966.

Stafford, Mallie. *The March of Empire*. San Francisco: Geo. Spaulding & Co., 1884.

Staples, Mary Pratt. Reminiscences and Related Papers, 1850–1862. The Bancroft Library, University of California, Berkeley.

Steele, Rev. John. *In Camp and Cabin*. Lodi, Wis., 1901. Reprint. Chicago: Lakeside Press, 1928.

Stern, Madeleine B. "Two Letters from the Sophisticates of Santa Cruz." *Book Club of California Quarterly News-Letter* 33 (Summer 1968): 51–62.

Stewart, George R. *The California Trail*. New York: McGraw-Hill, 1962. Reprint. Lincoln: University of Nebraska Press, 1962.

———. *The Opening of the California Trail*. Berkeley and Los Angeles: University of California Press, 1953.

———. *Ordeal By Hunger*. 1936. Reprint. New York: Washington Square Press, 1960.

Stillman, Dr. Jacob D. B. *Around the Horn to California in 1849*. San Francisco: A. Roman & Co., 1877. Reprint. Palo Alto, Calif.: Lewis Osborne, 1967.

Stoddart, Thomas R. *Annals of Tuolumne County*. Edited by Carlo M. De Ferrari. Sonora, Calif.: Tuolumne County Historical Society, 1963.

Stover, Jacob Y. "The Jacob Y. Stover Narrative." In *Journals of Forty-Niners, Salt Lake to Los Angeles*, edited by LeRoy R. and Ann W. Hafen. Glendale, Calif.: Arthur H. Clark Co., 1954.

Stratton, R. B. *Captivity of the Oatman Girls*. New York: Carlton & Porter, 1857. Reprint. Lincoln: University of Nebraska Press, 1983.

Street, Franklin. *California in 1850 . . . Also a Concise Description of the Overland Route . . . including a Table of Distances. . . .* Cincinnati: R. E. Edwards & Co., 1851. Reprint. New York: Promontory Press, 1974.

Strentzel, Louisiana. "Letter from San Diego, 1849." In *Covered Wagon Women*, vol. 1, edited by Kenneth L. Holmes. Glendale, Calif.: Arthur H. Clark Co., 1983.

Taylor, Bayard. *Eldorado, or, Adventures in the Path of Empire*. New York: George P. Putnam, 1850. Reprint. Glorietta, N.M.: Rio Grande Press, 1967.

Taylor, Rev. William. *Seven Years' Street Preaching in San Francisco, California; Embracing Incidents, Triumphant Death Scenes, Etc.* New York: Carlton & Porter, 1856.

Thompson and West. *History of Nevada County, California*. Oakland, Calif., 1880. Reprint. Berkeley, Calif.: Howell North Books, 1970.

Townsend, Susanna Roberts. Correspondence, 1838–1868. The Bancroft Library, University of California, Berkeley.

Tuck, Abigail. Letters. Marsh Family Papers. The Bancroft Library, University of California, Berkeley.

Tullidge, Edward W. *The Women of Mormondom*. New York: Tullidge & Crandall, 1877.

Underhill, Reuben L. *From Cowhides to Golden Fleece: A Narrative of California, 1832–1858*. Palo Alto, Calif.: Stanford University Press, 1939.

Unruh, John D., Jr. *The Plains Across*. Urbana: University of Illinois Press, 1982.

Unsigned letter to Catherine D. Oliver, San Francisco 1850. Manuscript 1596, California Historical Society, San Francisco.

Walker, Wyman D., ed. *California Emigrant Letters*. New York: AMS Press, 1971.

Walsworth, Sarah A. Letter, July 14, 1853. Walsworth Family Papers. The Bancroft Library, University of California, Berkeley.

Walton, Annie Esther. "Pioneer Letters." Edited by Gaylord A. Beaman. *Historical Society of Southern California Quarterly* (March 1939): 27–29.

Ward, Harriet S. *Prairie Schooner Lady: The Journal of Harriet Sherrill Ward, 1853*. Edited by Ward G. and Florence Stark DeWitt. Los Angeles: Westernlore Press, 1959.

Ware, Joseph E. *The Emigrant's Guide to California*. St. Louis, Mo.: J. Halsall, 1849. Reprint. Princeton, N.J.: Princeton University Press, 1932.

Wells, Evelyn, and Harry C. Peterson. *The '49ers*. New York: Doubleday & Co., 1949.

Whipple, A. B. C. *The Challenge*. New York: William Morrow & Co., 1987.

Wienpahl, Robert W., ed. *A Gold Rush Voyage on the Bark Orion*. Glendale, Calif.: Arthur H. Clark Co., 1978.

Wilson, Luzena Stanley. *Luzena Stanley Wilson, '49er: Memories Recalled for Her Daughter, Correnah Wilson Wright*. Mills College, Calif.: Eucalyptus Press, 1937.

Wright, Doris Marion. "The Making of Cosmopolitan California: An Analysis of Immigration 1848–1870." *California Historical Society Quarterly* (December 1940): 323–338; (March 1941): 65–79.

Woodson, Rebecca Hildreth Nutting. A Sketch of the Life of Rebecca Woodson. California State Library, Sacramento, California.

INDEX